D1272415

ELITES IN
THE MIDDLE EAST

Sponsored by the Joint Committee on
the Near and Middle East of the
American Council of Learned Societies and
the Social Science Research Council

Edited by
I. William Zartman

ELITES IN
THE MIDDLE EAST

PRAEGER

PRAEGER SPECIAL STUDIES • PRAEGER SCIENTIFIC

Library of Congress Cataloging in Publication Data

Main entry under title:

Elites in the Middle East.

    Bibliography: p.
    1. Elite (Social sciences)--Near East--Addresses,
essays, lectures. 2. Elite (Social sciences)--Ad-
dresses, essays, lectures. I. Zartman, I. William.
HN656.Z9E43   301.44'92'0956   79-22932
ISBN 0-03-055961-8

Published in 1980 by Praeger Publishers
CBS Educational and Professional Publishing
A Division of CBS, Inc.
521 Fifth Avenue, New York, New York 10017 U.S.A.

© 1980 by Praeger Publishers

0123456789   038   987654321

Printed in the United States of America

To Louis Fougère

ACKNOWLEDGMENTS

This book has been prepared under the auspices of the Joint Committee on the Near and Middle East of the Social Science Research Council and the American Council of Learned Societies.

CONTENTS

LIST OF TABLES AND FIGURES

ELITES IN
THE MIDDLE EAST

1

INTRODUCTION

I. William Zartman

Elite studies developed in early twentieth century European scholarship as an alternative to Marxist emphasis on class and as a corrective to the egalitarianism of democratic philosophy. The approach began with a basic reaffirmation: in any political system, power is inevitably concentrated in the hands of the few. If some people have more power than others, it becomes important to know who they are and how they acquire power and, also, to find terms for analyzing the differences among political systems within the universal characteristic of power concentration. In their now classical works, Mosca, Michels, Pareto, and, to some extent, Weber were sometimes excessively fascinated with this basic discovery of power concentration, but, at other times, were able to move toward the identification of concepts for explaining distinctions among elites. These concerns were further pursued toward the middle of the century, notably by Lasswell and Lerner in the United States, but the primary focus of elite studies came to rest on the degree of concentration of power within American democratic society.

THE DEVELOPMENT OF MIDDLE EAST ELITE STUDIES

The contribution of studies of Middle East elites, beginning with the seminal works of Berger on Egypt and Frey on Turkey, has been to return to the question of elite circulation and to relate it to another topic of interest to social scientists: political, social, and economic development. However, these studies have been limited to single countries, and it has only been very recently that comparisons of Middle East elites have been undertaken.

The early studies of Middle East elites found that the dramatic transformation of the political system associated with development was accompanied by the replacement of traditional sources of power—such as land, market, and palace connections—by education, technical skills, and local position as criteria for elite recruitment. At the same time, attitudes on professional performance, related to achievement rather than ascription, were held and propagated by modernizing elites. These elements, in turn, were found to give rise to two themes governing the process of elite circulation under modernization. In one, education and experience vied with local ties as criteria for selection and promotion, until two groups of competing elites came into being; the success of the first in establishing a unitary, tutelary system prepares the way for the second to rise and form a pluralistic, competitive system. In the other, the stability of a polity under transformation has appeared to depend on the system's ability to absorb new rising elites created by the incumbents' policies of change. Later studies have elaborated on these characteristics of elite circulation, notably under monarchial, bureaucratic, and revolutionary variations of the tutelary approach to development.

Such findings were possible because the studies pioneered in the application of new methods for generating data. Middle Eastern elite studies have shown that detailed background data and opinion surveys can be gathered in the most unlikely places, to supplement more conventional sources of information, and can be subjected to sophisticated types of analysis.

Some questions, however, have either been left unanswered or have been brought to light by these studies. Discussions of circulation have left much of that process untreated and have really dealt only with mechanisms of recruitment. The dynamics of factionalism and networks within elites remain poorly understood, and there is still no satisfactory way of conceptualizing these groups and ties. The boundary problem has never been solved, and, while social scientists need not feel uncomfortable living with unbounded concepts, a clear boundary is a necessary prelude to satisfactory treatment of such other important matters as elite size, elite-mass relations, and even elite characteristics and behavior.

It is not even clear whether these questions are empirical or theoretical. To the extent that they have been faced at all, they have been argued on theoretical grounds, but it may be that they are best answered simply by better data or by data better focused on the particular questions. Middle East elite studies have not wanted for information. On the contrary, their data-generating techniques have sometimes produced more than one ever wanted to know, but have failed to relate these data to questions of significance or to establish relationships between various data in order to provide explanations. Rich in description, the studies have often tended to be thin in explanation or to provide explanations that were simply descriptive reiterations.

This is not the place to repeat these descriptions, particularly since most of them are organized in country-specific categories. But a general notion of some common features of contemporary Middle East elites and of their political dynamics can be provided by these studies. The focus is on national political elites identified *in institutional terms*. These are people who occupy the top positions in their political systems and who are thereby assumed, with reasonable accuracy, to have power. Their emergence has been associated with one of two usually-successive issues of political structure: independence from colonial or imperial rule and overthrow or continuance of monarchial rule. In organizational and role terms, the first issue is important because it brings to power the leaders of a nationalist-movement-turned-political-party, as in Egypt and Turkey in 1922 (Wafd and Republic Peoples parties, respectively); Syria in 1946 (National Bloc); Israel in 1948 (Mapai and others); Sudan, Morocco, and Tunisia in 1956 (Umma and National Union, Istiqlal, and Neo-Destour parties, respectively); and Algeria in 1962 (National Liberation Front). The second issue, on the other hand, brought to power consolidating monarchies (in Egypt, Iraq, Libya, Jordan, Iran, Morocco, and Saudi Arabia) that broke up and tamed the nationalist party elites where they existed. Many of these monarchies, as in Egypt, Iraq, and Libya, were overthrown, in turn, by a new group of military rulers who tried rather unsuccessfully to set up new parties of their own. As in any attempt to categorize reality, there are also some important mixed cases that may stand as prototypes of new patterns: progressive military reformers without a monarchy as in Africa, Syria, Turkey, and Sudan; non-military revolutionaries against a monarchy as in Iran; and institutionalized post-military regimes as in Syria, Egypt, Algeria, and Turkey. For these elites, the structural issue is one simply of finding appropriate political institutions.

Nationalist party elites in politicians' roles have not fared well in any case. From Morocco to Iran and from Syria to Sudan, contemporary Middle East elites have been primarily bureaucrats and technicians instead of politicians, occupied with the allocation of outputs rather than with demands and inputs, with power flowing downhill rather than uphill. They have attempted to control rather than to generate participation, in a system where exaggerated demands can be destabilizing (a fact they well know since they themselves came to power to replace regimes overtaxed by the demands placed on them). Their power comes from their control of the state, from above rather than below, and, even when elected, they present themselves as agents at court, as intercessors and intermediaries rather than as mandatories and monitors.

Yet behind such standard political terms, other characteristics and changes appear. Not only are there rivalries and replacements among institutions and roles, but new individual and social attributes are also being brought into politics. *In socioeconomic terms*, the new elites are clearly "modern" rather than "traditional," in the sense of being more educated, more dependent on salaried income, and more secular than their predecessors, often only a generation away from very different social backgrounds from which they have been raised through education. If independence after World War I or II created the revolution in political structures, education has created the sudden changes and opportunities in social promotion, permitting new roles, creating new classes, providing the basis for new struggles for succession and policy direction. *In attitudinal terms*, on the broadest level, the past century has been the stage for a succession of dialectical struggles between modern-Western and traditional-national attitudes in which each successive modern-national synthesis is attacked by a neotraditional counterelite for being too pro-Western. The attempt to create an authentic culture that is both national and modern, proceeding by reactive phases, has provided a powerful dynamic for elite politics.

Nationalist organization, bureaucratic and technocratic professionalization, educational promotion, and modern-nationalist culture have been the characteristics of a new middle class of elites who have worked to centralize and consolidate political control over new political systems in the Middle East. But as these elites come to power, they also accomplish a significant expansion of participation in politics. Through successive integrative revolts—more than coups but less than revolutions—politics has been removed from the hands of an aristocracy (in several senses) and taken over by the representatives of small townpeople and villagers, no more than a generation from the soil. Sometimes this process has been sudden; in other cases, it is spread over a longer period of time, and, in a number of important cases, we are simply still waiting for the returns to come in.

In Egypt, the sons of middle peasants came to power in the military coup of 1952, after having taken advantage of the opening of the military academy in 1936 to Egyptian Muslims as a channel of rapid social promotion. In Algeria, a new elite from small towns and villages eliminated the colonial rulers in 1962 and then came to power as a homogeneous group in 1968, "peasants' and workers' sons," as President Houari Boumedienne put it, who had been raised to positions of technocrats through university education. In Tunisia, the Neo-Destour party, which came to power in 1956, was centered above all in the rural villages of the Sahel, although Sahlis came into a majority in the political elite only in 1970. In Syria, the process was even more dramatic, although spread over a longer period; the hold of the old land-and-money families was broken by the union with Egypt in 1958–61, and a new group of villagers' sons, benefitting from education in teachers' training and military schools, broke through in 1963–66 and consolidated its stable control over government in 1970.

In other cases, the information is less complete. Libya and Sudan appear to have benefitted from a sudden rural influx through their military coups of 1969. In the absence of detailed information on a number of other important countries, the notable exceptions seem to be Iran, Israel, and Morocco, where the elite comes from the old city (Teheran, Jerusalem, or Fes) or from other large urban centers, although otherwise the countries are rather different.

Once the village has taken over the capital, the new elites create new institutions to suit their purposes—a process that usually does involve some increase in participation for the general population—and proceed to implement policies of social change suggested by their own origins. The roles for politicians, however, remain distinctly subordinate to those of technicians; the villagers' sons become the new capital dwellers, where they have preferred access to education and hence to government positions, and power remains in their hands, to be passed on to their children. Their position in the political sector is used to reinforce their social and economic position. The major policy mechanism for this process is the elimination of former wealth, power, and privilege through nationalization, which also concentrates economic resources and decision-making power in state hands for development. Initially, the state sector absorbs the new elite, leaving few personnel left over for private economics (business) or politics (party). As time passes—usually about two decades—the state sector becomes saturated and clogged, and new and better talent moves to the private sector, which the state-dominated system is forced to legalize in order to reduce pressure and dissatisfaction. The new private sector expands rapidly, moving the society toward competitive economies and publics. If Mohammed Ali is the prototype of this evolution, Republican Turkey and Republican Egypt are his followers, and Algeria, Syria, and others may join in time.

The new elite has a conscious policy choice between expanding and integrating new elements, on one hand, and facing another round of integrating revolts, on the other. The old political system, imperial or colonial, was unable to survive because, by its nature, it was not able to absorb the new elites it created. The new polity does not yet have such structural impediments to the continued absorption of elites the political, economic, and social systems produce. But accumulating social changes and aggravated economic deficiencies will produce real strains on a smooth integrating process, even if that is the policy of the incumbents, and will sharpen the pressure for new integrating revolts if the incumbents make no effort at new absorption. In this case, the dialectical struggle for the creation of a modern national culture provides the recurrent ideology for revolt against a concentrated, corrupt, defensive incumbent elite. Islamic fundamentalism is the local form of this cyclical struggle, but the constant element is the search for a national culture and the entrenched nature of a recent incumbent group, not Islam. Ibn Khualdun has described this process as a pact era, but the Muslim Brotherhood was a more recent manifestation, and the revolts of Qadhdhafi and Khomeiny are more successful cases. Thus, village influx, nationalization policies, and cultural dialectic are the ingredients of the cycles of integrating revolt and incumbent consolidation that characterize postwar Middle East elite circulation.

THE CHALLENGE OF MIDDLE EAST ELITE STUDIES

Hitherto, few elite studies have given more than facts about those in power, and few have prepared us for the phenomena of Sadat, Qadhdhafi, Khomeiny, Bonmedienne, or Begin. It is not always clear what is really known when one has a table full of fascinating facts about supposedly powerful people. Facts alone are merely the raw material for relationships and explanations in social science, and ways of describing elites are merely the preliminary steps for explaining the relationship between who they are and what they do (including how they get to be elites). Furthermore, there is a whole subject area in between these two variables, comprising the attitudes that grow out of social origins and underlie political action.

Thus, the description of elites' social background tells only what they were before they became elites, leaving their attitudes, attitude formation, and their behavior and its causative influences unexamined. Even outside the Middle East, such matters are not fully elucidated, although here and there some hypotheses have been formulated. Moreover, such preliminary findings only raise a further question: Are hypotheses about elite attitude and policy formation applicable to the Middle East if based on American political socialization, European recruitment, Western personality, or, for that matter, mathematical coalition studies?

Such were some of the questions raised during an initial workshop held in Belmont, Maryland, in March of 1972, which brought together elite specialists, methodologists, and students of the Middle East. Pairs of scholars, one with a Middle East specialization and one working on theories and concepts of elite studies, examined such related aspects of elite politics as coalitions and alliances, technological change, political structures, mass linkages, recruitment and retirement, socialization and formation, personality, and ideology and political culture. The discussions showed further ways of dividing and organizing the subject, not always explicitly spelled out and sometimes confused with each other. Thus, elites are generally studied not as individual biographies or as shadings in a total undifferentiated society, but as groups of people or as aggregates of roles, and yet these latter approaches have different implications and are not always clearly separated. Too often it is assumed that specific groups, such as lawyers or the new middle class or capitalists, have fixed specific behaviors, as if the relation between 'who elites are and what they do were already determined and immutable.

Another distinction emerged from the Belmont conference. Inside and outside the Middle East, elites can be studied through a number of related processes: *absorption*, or the strategies of blockage, recruitment, promotion, and dismissal adopted by incumbents toward aspirant elites; *socialization*, or the experiences of background preparation, attitude formation, and on-the-job training undergone by the elites; and *decision*, or the policies, behaviors, and organizations produced by elites. The study of these three processes can be carried a step further by relating them to each other. What effect do attitudes toward elites (absorption) and attitudes of elites (socialization) have on elite decisions? What are the feedback effects of decision on absorption and socialization? What are the effects, and in which way do they run most strongly, between socialization and absorption processes?

On the other hand, a second and rather different approach regards elites as actors wielding power within organizational structures and acting to stay or rise in their position, with the structures and positions standing as independent variables explaining attitudes and behaviors. The two approaches differ in important ways. In the first, decisions are perceived as resulting from the nature and experience of those who make them, no matter (within limits) where they are. In the second, they are thought to result from the position of the policymakers within a set of political relations, no matter who they are.

Although each approach provides useful answers when pursued rigorously, keeping all other things equal, both approaches are analytical caricatures. Elite studies need to combine the questions of structure and process to explain what happens when particular types of people act in particular positions. Although it is unlikely that any single effort would be able to put such a welter of questions and concerns in order, after the Belmont conference a smaller group was called together to address parts of the subject from two complementary angles. How can political elites best be studied in the Middle East? What conceptual and empirical findings from the study of elites in the Middle East and elsewhere can be employed to further the study of elites anywhere? The group changed its membership over the years, but the focus remained the same. It was decided to orient the collective effort toward a general concern with the process and dynamics of elite functions with an eye toward developing elite studies as a means of grasping the whole political system rather than as an isolated phenomenon in itself.

The whole-system approach to elite studies is a particularly crucial starting point, for anything less abstracts political elites from the context that gives meaning to their actions. In fact, understood in this way, most whole-system studies are in reality elite studies without being explicit about their nature. Disproportionate attention is given to elites, and yet the analytical subdivisions of the subject are not spelled out nor is the elite's relation as such to the rest of the polity or to its institutions and outcomes.

In the developing world, elites as the focus of whole-system studies possess another advantage, since they provide units of analysis when the standard indicators of change and stability that parties and elections offer are not present. The characteristics of elites—social backgrounds, promotion patterns, geographic or ethnic origins, ideological groups, generational cohorts—constitute sensitive data by which to measure reactions to social change and to test processes leading to outputs such as policies and strategies. Rather than trying to refine the use of these characteristics as predictors, the group of scholars meeting after Belmont decided it was more helpful to create a framework for understanding their position within broader and more dynamic processes of elite circulation.

In reviewing the potentialities of elite studies, the group did not envisage simply a cookbook on how to slice, strain, and serve the top political strata in the Middle East, but rather a collection of related essays that would both survey current advances in elite and Middle East studies and open up new perspectives. The result is not a work of new theory—the term is much too pretentious for most of even the good studies in current social science—but rather at the same time a stock-taking and an indication of new directions out of which better conceptual understanding might arise. The final review stage in the preparation of the volume took the form of a workshop, in March of 1975, organized for the Joint Committee by the Center for Near Eastern Studies at New York University. Component chapters were discussed and their usefulness evaluated by a number of historians, political scientists, and sociologists, who were themselves doing research on related Middle East topics under the auspices of the Joint Committee. Hopefully, the preparation behind this collection and its exposition of opportunities for useful analysis in the Middle East, combined with the current public attention given to the area, will promote further advances in the study of elites and will contribute to making the Middle East an academically more attractive place to study.

THE ORGANIZATION OF NEW MIDDLE EAST ELITE STUDIES

Chapter 2 by Charles Butterworth sets the philosophical context for the rest of the work. The author examines and contrasts the philosophical traditions that underlie both the subjects and the analysts. Even contemporary modernized Middle East elites grew up in a culture that legitimizes elite government, whereas both the cultural context of the analysts and the classical writings of elite studies are based on the necessity of controls over the abuse of power, the importance of interactions between the top and the bottom, and the conditions of the social contract.

In Chapter 3, Iliya Harik takes up the argument by examining the assumptions of the most recent tradition of elite studies, of Lasswell and his followers. He reviews and criticizes elite studies inside and outside the Middle East to date, finding them excessively descriptive and "elitist" in their handling of the concept of power. He calls for a reorientation of elite studies to emphasize elite behavior and outputs, elite circulation as part of the process of power generation, and power within a changing field of social forces.

I. William Zartman attempts to meet this challenge in Chapter 4, by developing some theoretical concepts into a model of elite circulation. In his mode, he conceives of elites as spokesmen for demand-bearing groups that form along four dimensions—geopolitical, ideopolitical, sociopolitical, evipolitical (age)—in response to needs and changes in society. Each dimension has its own dynamic; combined, they produce issue realignments and critical shifts in political elites and in their policies, related to specific issues, policies, and elites in the Middle East.

In Chapter 5, Leslie L. Roos, Jr. develops new methods of data generation and analysis that are particularly well suited for portraying and testing concepts of change and circulation. By specifically focusing on methods of causal modeling and quasiexperimentation (controlled use of nationally-generated data), the analyst can turn descriptive data to explanatory use. Such methods are appropriate for the type of data that can be gathered in the Middle East and for making tests of comparison and universality with other areas of the world.

In Chapter 6, Marvin Weinbaum applies some of the preceding notions to a function not usually perceived as being an elite activity, that of mediation, and he broadens the scope of his examination to include mediating elites operating both among elites themselves and between the summit of power and its lower relations. Mediation is a specifically, if not uniquely, Middle Eastern function, illustrated by a wealth of Middle East data. It can be broken down for analysis into positions and roles, providing a series of correlations by which to gauge power as social interaction.

Russell Stone closes the study in Chapter 7 with a review of knowledge to date on the subject of elite outputs or the decision process regarding the social consequences of elite behavior. The actual effects of policy and its determinants have been the subject of little study to date, within the Middle East or without. A reorientation of inquiry in this direction, on the basis of a number of different approaches already available, provides a new thrust to elite studies. Different from descriptive background analysis, the approach nonetheless builds on previous work to supply new answers to more interesting questions about elite behavior. This book only begins that new search, of course, but it does aspire to provide a coherent rationale and guideline for it.

2

PHILOSOPHY, STORIES, AND THE STUDY OF ELITES

Charles E. Butterworth

INTRODUCTION

Part of the attraction the Middle East and North Africa have for Westerners derives from the unique blend of old and new encountered there. City streets are thronged with men wearing somber robes and traditional headdresses, or the latest Italian cut in business suits, or bright sports clothes as well as with women decorously clad in long simple dresses or jauntily decked out in the current suggestive trend in skirts or trousers. Wooden-wheeled carts decorated with Quranic verses and pulled by donkeys vie with powerful Mercedes and raucous Alfas for right of way. Centuries-old city walls stand proudly opposite garish new cement office buildings. Groups of children hurry to the local mosque to sit at the feet of a revered sheikh and learn to recite the Quran, while their brothers and sisters rush to secretarial or computer school to learn skills that can be placed at the service of modern technology. On street corners, the great literature of the past, printed in sedate but inexpensive paper-covered volumes, is displayed alongside brightly colored magazines proclaiming new insights into the news and mores of the day.

My concern here is with this last aspect of the blend between the old and the new, the continued influence exercised by the best literature of the older tradition at the same time that modern, Western modes of thought ignorant of that literature make increasing demands for the attention of Middle Eastern and North African peoples. Along with their first lessons about the history of the Islamic empire, school children are introduced to the formal theory of the state

I am especially grateful to Stephen L. Elkin for his judicious criticism of this chapter.

that takes its fundamental principles from Quranic injunctions and traditionally accepted sayings of the prophet. The literature dedicated to teaching monarchs how to rule well—Nizām al-Mulk's *The Book of Government*, Kai Ka'ūs's *A Mirror for Princes*, and the fascinating stories of the *Kalilah and Dimnah* or of the *Thousand and One Nights* collections—is read in secondary schools and universities throughout the Middle East and North Africa. Similarly, university students are exposed to more thoughtful accounts about the advantages of rule by one or a few. They read Alfarabi's *Virtuous City* and his *Political Regime* or *Book of Religion*, as well as Averroes's *Decisive Treatise* and *Uncovering of the Clear Paths*, in addition to the basic writings of authors like al-Māwardī, Ibn Taimiyyah, and Ibn Khaldūn. In this tradition, however, there is no John Locke who might insist that "the liberty of man in society is to be under no other legislative power but that established by consent in the common-wealth" (Locke 1960, para. 22). Nor is there a Jean-Jacques Rousseau who might define the fundamental political problem as one of "finding a form of association which defends and protects the person and goods of each associate with all of the common strength and by which each person in binding himself to all the others obeys only himself and remains as free as before" (Rousseau 1964c, 1.6). And it is only rarely, almost exclusively in advanced university courses, that students are taught about the political literature of the West, which sets itself in opposition to the older idea that rule by one or a few is best.

Thus, even though we are aware of the deep interest in Western constitutionalism that developed during the latter part of the last century and of the more recent interest in socialist models, it seems reasonable to assume that the teaching of the traditional literature lives on in the minds of contemporary Middle Eastern and North African peoples. However, I do not propose to embark upon a detailed study of the political socialization of potential or actual rulers in order to show the influence of that literature. My goal is more modest. Since at the very least this traditional literature provides a common set of opinions to which most Middle Easterners and North Africans are exposed and which they seem to hold, I propose to look at the basic themes of this literature and to explain the kind of reasoning that prompts those themes. Such an approach should permit us to appreciate the cultural background of the people whose political environment we are seeking to describe.*

Still, in keeping with my earlier evocation of the unique blend between the old and the new in the Middle East and North Africa, there is another important body of literature I dare not ignore. This literature—the political and sociological treatises basic to modern social science—is significant for a number of reasons, but

---

*For an example of this approach with respect to more contemporary literature, see Leites (1953, pp. 21–22).

especially for the role it plays in relation to the kind of studies set forth in the rest of this volume. Although the debt is not always explicitly acknowledged, contemporary interest in the study of elites is primarily derived from the compelling analyses of the great social theorists of the late nineteenth and early twentieth centuries: Pareto, Mosca, and Michels. In formulating their own views, they, in turn, were deeply indebted to earlier political and social thinkers of the Western tradition: Machiavelli, Hobbes, Locke, and Rousseau.

Now the basic difference between this literature that lies behind modern social science and the traditional literature of the Middle East and North Africa is that, in the latter, rule by one or a few is self-consciously favored whereas, in the former, there is a tendency to blame that kind of rule. In the West, this difference is reflected in the extent to which current studies about rule by small groups or elites are motivated by a desire to show that, whatever may formally be said about the democratic character of a given regime, power is really concentrated in the hands of a few who rule without regard to the wishes of the many. In the Middle East and North Africa, this difference finds expression in the extent to which such practice is accepted, in a matter-of-fact manner, as normal. While most of us who study the political regimes of the Middle East and North Africa are aware of the basic difference between these two bodies of literature, we are reluctant to do more than recognize that it exists. Or, if we do give it more than passing recognition, we seek to explain its existence in terms of external forces that influence ideas or account for the persistence of patterns of ideas. Yet precisely because our own thought about politics can be traced to the same sources as that of the Middle East and North Africa, Plato and Aristotle, we cannot adopt a mode of explanation that presupposes the merit of one or the other tradition. What is needed is an explanation of each tradition as it presents itself, an explanation that pays careful attention to the dialogue going on between those who contributed to each tradition. Thus, in an attempt to arrive at such an explanation, I will follow my analysis of the basic themes of the traditional literature of the Middle East and North Africa with a general analysis of the literature leading to modern social science and the current interest in the study of elites. In other words, the attempt to appreciate the cultural background of those whose political regimes we study will be complemented by an attempt to appreciate our own cultural background and especially those aspects of it that influence our study of other people.

THE PHILOSOPHIC TRADITION IN ISLAM

The historical pattern of rule in Islamic communities has been monarchic. When Muhammad first began to control the affairs of the early group of believers in Medina, he did so along monarchic lines. After his death, the crisis of leadership was resolved by the most respected members of the early group of believers agreeing to name one person as his successor or *khalīfah*. This idea of a *khalīfah* to Muhammad was accepted to such an extent that subsequent political disputes arose because of disagreements over the identity of the legitimate successor, rather than because of disagreements about what form of government should be adopted.

Although all members of the regime agreed that the supreme authority was the divine law *(sharī'ah)* revealed to Muhammad and that all political decisions had to conform to the tenets of that law, it would be misleading to think of this regime as subject to popular will in any way. If there was any kind of compact that bound the members of the community, it was one that justified sovereignty being held in the hands of one ruler: the Commander of the Faithful *(amīr al-mu'minīn)*.* Other factors also helped to ensure that authority be exercised by a few. Whereas Muhammad had been faced with the task of forming the small group of early believers into a community that could withstand the attacks of those opposed to the new religious movement, his successors had the tasks of preserving an already established community and of ensuring that it adhere to the letter and spirit of Muhammad's prescriptions. Since those prescriptions had been set forth in a text considered sacred as well as in verbal utterances held to be second in importance only to the sacred text, it was inevitable that a group of people schooled in interpreting the text and in assessing the validity of the utterances arise.† Consequently, what began as a simple community ruled by a unique individual, or by an intimate associate who understood the goals of that individual, gradually grew into a complex and intricately ordered community comprising different groups of select people who exercised varying degrees of power, but who were nonetheless subordinate to the will of the supreme ruler.

For a number of reasons, the authors who concern us here accepted this kind of community structure as sound and tried to explain what justified it or to suggest how it might be improved. These authors fall into two distinct groups. One, comprised of thinkers like Alfarabi and Averroes, discerned deep philosophical wisdom in the teaching of the ancient Greeks and tried to pass that teaching on to the Islamic community. The other, represented by people like Nizām al-Mulk and Kai Ka'ūs, was content to limit itself to conventional wisdom and to explain its practical worth for better rulership.

---

*See Khadduri (1969, pp. 7–18) and Hobbes (1972, 1.6–11).

†See Māwardī (1966, pp. 3–4, 21), Laoust (1970, pp. 14–22, 230–79), and Rosenthal (1958, pp. 24, 26).

Alfarabi

During the first half of the ninth century, the caliphs al-Ma'mūn (813–833) and al-Mu'tasim (833–842) encouraged the translation of ancient Greek works. Among the works translated were Plato's *Republic, Laws,* and *Timaeus*; Aristotle's *Organon, Physics, De Anima, Metaphysics,* and *Nicomachean Ethics* as well as all of his smaller physical works such as the *De Caelo* and the *Parva Naturalia*; and most of Galen's logical and medical works.* The works of Plato and Aristotle were widely read and commented on, as were those of Galen, but Alfarabi (870–950) was the first to make their teaching an integral part of a wider Islamic philosophy. His subtle use of Plato and Aristotle to explain the grounds of the Islamic regime, that is, to show under what conditions it can be said to be a good regime, is best displayed in his *Book of Religion*.

The *Kitāb al-Millah* or *Book of Religion* opens with a definition of its subject, *millah*: "Religion consists of opinions and actions which are determined and restricted by the conditions prescribed for a community by its first ruler" (Alfarabi 1968a, p. 43). That definition is followed by an explanation that the size of a community may extend from a group as small as a tribe to an association of people as large as many nations. But, whatever the size of a community, Alfarabi insists upon the necessity of distinguishing the kind of goals the first ruler sets out for the community and of judging their merit. From the very beginning, then, there is an attempt to speak of religion in the same terms in which one normally speaks of political rule. And, by the way he enumerates the goals the first ruler must prescribe for the community, Alfarabi makes an even closer link between religion and political rule. Throughout this introductory explanation, the whole problem of establishing a religion for a community is presented as being the same as that of exercising the craft of ruling.

This identification of religion and political rule is achieved in yet another way. Since religion is always associated with revelation from God, Alfarabi tries to explain how his first ruler comes to an awareness of the opinions and actions he will set down for the community. Here, the argument is made that revelation either provides the first ruler with a set of opinions and actions already determined for the people of the community or that it provides him with the faculty for determining what opinions and actions are needed (Alfarabi 1968a, p. 44). In other words, the only thing that distinguishes a prophet from a king is the way in which one comes to an understanding of the opinions and actions that must be prescribed to the citizens of the community; whereas the prophet receives these opinions and actions as determined by God, the king uses his practical reason to arrive at the opinions and actions suitable for his people. As his enu-

---

*See Walzer (1962, pp. 5–8).

meration of these opinions and actions clearly demonstrates, Alfarabi considers them to be the same for all wisely governed regimes and for all virtuous religions. The reason Alfarabi is less concerned about whether revelation is direct or indirect than about religious and political rule is that he wants to show that the end of virtuous political life is the same as the end of virtual religious life: ultimate happiness.

While it cannot be denied that Alfarabi's argument has a familiar ring of pious conformity to established doctrine, there is a greater depth to the book than such a judgment would reveal. In addition to the surface argument, which clearly provides theoretical justification for the community established by Muhammad and carried on in an expanded version by his successors, there is another, less apparent theme. By defining revelation as being of two kinds, Alfarabi prepared the ground for thinking critically about the way the opinions and actions of virtuous religion should be determined. After all, if the first ruler could have acquired his own understanding of these opinions and actions by means of a rational capacity given to him by God, we can submit the prescriptions of any given first ruler to investigation in order to understand better what he was trying to achieve. Before setting about such an investigation, Alfarabi first shows that the very goals endorsed by virtuous religion and the means it uses to achieve those goals make it subordinate to practical philosophy and especially to political science (Alfarabi 1968a, pp. 46–47, 51–52). He then investigates what political science seeks to achieve and eventually shows that the intellectual faculty guiding political science is practical wisdom or prudence (Alfarabi 1968a, pp. 50–66, esp. 54–61). In this way, Alfarabi shows that the second type of revelation is really nothing but prudence. The philosophically-minded man is thus just as capable of being a first ruler of a community as is the prophet. Or, differently stated, the philosopher is a prophet in the most important respect. This theme is supported by Alfarabi's attempt to show in the closing pages of the treatise that the first ruler must have a view of the natural order of the universe and bring his prescriptions into conformity with that order.

Whatever the ultimate implications of this involved argument, it is at the very least clear that Alfarabi was intent upon showing the necessary relation between wisdom and political rule. Whether the founder of Islam be considered to have received direct or indirect revelation, it is clear that his prescriptions are in accordance with what reason would teach. Moreover, it is also manifest that his successors need to be able to understand those prescriptions in all their depth, or have access to someone who can explain them, if they are to carry out those prescriptions according to the intention of the first ruler. And, according to the argument of the treatise as a whole, it is impossible to reach such an understanding without having acquired a deep awareness of the order of the universe and of its various parts.

This same kind of argument occurs in Alfarabi's other works, and his general argument seems to be that good political rule requires extensive knowledge of nature as well as of the order of things to be discerned in nature (Alfarabi 1968b, pp. 69-74). The reason for such an argument is that political decisions must be made with respect to ultimate goals, and these can best be decided upon when proper attention is paid to the natural order. In one work, Alfarabi illustrates the various errors that can be made with respect to deciding upon the goals of political life by enumerating the kinds of political association that deserve blame. In his view, there are three basic kinds of blameworthy political associations. These associations are distinguished from the correct kind of political association because their citizens aim at some end other than ultimate happiness, due to ignorance of what ultimate happiness really is, or because they have rejected the goal of ultimate happiness and tried to obtain something else, or because they have an inadequate grasp of what ultimate happiness is (Alfarabi 1964, pp. 87-104). According to this schema, rule by many is blameworthy because the citizens of such an association refuse any hierarchy and value only freedom (Alfarabi 1964, pp. 99-102). Since, in the earlier part of this work, Alfarabi has demonstrated the way in which the political order of the community should imitate the natural hierarchy of the universe and since he thinks freedom is properly exercised only when it is in the service of ultimate happiness, he rejects the goals of that association.

In sum, Alfarabi favors the rule of one or a few because he thinks it unlikely that many people will have enough discernment to choose the proper goals for the political community. He is equally pessimistic about the ability of most human beings to understand what must be done to preserve good laws or to keep harmful changes from occurring. Whether it is a question of founding a regime—in which case the arguments relative to the character required for a first ruler are applicable—or one of preserving the regime founded by a first ruler, Alfarabi thinks it essential that the few most intelligent men or the one most intelligent man be looked to for leadership. And, since the people are so incapable of understanding what is in their best interests, it is often necessary to use a special kind of language to address them or to explain to them what is being attempted. While this language is not simply false, it is not simply true either. It is designed to lead people gently, by means of images they can easily grasp, from one set of opinions to another set closer to the truth.* Precisely because Alfarabi thought it necessary to take such precautions with most of the citizens, he could never endorse a regime that deferred to those citizens for political guidance. Like Socrates and Plato, Alfarabi thought that intellectual acumen was the greatest natural scarcity. As a result, he devoted his efforts to explaining the grounds of political rule based on the superior understanding of nature and people's place in nature, which might be acquired by the careful study a few could undertake.

---

*See Alfarabi (1968a, pp. 44-45, 47-48; 1964, pp. 85-87).

Averroes

Averroes (1126–1198) continued Alfarabi's basic argument, but looked at the political order from a slightly different perspective. Persuaded, as was Alfarabi, that there are clearly discernible differences in the intellectual capacities of the various groups of citizens, Averroes labored mightily to persuade others that those differences needed to be respected. One aspect of his activity was the attempt to prevent theologians and jurists from exercising too much power over the simpler citizens or over the rulers. To a certain extent, this effort was a response to a unique difficulty that had become acute in his lifetime. However, the grounds on which Averroes solved this temporal problem were the same as the ones on which he based his more theoretical teaching. For him, as for Alfarabi, it was essential to keep in mind the intellectual inequality among human beings and to ensure that political rule would be in the hands of those who could combine theoretical knowledge with practical wisdom.

The unique difficulty Averroes had to meet can be traced to the character of the political regime under which he lived in the Maghreb. Shortly after his birth, followers of the zealous religious leader Ibn Tumart succeeded in overthrowing the Almoravide dynasty and in establishing their own Almohade dynasty. In keeping with the origins of this dynasty, the rulers tended to be quite strict in matters of religion. As a result, pious men, ascetics, masters of tradition, jurists, and theologians came to enjoy an especially favored place in the dynasty. Their power was such that, even though Averroes's personal merit earned him the distinction of serving as political advisor, physician, and chief judge to two rulers who were quite learned and who greatly enjoyed talking about deep philosophical questions with him, the religious faction was able to have him banished to a remote little village shortly before the end of his life on vague charges of impiety.* Nonetheless, it was not the abuse the religious faction made of its power when it attempted to blacken his own reputation that troubled Averroes, but the completely mistaken manner in which it tried to instruct the populace about religious questions in order to increase popular support of its own beliefs. Convinced that this issue posed immediate practical questions as well as deeper philosophical problems, Averroes had combated the religious faction long before his own moment of ignominy.

His admittedly popular and political works are especially dedicated to showing what was wrong with the approach of the religious faction.† In these works he accepts the Islamic revelation as true and then tries to explain its significance for the different members of the community. His two basic arguments

---

*See Marrākushī (1893, pp. 154–68, 194–214, 226–67), Goldziher (1903, passim), Dozy (1932, pp. 137–66), and Renan (1949, pp. 25–54).

†See Averroes (1954, pp. 209–10, 358, 427–28; 1959, p. 18; 1963, pp. 132–33).

are that God had especially chosen some men to whom He had revealed His
wisdom and that this revelation of His wisdom admits of a twofold division.*
When Averroes says that God had especially chosen some men to whom He had
revealed His wisdom, he means that God had enabled these men to understand
His law and to follow its prescriptions. Averroes is not thinking of prophets here,
but of those who come after a prophet. He contends that God gave these select
individuals the ability to grasp that part of His knowledge hidden from the rest
of humanity and helped them understand the intention of the message brought
down by His prophet. In keeping with this special gift, God has made clear to
these select men the errors and distortions into which other men fall and has
explained to them that certain interpretations of His law are simply not permissible. This last injunction is closely related to Averroes's argument that the
divine law admits of a twofold division. His point is that the law can either be
understood in its most obvious and apparent sense or that it may be subjected to
interpretation. However, because of their intellectual limitations, the populace
should accept the whole of the law in its apparent sense and not seek to interpret it. Even the wise should not seek to interpret all parts of the divine law, but
should accept some parts according to their apparent meaning and interpret only
those parts clearly open to interpretation.†

The political thrust of Averroes's arguments is that God's intention with
respect to His community had been neglected. By providing Muhammad with a
divine law and explaining that different kinds of men would have to understand
parts of that law in different ways while agreeing on major parts of it according
to its apparent sense, God sought to provide the faithful with a clear plan for a
good and decent life. That intention had been neglected, and a grave danger had
arisen that Averroes sought to combat. However, even though the immediate
danger had its source in the religious faction of his own community, Averroes
tries to raise the issue to a more general level and to speak of the way it was
reflected in Islam as a whole. He thus contends that, because people have strayed
from the proper understanding of the law, erroneous sects have arisen and that
each sect has introduced new arguments and innovative interpretations of the
divine law. On the basis of these interpretations, each sect has advocated and
permitted the labeling of those who disagree with its understanding as innovators
or heretics. Moreover, by attempting to teach the populace about matters clearly

---

*See Averroes (1963, pp. 132-33, 181-82). This work is the third part of a trilogy,
whose first and second parts are the *Damīmah* and the *Kitāb Fasl al-Maqāl*; see Mahdi
(1964, pp. 117-25).

†Averroes (1959, pp. 7-8, 13-18). In this work, Averroes explains that the divine law
has a threefold division. There are passages that must be taken literally by all, passages that
must be taken literally by most but which the learned can interpret, and passages about
which there is some doubt as to whether they should be taken literally or be interpreted.

beyond their comprehension, the adherents of these sects have induced the populace to scorn all philosophical investigation and have constructed unnecessarily complex and confusing arguments about the basic articles of religious faith.

Still keeping the argument at a certain level of generality, Averroes seeks to solve the problem first by expounding the apparent aspects of the beliefs to which the populace must adhere in order to conform to the intention of the divine law and then by explaining the necessary beliefs by which faith is completed. To accomplish his first goal, he investigates Muhammad's intention with respect to apparent beliefs. To accomplish the second goal, Averroes looks again at Muhammad's intention and seeks to explain the root of the divine law, a process that enables him to show what is incorrect in the interpretations of the necessary beliefs set forth by each sect. Throughout his discussion, Averroes uses principles of philosophic reasoning and alludes frequently to basic logical propositions, thereby proving how useful philosophy can be in matters of faith. He also insists repeatedly on the basic limitations of the different classes of the people and reminds the reader over and over of Muhammad's own awareness of those limitations and of his injunctions to speak to different people according to their level of understanding (Averroes 1963, pp. 136-46, 148, 153-54, 157-58, 162-63, 166-67, 170-75, 178-81, 182-85, 186-88, 189-93, 203-6, 228-30, 241-44, 244-51).

Even though this aspect of Averroes's teaching is addressed to a specific problem, it is in basic agreement with his more theoretical teaching. His theoretical teaching as it relates to politics is set forth most clearly in his commentaries on Plato's *Republic* and on Aristotle's *Nicomachean Ethics* and *Rhetoric*. In these commentaries, Averroes argues that there is basic agreement between Plato and Aristotle about the necessity for the best regime to be ruled by the one person who is truly wise or by the few people who are of such a character. It is his contention that the kind of wisdom which gives a person the right to rule is theoretical knowledge of the whole universe and that the person who possesses this kind of knowledge is necessarily a sound ruler.

While there is little question that such an argument accords with the major thrust of the discussion in Books V-VIII of the *Republic*, there is room for much doubt as to whether it accurately captures Aristotle's argument about the relationship between theoretical knowledge and practical wisdom in Book VI of the *Nicomachean Ethics* or his general statements about the value of rhetoric in the opening chapters of the *Rhetoric*. Celebrated even until our time as *the* commentator, primarily of Aristotle but also of Plato, Averroes never perceives his task to be limited to a simple restatement of Aristotle's or Plato's arguments. Indeed, he frequently uses his commentaries to set forth his own teachings, without indicating a basic difference between his ideas and those of the author upon whom he is commenting, and does so in such a skillful manner that it is not easy to determine whether he has accurately reflected his author's opinion. For example, in his commentary on the *Nichomachean Ethics*, Averroes argues that the virtue of the rational part of the soul, which gives the truth appropriate for right principle in moral actions, is intelligence. Once he has established this point, it is easy for him to show that practical wisdom is subordinate to theoretical knowledge. Similarly, in his commentary on the *Rhetoric*, he agrees with Aristotle's arguments about the limitations of rhetorical speech, but goes on to suggest that the only person who can use rhetoric correctly is a philosopher. And in his commentary on Plato's *Republic*, Averroes ingenuously explains that he has decided to follow his commentary on Aristotle's *Nicomachean Ethics* with this commentary, because Aristotle's *Politics* has not yet come into his hands and because there is very little difference between the *Republic* and the *Politics*.*

The problems inherent in the position he takes with respect to the *Politics* and the *Republic* are far-reaching, especially because of the question that arises from Aristotle's qualified endorsement of rule by many in Books III and IV of the *Politics* as contrasted with Socrates' provocative arguments in Books V–VII of the *Republic* in favor of rule by a few men thoroughly trained in philosophy. By his peculiar reading of Plato and Aristotle, Averroes manages to present them both as authorities for his view that rule should be in the hands of one person of intelligence or in the hands of a few such people. However, given the perspective adopted at the beginning of this essay, there is no reason to devote greater attention to Averroes's interpretations of the *Republic* and the *Nicomachean Ethics* or the *Rhetoric*. Due to highly unusual circumstances, neither the commentary on the *Republic* nor that on the *Nicomachean Ethics* seems to have survived in Arabic. Because the only extant versions we have of them are Hebrew and Latin translations, it is only due to recent interest in Averroes in the West that even one of these works has been edited and translated into a modern language. Thus, very few Middle Easterners and North Africans have had any awareness of the views he sets forth in either of these works. The fate of his commentary on the *Rhetoric* was different, but did not lead to that work being any more widely read. It was preserved in Arabic and even edited in 1960. However, it was never studied very much, because interest in the Islamic world in rhetoric was directed more to studies of Quranic rhetoric *(balāghah)* than to classical rhetoric. For all these reasons, the Averroes read and studied in the Middle East and North Africa is the Averroes of the popular or political works, but an Averroes whose views accord completely with the Averroes of the theoretical works.

---

*See Averroes (1562, folios 90 D–F, 93 E–F; 1960, pp. 9–10, 247–49; 1974, pp. 21–24 Rosenthal pagination).

CHARMING TALES AND PRINCELY WISDOM

Both Alfarabi and Averroes give explicit reasons for proposing that ruler-ship be in the hands of one person or a few people. Ultimately, those reasons can be traced to their understanding of human nature, and their understanding of human nature is itself part of a more comprehensive view they both had about the universe. In their approach to human matters, they continue the general line of thought expressed by Plato and Aristotle and demonstrate an exceptionally fine understanding of those two philosophers. And their work is faithful to that of Plato and Aristotle in an even more important respect: Alfarabi and Averroes are more philosophic than pragmatic. Their thinking about rulership is addressed to questions larger than that immediate one of who or how many should rule. For them, as for other political philosophers, the quest was truth about the fundamental political questions.

Nizām al-Mulk and Kai Ka'ūs, on the other hand, were interested in the immediate, practical questions of political life. Even though it is possible to discover their reasons for preferring the rule of one or a few, they are not concerned with defending that preference. They accept rulership by one as a given and then set about advising the ruler on how to make sound decisions when confronted with difficult situations or on how to organize his regime so that difficulties will not occur. When they do refer to human nature to make a point, they refer to a popular view of human nature. And when they go beyond human things to a broader view of the universe, they have recourse to the view set forth in the revelation accorded Muhammad.

Nizām al-Mulk

The *Siyāsat-Nāma* or *Book of Government* by Nizām al-Mulk (1018–1092) is the more interesting treatise. According to Nizām al-Mulk, the book was written in order to explain the basic things a ruler would have to take into consideration and to illustrate the qualities required of a ruler. As this goal is pursued, it becomes clear that only rare individuals can acquire such qualities or correctly weigh the numerous considerations to which Nizām al-Mulk alludes. Consequently, his book serves as a defense of rule by one or a few highly competent individuals and as a criticism of rule by many.

Formally, this argument is set forth in fifty chapters, divided into two parts, that discuss different principles of rulership. Although there does not appear to be any order to the way the book is divided into chapters or any significance to its being divided into two parts, the number of stories used to illustrate the principles of rulership is striking. Fully one-half of the chapters contains stories and even stories within stories. Their importance for the interpretation of the book arises from the broader perspective they lend to the narrative. Frequently, the stories raise issues that Nizām al-Mulk does not directly address and thus challenge the reader to think about their fuller implications as well as to raise broader questions.

For example, Nizām al-Mulk's stories about the need to have information concerning the conduct of landlords, tax collectors, judges, and other appointed officials are as instructive about the evils of greed as they are about the need for the ruler to gain information (Mulk 1960, chaps. 5-7, esp. 6.2-13, 7.9-23). As these stories make clear, the problem with greed is that it drives people to seek self-interest even to the extent of neglecting duty. Judges seem most susceptible to it, for their position is such that people trust in them and ask them to hold valuables in safekeeping when they go away on trips. Ostensibly, the stories simply stress how important it is for the ruler to be aware of the force the passion of greed exerts on people, especially on those who hold offices of trust, and for him, therefore, to devise ways of knowing when they are under its sway. But this ostensible teaching is not the only moral of the stories. To the extent that they are stories about greed, they beg to be read in conjunction with the other stories in the volume about greed. When that is done, Nizām al-Mulk's teaching expands from a simple set of principles about how a ruler should handle greedy judges to more general reflections about the evils of popular rule. After all, the passion of greed is not only a vice of those who have power. Indeed, the greed of the common people is such that it makes them want to break down all distinctions of property and of private relationships, even those of husband and wife. Arguing that property distinctions and private relationships need to be maintained for the sake of order, Nizām al-Mulk blames this desire on the people. His contention is that because such a desire is so strong among the people and will therefore always manifest itself when they have political power, they should never be given such power (Mulk 1960, 44.4-13). The assumption that leads to this judgment is that moral virtues, not moral vices, must guide rulership. But because he is also persuaded that it is not easy to acquire moral virtues and that very few individuals are capable of acquiring the moral virtues necessary for wise rule, Nizām al-Mulk believes power should be given only to a few.

The other stories in the treatise illustrate both the need for these qualities and the difficulty of acquiring them. For example, it is readily evident that good rulership requires a special kind of cleverness not available to many people. The ruler must be quick to recognize and punish wrongdoers, but he must be ever mindful that the populace recognizes the justice of his punishment. Even if he is convinced one of his judges has cheated a citizen out of money, the ruler must be sure the people see that the judge did cheat and that they do not think the ruler punished the judge because of jealousy. To illustrate the difficulty of being sufficiently clever, Nizām al-Mulk relates a tale that poses an extraordinary problem: what would a wise ruler do if a merchant presented himself and complained that he had placed 2,000 dinars in a sealed brocade purse and given it to a prominent judge for safekeeping, but had received his purse back perfectly intact with 2,000 coppers in it instead of the dinars? Sultan Mahmūd ibn Sabuk-tigin was faced with such a dilemma and surmised that, if the merchant were telling the truth, the purse must have been cut open so that the dinars could be replaced with coppers and then repaired by a very skillful mender. Not knowing how to locate such a mender without arousing suspicion and thereby giving the crafty judge time to escape or prepare an excuse, Sultan Mahmūd secretly rent a precious bed coverlet made of gold thread and then watched to see how his servant, fearful that he would be blamed for the damage if he did not restore the coverlet to its original condition, would have it repaired. Once the mender of the coverlet was identified and acknowledged having mended the purse, Sultan Mahmūd could confront the judge and punish him (Mulk 1960, 13.15-19, 13.2-14). When we read Nizām al-Mulk's tale as a problem, it becomes abun-dantly clear that this kind of cleverness is not easily acquired and thus not possessed by many people.

Similarly, the ability to exercise the cruelty or ruthlessness that a ruler threatened by rebellious citizens must have in order to maintain his power is rarely found among people and is very difficult to acquire. Nizām al-Mulk's story of the manner in which Nushirwan the Just punished Mazdak and destroyed all of his followers depicts a ruler who far exceeds Machiavelli's Oliverotto in sheer brutality. When Nushirwan had discovered that Mazdak's claim to be a prophet was completely fraudulent and had shown his father, King Qubad, how Mazdak had managed to trick people into thinking that the sacred fire of Zoro-aster could talk to him, a major problem remained to be solved. Nushirwan had to seize not only Mazdak, but all of his followers as well, and he had to make sure that none of them would escape and then attempt to carry on Mazdak's project elsewhere in the kingdom. Nushirwan's solution follows.

First, alleging that he was about to convert to Mazdak's belief and needed only to be shown the magnitude of his retinue to become fully persuaded, Nushirwan had his father ask Mazdak to make a list of all of his followers. He invited Mazdak and all of his followers to a special feast that would mark his conversion and made such extravagant preparations for the feast that none of the followers would wish to be absent. When the day of the feast arrived, Nushirwan provided an abundance of food and followed the eating with a drink-ing party at which everyone was induced to consume a great deal of wine. Once the drinking had progressed to the desired point, he arose and announced that he wanted to present each of Mazdak's followers with a robe of honor. Since they were so numerous, Nushirwan suggested that groups of twenty or thirty pass into an adjoining room to be fitted for the robes and then proceed to another reception hall where everyone would gather for more festivities as soon as all the robes had been distributed. As each group of Mazdak's followers passed into the adjoining room, its members were seized by Nushirwan's soldiers and carried out to a parade field behind the castle where shallow pits had been dug. Thrust head-first into these pits, they were buried up to their waists in orderly lines. Under the pretense of according Mazdak even greater esteem, Nushirwan insisted that he be the last to pass into the adjoining room for his robe of honor. Then he, too, was seized and brought out to the parade field. But instead of being buried head first, Mazdak was buried feet first in a pit so situated that he was forced to gaze upon the legs of all of his followers grotesquely pointing up toward the sky. Scornfully urging Mazdak to command them in death as he would have commanded them in life, Nushirwan invited the people of the kingdom to come behold Mazdak in his terrible plight.* Part of Nushirwan's goal in permitting the people to taunt and ridicule Mazdak was to alert them to the terrible fate that befell those who challenged the established order and to show them that no one could escape his punishment. Finally, sensing that his father's gullibility in the whole affair was a sign that he was no longer fit to rule, Nushirwan asked him to transfer the power to him.

While the cruelty of Nushirwan's action cannot fail to impress us, Nizām al-Mulk seems more intent upon stressing the practical moral of the story, which is that exceptional threats to otherwise commendable rulership need to be countered with exceptional cleverness and cruelty. In this way, he brings us face to face with all of the problematic questions in political life. Yet not all of his stories set forth the qualities needed for sound rule in such a harsh pedagogical manner. Many of the stories illustrate the faults a ruler may have and thus serve as negative examples of the qualities of character and, above all, of judgment that rulership demands. There are also subtle allusions to the cleverness of women and, thus, something of a suggestion about the way rulership really functions at times (Mulk 1960, 4.5-24, 10.2-16, 40.10-12, 41.21-31, 42.3-6, 46.8-17).

Despite these leitmotifs, the constant theme in Nizām al-Mulk's treatise is that, because those who hold supreme power are often the wisest and most courageous men in the kingdom and have earned their posts of authority by dint of their excellence, rule by one is good and desirable. In this respect, his stories confirm the idea that those who rule deserve to rule, that is, that in what really counts the universe is well ordered. And since Nizām al-Mulk was careful enough to recount more stories about a good ruler ruling well than about a bad ruler making mistakes, his work testifies to that order. One example of this is the story of how Alptigin rose from the rank of slave to the post of army commander and gained a wide reputation for courageous actions as well as for irreproachable honesty. Another example is the way Sabuktigin, the father of Sultan Mahmūd, rose from the rank of slave to replace Alptigin and went on to accomplish such great deeds that he was given special honor by the caliph (Mulk 1960, 27.3-4, 5-21).

---

*See Mulk (1960, 44.1-26, esp. 44.15-26, 46.8-17) and Machiavelli (1950, chap. 8).

Yet another example, this one of a somewhat different order, is the one set forth in the story about the humble tailor of Baghdad who could compel powerful judges and nobles to turn away from evil ways simply by warning them that he knew of their wrongdoing. The tailor's remarkable power derived from the respect the caliph accorded his judgment, respect he earned in the following way. One afternoon the tailor had seen a Turkish noble dragging a married woman into his house against her will. Even though the tailor and the elders of the quarter remonstrated with the Turkish noble, he would not release the woman. Later in the evening the tailor, who also happened to be the muezzin of the neighborhood mosque, hit upon the idea of going up to the minaret and calling to morning prayer in order to trick the Turkish noble into thinking a new day had broken and thus into sending the woman out of his house. However, it happened that the caliph al-Mu'tasim heard the call to prayer and, concluding that anyone who would call to prayer at the wrong hour must be seeking to undermine the faith, angrily sent a guard to bring the guilty muezzin before him. After the tailor had explained the reason for this extraordinary call to prayer, the caliph rescued the woman, interceded with her husband on her behalf, and had the Turkish noble brought before him. As punishment for this ignoble deed, al-Mu'tasim ordered that he be placed in a sack and flailed with heavy clubs by two large men until he was smashed to smithereens. The sack of bone splinters was then hauled ostentatiously through the streets and thrown into the Tigris. Once reports of this incident spread to members of the court, there was no one who did not fear the little tailor nor studiously avoid giving him cause to report individual wrongdoing to the caliph. Consequently, it was enough for the tailor to inform a judge or noble of a complaint that had come his way for the injustice to be corrected.*

Like the other stories, this one has a number of themes beyond the obvious one of illustrating the ruler should take care to have judicious informers like the tailor. It also reminds us that, in a good regime, the caliph or sultan will have such informers and that we will thus always be able to receive justice. And through the description of the tailor, it emphasizes the qualities we should look for in a good ruler. The latter point is made more persuasive by Nizām al-Mulk's use of a story within a story to tell us about the tailor and his power. Only because of the insistent curiosity of someone whom the tailor had helped does he agree to relate the involved tale about how he acquired his unique power. From that tale we learn how the tailor's own insistence on remaining in his humble position and on verifying any complaint brought to his attention before

---

*See Mulk (1960, 7.9–23, esp. 19–23). According to Andrew Hacker, the humble tailor ploys a different trade in the contemporary United States, but has power similar to Nizām al-Mulk's character. See Hacker's contention that "it is entirely possible to engage in rule without being part of a ruling class" (1975, pp. 9–13, esp. 13).

acting upon it especially increased his power. In other words, the form of the tale shows us that he bore perfect witness in the most important respect to the qualities all would wish to see in a ruler: he neither profited from his power nor used it unwisely.

These few examples must suffice to indicate the way in which Nizām al-Mulk's stories frequently have a deeper significance than the one he explicitly draws from them at the moment of recounting them. This does not mean to imply that they contribute to a secret teaching that is in some important manner opposed to the superficial argument of the text. There is no evidence of such a teaching. It does mean, however, that they merit closer examination in order to see what they indicate about the problems of ruling above and beyond the limited lessons Nizām al-Mulk uses them to illustrate. It would be wrong to object that such reflections are unwarranted here, since it is unlikely that many people have ever read Nizām al-Mulk in such a light. Even if most of those who read his book as schoolchildren in the Middle East and North Africa have been taught to read it strictly as a simple apology for rule by one or a few, it is by no means impossible that some see the very implications alluded to here and thus become even more persuaded that rule by one or a few is good.

Kai Ka'ūs

As has already been stated, the *Qābūs-Nāma* or the *Book of Qābūs* by Kai Ka'ūs (1021-1098) is neither as interesting nor as suggestive as Nizām al-Mulk's *Book of Government*. According to what he says in the preface, 'Unsur al-Ma'ālī Kai Ka'ūs ibn Iskandār ibn Qābūs ibn Washmgīr wrote this book in order to provide his son, Gilānshāh, with general advice about life. The book consists of forty-four chapters that seem to fall into three major groupings. The first four chapters are dedicated to the religious beliefs Gilānshāh should hold and the pious actions he should perform. These chapters are followed by twenty-six chapters that examine the practical or worldly matters he must know about. Kai Ka'ūs's counsels range from basic instructions about the amount of sleep proper for a human being to general rules about eloquence. The last fourteen chapters are devoted to an examination of the possible ways in which Gilānshāh might make a livelihood and cover such disparate pursuits as kingship, sufic devotion, farming, and astrology.

Kai Ka'ūs's treatise, like that of Nizām al-Mulk, is replete with illustrative tales. More than half of the chapters in the work, twenty-four, contain such tales. While they are nowhere so enticing or so involved as those recounted by Nizām al-Mulk, they do serve a distinct pedagogical purpose. With one exception, topics that can be spoken of in definite terms or subjects about which little confusion can arise are treated in a direct manner. For example, no illustrative tales are used by Kai Ka'ūs in his discussions about when and how to engage in sexual relations, about ways to acquire wealth, or about things to consider when buying slaves or horses or—which may also be a kind of purchase—when choosing a wife.*

In general, Kai Ka'ūs is very sensitive to what is seemly according to common opinion. His advice is usually based on a consideration of what other people think of a person or on what conventional moral teaching and conventional religious wisdom teach. All of these considerations can be reduced to one thing, Kai Ka'ūs's overweening concern with what other people will think. Repeatedly he justifies his advice in terms of how the action he favors will enhance his son's reputation, and he always explains the practical benefit of the advice he sets forth. In his eyes, even acts of worship have a private and public side; they bring private and public advantages when practiced correctly (Ka'ūs 1951, chap. 3). This same kind of reasoning leads him to praise eloquence as the best human accomplishment (Ka'ūs 1951, 6.22–23, chap. 7).

Throughout his work, Kai Ka'ūs assumes that rulership will continue to be about the pursuits he might profitably follow. Of the sixteen pursuits enumerated in the last fourteen chapters of the treatise, kingship is the one he most desires for his son (Ka'ūs 1951, 31.145–46, 41.221). Nonetheless, in keeping with the pious tone that marks the book as a whole, Kai Ka'ūs claims that pursuit of the religious sciences is simply the highest pursuit. His reasoning is that the reward for such a pursuit is eternal happiness in the life to come, whereas the reward for pursuit of all of the other professions depends upon another craft. Consequently, he begins his discussion of the professions with jurisprudence *(fiqh)* based on the divine law *(sharī'ah)* and terminates it with a discussion of the sufic way. Similarly, he subordinates the science of medicine to the science of astrology on the grounds that astrology is "one of the miraculous possessions of apostleship and therefore indubitably a science linked with prophethood."† These explicit remarks notwithstanding, I think Kai Ka'ūs's ordering of the professions shows he prizes kingship above all.

The reason he gives for presenting a summary account of so many professions is his awareness of the transitory nature of things in this world or, as he says, his awareness "of the accidents of fate and the vicissitudes of fortune." He desired to give his son an idea of the professions that he would need if he remained a ruler or that he might be forced to exercise if unfortunate circumstances should befall him. In order to account for the numerous professions he is going to discuss, Kai Ka'ūs begins by proposing a means of classifying them. As he sees it, professions fall either into the category of a science linked with a craft, into the category of a craft linked with a science, or into the category of an independent craft (Ka'ūs 1951, 31.145). To illustrate what he means, Kai Ka'ūs

---

*See Ka'ūs (1951, chaps. 15, 21, 23, 25, 26). Other chapters not containing illustrative tales are 8, 11, 16, 17, 24, 33–36, 41, 44; chaps. 1–4 constitute the exception.

†See Ka'us (1951, 31.146; 32.156, 165; 33.175) and Plato (1968, 341^d–342^d).

indicates that he considers geometry, medicine, surveying, and versification, that is, the professions discussed in Chapters 33–35, as belonging to the first category. In the category of professions consisting of a craft linked with a science, Kai Kaʻūs mentions music, the subject of Chapter 36, and three other professions he never discussed in this work—the veterinary art, architecture, and the construction of underground channels. He gives no example whatever of what he means by an independent craft.

The simple and obvious conclusion is that this classificatory schema is not exhaustive. It only accounts for five of the sixteen professions enumerated in this work. Even by trying to apply the categories set up by Kai Kaʻūs to the other professions, several problems remain unsolved. To be sure, it would be possible to place jurisprudence or religious science, the subject of Chapter 31, and the pursuit of the sufic way, part of the subject of Chapter 44, into the category of professions consisting of a science linked with a craft. Similarly, secretaryship (Chapter 39), military command (Chapter 41), agriculture and craftsmanship (Chapter 43), and knighterrantry (part of the subject of Chapter 44) can be placed in the category of professions consisting of a craft linked with a science. And the art of the merchant (Chapter 32), as well as that of the vizier (Chapter 40), seem to be best described as independent crafts. But the art of kingship (Chapter 42), not to mention the pursuit of service to the king (Chapter 37) and that of boon companionship (Chapter 38), defy classification according to this schema. What is more, this schema does not allow for a hierarchical ordering of the professions. Although the professions consisting of a craft linked with a science ought to be subordinate to those consisting of a science linked with a craft, Kai Kaʻūs does not clearly order the professions in this way.

He does not do so because this classificatory schema is not that important to his argument. The order he really imposes upon the professions arises from the way he enumerates those a king or ruler needs to know about in order to exercise his rule, then discusses kingship itself, and finally tries to account for the professions that are not important for rulership and are almost antithetical to it.* But to state that order openly would have required Kai Kaʻūs to mitigate his pious proclamations, and, just as he wishes to give subtle advice about the importance of deceptiveness and cheating without having to drop his cloak of general decency, so too he wants to indicate the supreme importance of kingship without having to renounce his formalistic pronouncements of piety (Kaʻūs 1951, 39.204–08, 209–10). Kai Kaʻūs's preference for rulership needs to be played down for another reason as well: he cannot justify kingship in any terms other than those of self-interest. The advice he gives for the pursuit of the pro-

---

*See Kaʻūs (1951, chaps. 21–44, 38.196–98).

fessions that are ultimately in the service of the king, as well as the advice he gives to the king, is founded upon self-interest rather than upon higher considerations. What is more, although he enumerates general qualities a king should strive to acquire, he can identify no moral quality that is proper to kings or that sets kings apart from all other men. Whereas Alfarabi and Averroes explicitly likened a virtuous ruler to a prophet or *imām*, and Nizām al-Mulk suggested that a virtuous ruler had remarkable qualities, Kai Ka'ūs sees no necessary kinship between rulers and those who possess intellectual excellence.* Even the stories he tells about kings show his preference of kingship to be problematic. Almost every example is negative in that it shows how a ruler had to be instructed about his duties by those who came to seek his help.

The grounds of Kai Ka'ūs's preference for kingship are thus more formal than those behind Nizām al-Mulk's preference. Kai Ka'ūs argues that all of the professions contribute to the well-being of the kingdom and that it is therefore necessary to have someone at the head of the kingdom who understands the basic features of those professions. In his eyes, rule by one is justified not as much because only an exceptional person could master such a vast amount of learning as because only one person can coordinate all the different kinds of learning necessary for preserving a nation. It did not matter to him whether the king knew all of these matters or simply had an extremely competent vizier. What did matter, however, was that the king know how to employ his vizier correctly. In sum, Kai Ka'ūs tells us more about the practical problems arising from rule by one than about the theoretical grounds that justify such rule.

PHILOSOPHERS, STORYTELLERS, AND SOCIAL SCIENTISTS

The basic conclusion that must be drawn from the preceding discussion is that compelling reasons can be given for preferring rule by one person or by a few people. Even though we know there was a kind of patriciate elite that ruled cities and a series of monarchic rulers responsible for districts and regions, eventually culminating in a supreme ruler, that knowledge does not answer the most important question of why such rule is justified.† It is not enough to cite the historical fact of rule by one or a few and to infer from it that authors spoke in favor of such rule only because they lived in an age when such rule predominated. Moreover, these reflections on the writings of Alfarabi and Averroes

---

*See Kaus (1951, 40.213; 42.229; compare also 40.231, 235 with 44.242,255,256).
†See Bulliet (1972, pp. 20, 26–27, 46, 56–58, 61–62, 72) and Lapidus (1967, pp. 5, 44–50, 79–85, 91–92, 95–97, 108, 113).

permit us to discern elements of their arguments in more popular kinds of writing and thus to be wary of the facile conclusion that they had little or no influence on more traditional political thought.*

Once it is conceded that these authors and their predecessors may have had some significant thoughts about political life, it is possible to draw a more interesting conclusion from the foregoing analysis. The real point of what they said is that people used to think they knew what politics was. It was an art, just as navigation is an art. Thus, for the very reason that no one in his right mind would advocate turning the helm of a seabound vessel over to an unskilled sailor or to a farmer who lacked knowledge and experience of the sea, regardless of how successful he might be in his pursuit of farming, so no one in his right mind would advocate entrusting the helm of the ship of state to anyone unskilled in the art of politics. In either case, only a miracle could save the respective ships, crews, and passengers from utter destruction. The comparison with navigation is felicitous, too, for what it tells about the need for a potential ruler to have a certain kind of knowledge before daring to claim that he is ready to assume responsibility for the ship of state. These authors and their predecessors thought they knew what knowledge was needed and that it was extremely difficult to acquire. Moreover, because they held that politics was an art, they inferred that it had an end or a goal just as other arts have ends or goals. And that inference led to another important consideration about the art of politics, namely, that a good political regime could be distinguished from a bad one in terms of its goals.†

Although much more could be said about the significance of the way these authors and their predecessors viewed politics as an art, these remarks provide an adequate indication of the vast differences between their views and our own. We no longer think we know what politics is, much less what kind of knowledge is needed for rulership. More importantly, we no longer feel competent to discuss the ends of political regimes or to distinguish between good and bad regimes. The most we feel capable of striving for is a balanced discussion of the relationships between persons involved in political parties and similar kinds of groupings or of their behavior. We seek to identify those members of a particular regime who are most active politically and to explain what they do. Our goal is to understand the way that regime functions, and the test of correct understanding is the predictive capability of our descriptive explanation. Although we frequently do have reasoned preferences about what kind of political rule would be best for that regime, we differ from the authors just considered insofar as we studiously

---

*See Grunebaum (1961, pp. 171–72, 211–20; also pp. v–vi, 158 and n. 33, 324–25, 329–31) and Rosenthal (1958, p. 210).

†In addition to the previous reference, see Plato (1956, 216^{a-b}; 1968, 487^{e}–489^{c}), Thucydides (1954, 3.82), and expecially Xenophon (1965, III. vi. 1–18).

avoid expressing those preferences.* These differences are primarily due to the change in perspective that is the hallmark of modern social science, especially that facet of it concerned with the study of political elites, which can be traced through the major social and political thinkers of the modern Western tradition from Machiavelli to Michels and beyond. In what follows, I will try to explain how this change in perspective came about.

THE WESTERN RESPONSE
TO TRADITIONAL PHILOSOPHY

Machiavelli

Niccolò Machiavelli (1469-1527) is both closest to the core of the tradition we have just discussed and most removed from it. In a famous letter to his friend Francesco Vettori, Machiavelli explains his devotions to the ancients.

> As evening falls, I return home and enter my study. At the doorway, I take off my everyday garb which is covered with mud and straw and put on garments suitable for the royal or pontifical court. Then appropriately attired, I enter the ancient courts of the men of antiquity. Greeted affably there by them, I nourish myself with the food which is mine alone and for which I was born. I am not ashamed to speak with them or to question them about the reasons for their actions, and they, because of their humanity, reply. And for four hours at a stretch, I feel no annoyance, I forget all my troubles, and I cease to dread my poverty; even death does not frighten me. I am completely carried away by them.†

---

*See Schonfeld (1975, pp. 146, 156-58), Zartman (1974, pp. 465-67, 470-71, 486-88), and Dahrendorf (1967, pp. 217, 222, 268-69, 278-79).

†Machiavelli (1961, p. 304). Immediately after this account of the way he spent his time, Machiavelli goes on to say:

> And since Dante says that there is no knowledge unless one retains what one has understood, I have noted down what I think to be most important from my conversation with them [the ancients] and composed a little work, *De Principatibus [on Principalities]*, in which I go as deeply as I can into this subject and discuss what a principality is, how many kinds of it there are, how they are lost. And if any of my other scribblings has pleased you, this one ought not to displease you; and it ought to be accepted by a prince, especially a new prince.

Later in the letter (p. 305), Machiavelli exclaims:

As Machiavelli also explains in this letter, the fruit of the time thus spent with the ancients was a little book that he later entitled *The Prince*. Written in Italian, but given Latin chapter headings, *The Prince* is a remarkable blend of the old and the new. Because of the Latin chapter headings and the basic format of the treatise, it looks like yet another contribution to the "Mirror of Princes" literature. The abundance of references to ancient historical events also helps to give it that character. But within this traditional shell lurks a completely revolutionary doctrine.

Basically, the book explains how someone may become a prince, that is, how someone may acquire a principality and hold it. To this end, Machiavelli enumerates the different kinds of principalities and explains how they are acquired (Chapters 1-11). At no point in the argument does Machiavelli raise a question about the relative worth of a regime ruled by a prince. The good of the people is not his concern. Rather, his concern is with those who feel themselves capable of doing what all people would like to do: acquire power. Since it is natural for people to have such a desire, Machiavelli will show them how to realize it.* He is in no way concerned about what people should desire. To the contrary, for the purposes of this work, Machiavelli is only concerned with instructing those who are capable of carrying out the desire we all have. However, it is clearly not sufficient to acquire power; a competent prince must know how to hold what he has acquired. And when Machiavelli explains what actions must be undertaken to maintain power, the traditional shell of his teaching begins to fall away. At first, he considers simple and time-honored suggestions such as the prince taking up residence in his new principality or sending out colonial settlers, becoming the defender of the less powerful neighbors while trying to weaken the stronger ones, and keeping powerful foreigners from acquiring too much influence. But these suggestions are soon buried under more ruthless advice about the kinds of steps the ruler must take if he is to exercise his new power with any kind of security. Essentially, his advice is to destroy the customs and laws of the conquered people and to make them completely subject to his rule, a sign that Machiavelli has no esteem whatever for liberty, convention, or any kind of human rights.†

When this work is read, it will be seen that I have not slept or frittered away the fifteen years I have passed in studying the art of the state.

*See Machiavelli (1950, chap. 3, end): "To desire to acquire power is truly something very natural and ordinary. And whenever men do it who are able to, they will be praised and not blamed. But error and blame arise when they cannot do it and they want to do it at any cost."

†See Machiavelli (1950, chap. 3 with chaps. 4 and 5). For much of my interpretation of Machiavelli, I am deeply indebted to Leo Strauss's excellent study, *Thoughts on Machiavelli* (1958).

In the second part of the book (Chapters 12-26), Machiavelli pursues this argument from a different perspective. Here, he tries to explain the considerations basic to the ruling art and does so by looking at the way the prince should conduct himself with relation to his enemies (Chapters 12-14) as well as with relation to his subjects or friends (Chapters 15-23) and by explaining the importance that ought to be attached to prudence and chance in this regard (Chapters 24-26). When considering the way the prince should conduct himself with relation to his enemies, Machiavelli places supreme emphasis on the importance of good arms and even goes so far as to consider the quality of a prince's arms an index of the quality of his laws.

> The principal foundations of all states, new as well as old or mixed, are good laws and good arms. And since good laws cannot exist where there are no good arms and since wherever there are good arms it follows that there are good laws, I will leave the consideration of laws aside and speak about arms (Chapter 12, beginning).

In fact, Machiavelli never does get around to considering laws. He does not do so because he is concerned above all with enabling the newly established principality to endure. For him, its continuation is a more important consideration than the goodness or badness of the life citizens might be able to pursue in it. It is so important that the only time Machiavelli expresses any concern about the subjects of the principality is when he tries to explain the way their character may aid or hinder the development of an army that is the prince's own.

Throughout *The Prince*, Machiavelli's attention is focused exclusively on this single ruler and his survival. Yet, unlike any of the authors previously discussed, Machiavelli never offers an explicit justification of his preference for the rule of one. He does not do so because he denies the validity of the grounds on which such an argument could be made. Such an argument would have to be based on considerations of goodness and badness, and Machiavelli denies that those terms have any meaning in themselves. They have value only insofar as they facilitate self-preservation.

Machiavelli's intention in this work is to be useful to the one person who can profit from his advice, the person who can be a true prince. He thus refuses to fall into the error common to his predecessors, that is, to speak about political rule in terms of what ought to be rather than in terms of what is. Rather than chase after imaginary goods, Machiavelli pursues the effective truth of things and limits himself to telling the prince how to preserve himself and his rule.

> It now remains to see what ought to be the modes and ways of governing of a prince with respect to subjects or friends. Since I know that many have written about this, I am afraid that in writing about it myself I might be held presumptuous because I break away extensively from others in my discussion of this subject. But since my

intention is to write something useful for him who understands it, it seemed to me to be more appropriate to go straight to the effective truth of the matter than to what is imagined about it. For many have imagined republics and principalities which have never been seen or known truly to exist. There is so much distance between the way people live and the way they ought to live that he who rejects what people do in favor of what they ought to do brings about his ruin rather than his preservation; for a man who wants to do good in every matter comes to ruin among so many who are not good. Thus it is necessary that a prince who wants to maintain himself learn to be able not to be good and to use goodness or not use it as necessity demands (Chapter 15).

So the reason Machiavelli does not try to justify the rule of the prince in terms of what he might do for the sake of the subjects is that such considerations would lead to the pursuit of imaginary goods. The one good that is not imaginary, the pursuit of glory, does not add any meaning to the idea of striving for freedom and happiness as political goals. He knows that men strive for wealth and glory, and he is willing to explain how lasting glory might be sought (Chapter 25). But his view of what constitutes glory leaves no room for bettering the lot of the citizens.

To hold these views, Machiavelli had to reject the old idea that there was an order in nature that could be discerned by humanity and that showed how to lead a good human life. He also had to reject the notion that God had revealed to select individuals His intention regarding the way people should live. And in the place of these former standards, Machiavelli offers us the challenge of daring to follow our own desire for glory. Largely as a result of what he rejected, his view has come to dominate our opinions today. Mosca and Pareto frequently refer to Machiavelli for what they consider truths about the way men act, "effective truths" Machiavelli might say. And most of his immediate successors shared his basic criticism of former philosophy. They, too, wanted to be useful and to avoid speaking about imaginary goods or imaginary governments.

Hobbes

Thomas Hobbes (1588-1679) is a worthy successor of Machiavelli in at least two respects and an equally worthy opponent in at least two other respects. Like Machiavelli, he effects a radical break with the past. And like Machiavelli, he favors rule by one. Unlike Machiavelli, Hobbes seeks to defend his predilection for rule by one. Moreover, he differs from Machiavelli insofar as he thinks he can perceive an order in nature that helps us understand how to order human life.

The whole teaching of Hobbes starts from his thoughts about nature and natural law. Even though he admits that the life of most people consists of "a perpetual and restless desire of power after power that ceaseth only in death," Hobbes does not think that natural urge should be followed. To the contrary, it is his contention that natural human reason teaches how necessary it is to moderate that desire and to seek a much more modest goal: security from violent death.* Hobbes thinks that he has seen more clearly than any of his predecessors and that he alone will be able to contribute to the progress of moral philosophy because he alone has discovered the right way to handle the subject. The reason he thinks that no progress has been made in moral philosophy is that, at his time, there was great ignorance about natural law and continuous bickering between philosophers over its character. Such was the plight of moral philosophy because no one prior to Hobbes had thought to use an "idoneous principle of tractation," that is, to start as close to the beginning of the question as possible and reason from there.

For Hobbes, the beginning of moral philosophy is inquiry into the origin of personal right or ownership. This must be the beginning point, for moral philosophy is about natural justice and justice is concerned with giving to each what is his by right. According to Hobbes, all things are in common by nature. Difficulty arises in the natural state due to human propensity to try to take as one's own what is common to all. Such concupiscence leads to horrendous conflict. and ultimately results in a war of all against all. Only when reason or desire to avoid hurt teaches people how to put an end to this conflict and assign titles to appropriation does it become possible to escape the wretchedness of the natural state. According to this line of reasoning, personal ownership or right to property comes about by consent. Differently stated, Thomas Hobbes's application of an idoneous principle of tractation to the problem of natural justice leads to the conclusion that justice is not natural, but conventional.†

What Hobbes learns from his reflection on human nature is that it is necessary to control human nature. Basically, there are two passions at the root of human existence: the desire to possess and the desire to avoid hurt. Because these desires are natural, they cannot be eliminated. They can only be controlled by human artifices, that is, by conventions. Clearly, then, even though men need society, they are not naturally fit for it; they must be taught to live in society.

In direct opposition to his predecessors, Hobbes denies that all people need to do is to make laws for associating. They come together not by nature, but by accident. We do not live in society because we wish to be with other human beings, but because we see some profit or honor in associating. At the same time, because society is based only on profit or honor, it cannot be very stable nor longlasting. Only fear helps us to preserve this shaky structure, fear of

---

*See Hobbes (1968, chap. 11 with chaps. 13 and 14).
† See Hobbes (1968, chaps. 4 and 5) and Hobbes (1972, Epistle Dedicatory).

what each of us would be subjected to if there were no society (Hobbes 1972, 1.2). Now the point of Hobbes's argument about people being nonpolitical by nature is that nature is not benevolent to people. To survive, humanity must learn to conquer nature. Part of this act of conquering nature is to restrict human freedom: prior to the formation of society, humanity was radically free and utterly miserable; to escape that misery, radical freedom must be surrendered.

The means by which human freedom is surrendered is the social contract. Its realization requires that every person promise all of the others that he will not resist the person or council to whom all have agreed to submit themselves (Hobbes 1972, 5.7). Once Hobbes explains the formation of a society of this sort, he turns his attention to the question of how it should be governed. Since he insists that any form of government must be strong enough to provide for the security of the citizens by punishing wrongdoers, Hobbes does not distinguish between the different kinds of regime on the basis of the greater or lesser freedom to be found in one or the other. His primary criterion is efficiency: a single ruler is more likely to receive correct advice and to be spared egregious rhetoric than a multitude of rulers; moreover, factions cannot arise in a regime ruled by one person as they can in a regime ruled by a multitude (Hobbes 1972, 6.6, 10.8-18). Even though this kind of reasoning has something in common with the kind of reasoning that we saw in the traditional views about rulership, there is a basic difference. Hobbes does not argue that the ruler must direct the society in accordance with special knowledge that only rare individuals might acquire. He sees no end for society such as to require the ruler to have an extensive familiarity with nature and with human ways. Rather, he prefers the rule of one person because he thinks that such a ruler is less likely to be swayed by misdirected rhetoric. Hobbes's ruler need have no special talents. All he aims at is the preservation of the laws of the state and the preservation of the vigor of those laws so that the citizens will not be threatened with the kind of dangers they encountered in the state of nature.

Locke

The rejection of the teaching that had filtered down from the ancients or that accords in any way with revelation is particularly marked in the political arguments of John Locke (1652-1704). He begins his reflections on politics by looking for an explanation of why government exists. Since he can show why the notion that government exists by divine right is as fallacious as the notion that might makes right, he sets out to find another way of explaining its existence.*

---

*John Locke's major political work is the *Two Treatises of Government*. In the *First Treatise*, he considers Robert Filmer's arguments in favor of the divine right of kings quite

Locke argues that an adequate explanation must have two qualities. In the first place, it must account for the differences between a magistrate's rule over his subjects, a father's rule over his family, and a master's rule over his slaves. Because each of these kinds of association has different origins and ends, they are qualitatively so distinct that parallels cannot be drawn between them. Secondly, a proper explanation must show why the only warranted concern of a commonwealth is the regulation and preservation of property. Since all values relating to government are subsumed under Locke's idea of property, a regime loses its claim to the allegiance of its citizens when it threatens their property or fails to protect the nation from foreign injury.

Locke's explanation begins with an account of natural human condition. Like Hobbes, he sees that nature offers some suggestions about how we should order society. And like Hobbes, he does not think that nature offers sufficient guidance. Because natural human condition is not the best condition, it is evident that nature must be improved upon. Contrary to Hobbes, however, Locke denies that a war of all against all is inevitable in the state of nature. Rather, he sees the state of nature as a situation marked by the reign of peace and equity. People in the state of nature are free and equal, and their tranquility is assured to the extent that they are each one subject to the law of nature or of reason. The reason that they leave the state of nature and form society is that the possibility of war breaking out is ever present in that state, that is, it is always possible that one individual may try to seize the goods of another individual unjustly (Locke 1960, paras. 8, 10, 19-21, 31, 127). In other words, while Locke agrees with Hobbes's view that by nature people have a right to everything or that by nature all things are in common, he disagrees with Hobbes's notion that natural human concupiscence inevitably engenders a war of all against all. Locke disagrees because he thinks that natural human reason is strong enough to control desire, yet he admits that desire may overwhelm reason at any time and thus acknowledges that the formation of society is a sound way to preserve tranquility.

When society is formed, however, care must be taken that humanity is not worse off in society than in nature. Above all, nothing must be done to abridge natural human equality or freedom. Differently stated, no one can alienate his freedom to preserve himself (Locke 1960, paras. 22-24, 85, 172, 176, 178-79, 182, and esp. 196). But beyond this negative injunction, nature offers no guidance for telling us how society should be organized. In Locke's view, there is no

---

extensively and emphatically refutes them. To the best of my knowledge, Locke never makes an explicit argument against the assertion that "might makes right;" for a refutation of that view, see *infra*, p. 00. In the *Second Treatise*, that is, the *Essay Concerning the True Origin, Extent, and End of Civil Government*, he accepts his argument against Filmer as conclusive and goes on to offer his own account of government; see Locke (1960, paras. 1-3).

natural end of humanity that can be favored by a given social organization. Even though he recognizes a period that was so happy and blessed it could be likened to the golden age of humanity, he does not draw from it any idea of institutions or personal arrangements that might be imitated. He considers it simply as a stage through which we pass.*

Still, by thinking more carefully about the relationships that arise almost spontaneously among human beings and by remembering the importance of natural freedom, Locke is able to infer how society ought to be organized. Reflection about the parent-child and husband-wife relationships shows that each presupposes certain limits and has very definite ends and that neither could be cited in defense of an argument for absolute rule. Parents have a right—and even perhaps a duty—to raise their children, to educate their children to the age of reason. But once that task is completed, they have no more right to rule over them. They cannot even force their children to stay in the commonwealth of which they are citizens: the only reason children become citizens in their parent's country is to enjoy the property that might be passed on to them. The situation is similar with respect to the husband-wife relationship. In Locke's eyes, it does not give either party absolute power over the other. It is really nothing more than a compact voluntarily entered into by each party (Locke 1960, paras. 63, 65, 72-73, 75-76, 78-80, 82-83, 86).

Thus, if any arguments about the organization of society are going to be made by referring to these relationships, it is clear that they must be patterned on the provisions for voluntary association and for the freedom of the participants essential to these relationships. In other words, reflection on these relationships suggests the importance that must be attached to preserving human freedom. For this reason, Locke concludes that the origin of society must be the consent of all involved and that all decisions taken by society must be based on the willingness of most members of society—the majority—to agree to those decisions.† The practical consequence of Locke's emphasis on consent, both at the moment society is formed and for all decisions taken subsequently, is that the powers of government are limited. Although Locke admits the necessity of allowing the government sufficient strength to accomplish its goal (that is, to preserve the property of the citizens that was threatened by the injustice of others), he insists upon restraining that new creation. Unlike Hobbes, he saw no need to envisage this new invention as another Leviathan.‡

In this sense, Locke's distance from the teaching about rulership sketched out in the first part of this chapter is greater than that of either Machiavelli or

---

*See Locke (1960, paras. 110-111, 128) and Ovid (1960, I. 89-162).

†Cf. Locke (1960, para. 94 and reference to Hooker with para. 111; paras. 95-98.

‡Cf. Locke (1960, paras. 123-28 with 129-31, 98, 142) and Hobbes (1968, chap. 28, end) with Job 41:33-34.

Hobbes. With Locke, we enter into the kind of thinking so characteristic of Western democracy. People accept the restrictions of society in order to preserve things they hold dear, but they do not accept just any restrictions. All governmental decrees must be clearly directed to the end for which government was instituted. And each person may judge how appropriate those decrees are, for each is competent to judge. After all, it is our property that is at stake; our life, liberty, and goods are at stake. For such matters, we do not really need Locke's clear instruction that in questions of this nature "The People shall be the Judge;"* we know that we should judge when our own goods are at issue.

Rousseau

It is Jean-Jacques Rousseau (1712-1778), however, who administers the *coup de grâce* to the notion that one person or a few people can ever rule equitably or wisely for many. His whole literary effort is a lucid, but frequently impassioned, defense of the sentiments as adequate guides in moral and political matters. A writer with rare insight and exceptional stylistic ability, Rousseau is the most eloquent spokesman the people have ever had. In his books and essays, the enlightenment is denounced and the recourse to conscience or to right feeling rehabilitated. The necessary consequence of his defense of conscience or sentiment, passions common to all, is advocacy of popular sovereignty and rejection of any view of government that favors anything but the will of the people.

Rousseau's clearest statement of the reasons why he considered popular sovereignty the only basis for just government is the *Social Contract* and, since he says on a number of occasions that all of his works set forth the same argument, it seems fair to limit our discussion of Rousseau to this work.† In the *Social Contract*, Rousseau first tries to show why no argument for the foundation of civil society that does not provide for the sovereignty of the people is sound and then explains how a society founded according to popular sovereignty would work. The argument of the first four chapters of this work is devoted to the examination of the traditional explanations for human subjection to civil society as well as to their refutation, and the argument of the rest of Book One explains what Rousseau considers to be the only just grounds for civil society.

Like Locke, Rousseau rejects the argument that the natural authority which a father has over his children is analogous to the authority a king has over

---

*Cf. Locke (1960, paras. 123, 240 [emphasis in the original]) and Hobbes (1972, pp. 1.9, 3.13).

†See Rousseau (1969, p. 928): "I have written about diverse subjects, but always according to the same principles—always the same morality, the same belief, the same maxims, and, if you will, the same opinions." See also Rousseau (1959, pp. 932–35).

his subjects. Rousseau contends that a father's authority ceases once the children are able to care for themselves, because he thinks that natural law compels each person to look after his own preservation and to be the sole judge of what conduces to his preservation. Under no circumstances can people in society be likened to helpless children. What is more, there is a fundamental difference between a family and a kingdom: the father of a family strives to increase his wealth and preserve it so that he may pass it on to his progenitors, whereas a king strives to enrich himself and a few favorites at the expense of the people (Rousseau 1964c, 1.2). In the same vein, Rousseau denies that it is possible to view rulers as having a natural superiority over most people, if not that of a father at least that of a shepherd over his flocks. In the first place, the argument supposes a natural inequality among people about the most basic matters, an inequality not buttressed by any observation. In the second place, such an argument fails to take account of the end for which the shepherd watches over his flocks, that is, to devour them. Consequently, he maintains that arguments based on the notion of a kind of natural superiority of some men must be rejected.

Those arguments that seek to base the social order on the right of the strongest are also rejected by Rousseau. According to him, an explanation that society rests on the right of the stronger is an admission of the right for continual revolution. Strength entails no morality. At best, we give in to a stronger person because of the dictates of prudence. But prudence of that sort is no ground for duty (Rousseau 1964c, 1.3).

Rousseau uses a similar line of attack in refuting the argument that seeks to defend slavery as natural. His contention is that slavery could only be traced back to an original act of force. To cite the kind of inequality now existent among people is not sufficient proof for him, because it simply confuses the cause and the effect. Whatever kind of inequality now exists must be traced to the fact that these "natural slaves" have been born in slavery; it is because they have been brought up as slaves that they appear so slavish. Similarly, the arguments that defend slavery as a convention between the enslaved and the enslaver in exchange for a commodity, such as food, cannot be defended. It is not a reasonable convention, because one of the parties sacrifices too much. But even if it were admitted for an individual, it could never apply to a whole people because the enslavers, that is, the rulers, take more than they give, because the enslaved never gains calm by such an arrangement, but continual misery, and because one person cannot speak for the freedom of yet unborn children (Rousseau 1964c, 1.4). The crucial assumption for this whole argument is that the renunciation of our freedom is equivalent to the renunciation of our humanity. A human is a human because of his free will. If society is to be justified or made legitimate, it must respect a person's free being. The only way that can be done is for the individual never to be subject to any force that is arbitrary, that is, willed by someone else without regard to his own well-being.

Obviously, the simplest way to resolve this dilemma is to deny the necessity of society and to turn to a praise of anarchy. Rousseau does not choose that solution because he recognizes that people cannot provide for their self-preservation except by mutual association. He therefore seeks to formulate how they can unite the means by which they secure self-preservation, that is, their strength and their freedom, in order to provide for their mutual self-preservation without jeopardizing their right to anything that they put into the association. This argument leads to his formulation of the social pact as a means of founding a community that will act for the well-being of all without threatening the freedom of any. Everybody will maintain his own freedom because each decision of the community will require that the will of each participant be consulted. The individual is to see himself as part of a larger whole and to will for the sake of the larger whole rather than for his personal self-interest. But in thinking of the whole, his self-interest as a part is provided for: the well-being of the whole requires the well-being of the parts. Formulated in this manner, the foundation of society is seen to accord with natural law. In other words, each person provides for his self-preservation by striving for the preservation of all (Rousseau 1964c, 1.6, 1.8).

It is not important for Rousseau to determine whether the social contract has ever served as the basis for a society. Given his presuppositions, he proves that such a foundation of society is in accordance with justice. Still, the argument needs to be buttressed by more than an abstract proof for it to be convincing. In order to show why only a political society based on the social contract can be just, Rousseau must show how such a society will function. He also must prove that it will always enact just laws. The purpose of the analysis and arguments of Books 2–4 is to provide precisely such a proof. Above all, Rousseau needs to make a convincing argument that people can indeed will the general interest. For a number of reasons, Rousseau's argument is not completely persuasive, and, at one point, he actually concedes that the will of the people as people, that is, the general will, might fail to find proper expression.

There are three reasons such a failure may come about. If the people are mistaken about what is in their best interest, the fact that a general will results will not compensate for the disastrous errors it might bring upon the community. Then again, if factions and other divisions arise, the community will suffer because such factions will prevent the expression of the general will. For the will of the people to be indeed general, it must be a sum of the individual wills concerning the whole; any intrigue by groups destroys the general nature of the will of the people. But it is not simply factions and intrigues that might threaten the expression of the general will. Its expression might also be threatened by failure of each citizen to think of the larger whole when expressing his individual will (Rousseau 1964c, 2.3, 2.6). In order to resolve these difficulties, Rousseau admits that citizens must be educated in civic virtue and that some attention must be paid to preserving the salubrity of their ways. That admission leads him to speak about the need for a legislator to form the people and for censorship to preserve the legislator's efforts.* Contrary to what might be thought, these developments do not mitigate Rousseau's attempt to establish government based on popular sovereignty. The role of the legislator and of the censor is extrapolitical and is intended to favor the sound will of the sovereign people, that is, to educate the people to rule in full view of their self-interest, not to rule in their stead. In this sense, the overwhelming significance of Rousseau's arguments in the *Social Contract*, as well as in his other works, is their refutation of all opinions that favor the rule of one person or a few individuals (Rousseau 1964b, pp. 179-84). The force of these arguments was such that entirely new grounds had to be found if such rule was to be defended. And that is exactly what occurred.

FROM POLITICAL PHILOSOPHY
TO THE STUDY OF ELITES

Mosca

After Rousseau, political writing changed dramatically. Completely caught up in questions of political action or overwhelmed by a desire to set forth a theory that would serve as a universal history of humanity, thinkers turned their attention away from reflections about what might be in order to concentrate on the real world. Those whose writings are of most interest to students of elites directed their criticisms of actual politics at Rousseau and his praise of popular rule, but were primarily interested in showing what was wrong with the political activities Karl Marx's powerful pen had stirred up. As is well known, Marx started from the premise that the prevailing mode of economic production and exchange in any epoch determines the social and political organization as well as the political and intellectual history of that epoch. He insisted that all historical change could be explained in terms of class struggles between those who exploited the means of production and those who were exploited by them, and he subjected the economic system of capitalism to a thorough, critical analysis. Persuaded that his analysis revealed the proletarians or workers of his day to be the exploited and the bourgeoisie or owners of the modes of production to be the exploiters, Marx predicted the total defeat of capitalist economy and the eventual elimination of all exploitation. He envisaged an uprising in which the masses

---

*See Rousseau (1964c, 2.7, 4.7) and the last three paragraphs of Rousseau's *First Discourse* (1964a).

of workers would take power into their own hands and then form a classless society free of any rulership or politics. Response to his analysis and to his persistent attempts to hasten this defeat of capitalism was varied. While numbers of people accepted his analysis as valid and eagerly rushed forward to bring about a new stage in political economy, others tried to defend the existing order and to refute Marx's analysis. Gaetano Mosca (1858-1941) was one of these critics. However, like so many others, he directed his criticism at Rousseau rather than at Marx and insisted that Rousseau or anyone who shared his views was simply wrong to praise popular sovereignty as good. According to Mosca, popular sovereignty was both an erroneous foundation for effective government and a hopelessly idle dream. Whatever anyone might claim, it could not be shown to exist in his day and never would exist.

Mosca's argument is set forth in his treatise *Elementi di Scienza Politica*, a work he first published in 1895 and then published again in 1923 with an additional part consisting of six chapters. The reason he republished it is that, while he continued to believe in the validity of his method—the study of individual and collective human psychology—he had come to think it important to modify certain aspects of the argument of the First Part. His goal is to investigate the "tendencies that regulate the organization of political powers" (Mosca 1923, pp. vii-viii, 4). To accomplish his goal, he first explains what political science might be and why it has not progressed very far. Then he sets forth his view of the proper procedure to be followed in political science and shows how it helps him to understand those tendencies referred to earlier.

Political science has not made much progress since the time of Plato and Aristotle because no one has yet discovered a sound method or studied political phenomena according to an accurate perspective. His point is that method is not enough; it is also important to have sound assumptions about the subject matter (Mosca 1923, pp. 1-8, esp. p. 5 and n. 1). Two examples of the erroneous paths followed by previous thinkers are the attempt to interpret political phenomena in terms of an explanation that stresses the physical environment and one that stresses race. Mosca examines these views at some length, but simply dismisses in passing two other reasons for the little progress achieved by political science. The first is the tendency for people to justify an existing form of government by means of a rational theory, such as calling the government the free and spontaneous expression of the will of all or most of the citizens. The second is their tendency to justify existing regimes by a supernatural belief, that is, saying the government is part of God's will.* Although he says almost nothing about these

---

*See Mosca (1923, p. 7). For his continuing argument against popular sovereignty, see (1923, pp. 54-55, 141-48, 153-55, 258-65, 275-332, 338-39, 341-44, 386-87, and esp. 397-98 with n. 2).

views, the major objective of his political science proper is a refutation of the first view.

Mosca's contention is that political science will make progress as it learns to study social facts, an investigation that depends on having good histories of different nations. Such a procedure is possible now, because the major discovery of the nineteenth century has been the historical method and because we now have access to much more historical knowledge than was available to any of our predecessors. Mosca emphasizes the importance of the discovery of the historical method in the nineteenth century in order to defend his contention that the previous use of history by Aristotle, Machiavelli, Montesquieu, and others had not resulted in a "truly scientific system." In keeping with this new discovery, it is incumbent on researchers to be selective about the material they study. Not anecdotal and biographical detail, but the psychological laws that show forth in the lives of nations—especially developed nations—through their administrative and legal institutions are what must be subjected to study (Mosca 1923, pp. 42-47, 50-55).

When Mosca applies his method to the world around him, he discovers that there are only two classes in society: the ruling and the ruled. Others fail to see this as clearly as he because they attach too much importance to the idea that one person is the chief of state and that the discontent of the masses can occasionally sway the established ruler. If Mosca's analysis is correct, it follows that the old scheme for classifying political regimes—that is, the one followed by Aristotle and revised by Montesquieu—is wrong. What determines the regime is the makeup of the ruling class. Indeed, as Mosca looks again at history, he discovers that the ruling class has been modified over time. In an earlier age, it was the warrior class; as time went on, it acquired land and thus became the wealthy class (Mosca 1923, pp. 52, 56-62 [esp. 59-60], 68-69, 73-75, 335-38).

This observation leads Mosca to raise the question that preoccupies us today. If it is indeed true that a ruling class exists, it then becomes essential to understand why that class succeeds or, conversely, fails to maintain its rule.* His answer is quite straightforward: "Every new political edifice must more or less utilize the ruins of the one that preceded it" (Mosca 1923, p. 384). In other words, the ruling class perpetuates its rule insofar as it can appropriate to an eminent degree the qualities prevalent among the people of the society. Even though Mosca concedes that the mark of good rulers is the extent to which they introduce better principles of recruitment and organization into the ruling classes, he contends that there are limits to what can be achieved. The purpose of his work is to remind us of those limits and to show us that it will never be

---

*See Mosca (1923, pp. 339, 384-85), Zartman (1974, pp. 487-88), and Parry (1970, p. 14).

possible for the ruling classes to embrace the kind of radical political ideas that would threaten their very existence. Thus, there will never be a regime based simply on popular sovereignty. Regardless of what the ruling class says about its adherence to the noble spirit contained in such a project, it will never relinquish its own power (Mosca 1923, pp. 438-40, 442-44, 446-47, 472-73). From Mosca's perspective, both Rousseau and Marx are wrong. Rousseau errs because he fails to pay sufficient attention to the fact that people are more interested in ruling others than in ruling themselves, and Marx goes astray due to excessive confidence in his analysis of capitalist economy.

As a result, Mosca concludes his work with a plea to return to the political system "of our fathers." In his eyes, such a system necessarily entails censorship, limits on the freedom of association, and the ruling class being fully cognizant of its status as a ruling class. The point is that the political movements of the nineteenth century have resulted in admission to the ruling class now being open to all people, and Mosca wants to ensure that only those with superior talents will indeed rule (Mosca 1923, pp. 483-84, 486-87, 492-500, 501, 502-3 with n. 1, and 503-4). In other words, in Mosca we find very much the same kind of concerns as the ones that prompted those we studied as representatives of the traditional position: the originator of what has come to be known as elite theory is himself in favor of rule by elites—provided they are indeed elite.

Pareto and Michels

This problem of whether the ruling elements are really elites prompted Mosca to criticize Vilfredo Pareto (1848-1923) for using the term elite to describe the ruling class.* However, Pareto's use of the term is not value-laden. He sees the qualities that give admission to the governing class as relative. But he speaks of the members of the governing class as elite, fully aware that the term can be taken to mean best, because that is the way they are viewed by those who are not members of the governing class (Pareto 1916, paras. 278-79, 1152, 2029, 2031-36, 2047-50, 2237-78, 2411). Apart from this minor disagreement, Pareto and Mosca think along similar lines. Like Mosca, the major issue for Pareto is to understand why the governing class succeeds or fails. His answer is based on a very complicated theory of what he calls residues and derivations as constitutive elements of society and is very similar to Mosca's. The ruling class is composed of those who are best able to manipulate the dominant ideas in society for their own self-interest (Pareto 1916, paras. 842-43, 847-88, 2060, 2170-2236,

---

*See Mosca (1923, pp. 459, n. 1; 460, n. 2; 461, n. 2; 461-62) and Pareto (1916, para. 2026, n. 1).

2612). In one sense, however, Pareto differs from Mosca. In his approach to society, he is less willing to evaluate political movements. Even though he accepts the idea of society being governed by an elite, he does so because it is a fact. His refutation of movements that oppose rule by an elite, such as socialism, is based on the idea that such movements are bound to failure rather than on the idea that they are wrong.*

Robert Michels (1876-1936) approached the question from a much narrower perspective. By looking critically at democracy in action, at the way political parties function, Michels arrives at the conclusion that the masses are apathetic and need to be guided. The people are generally incompetent, have little interest in political issues, and are slow to act. What is more, they seem to be imbued with a desire to adore leaders. Consequently, democracy will never be possible (Michels 1959, pp. vii-viii, 25-26, 49-50, 64-65, 86-87, 151-52, 205, 235, 407-08). To the contrary, his analysis of political parties convinces Michels that all political organization, even that within political parties devoted to the goal of popular sovereignty, tends toward domination by a few or what he calls oligarchy. For these reasons, he accepts Mosca's ruling class explanation of society and, with some reservations, aligns himself with Pareto's views about the circulation of elites within a given society (Michels 1959, pp. 11, 32, 42-43, 365-66, 377-78, 381-83, 390-91, 401). In many respects, Michels represents a return to the ancients and their statement about rule by many. But there is a crucial difference. The ancients told us about the evils of rule by many in order to teach us that we should follow another kind of rule, whereas Michels simply tells us about what is and attempts to predict what will be.

CONCLUSION

These, then, are the thinkers and the thoughts we must consider if we wish to understand our own intellectual background as well as that of the peoples in the Middle East and North Africa whose regimes are our dominant focus. As was mentioned at the beginning of this chapter, there is a common root in our background and theirs, that represented by those two giants who stand at the origin of political and philosophical inquiry—Plato and Aristotle. Now, however, it should be clear that not the least of the differences between us and the peoples of the Middle East and North Africa is the different way these two thinkers have been treated in each tradition. It should also be clear that our current interest in the study of elites and our trust in the correctness of the goals of social science derive from the different way we have interpreted their teachings.

---

*However, see Pareto (1964, para. 837).

Alfarabi and Averroes as well as Nizām al-Mulk and, to a certain extent, Kai Ka'ūs are in substantial agreement with Plato and Aristotle. In the first place, all of these thinkers concur that it is extremely difficult to achieve sound political rule and highly unlikely that more than a few citizens will ever be capable of governing well. Each of them, with the possible exception of Kai Ka'ūs, is of the opinion that it is especially important to reflect upon how good rulers can be formed and upon the institutions that promote the development of individual and political excellence. As a consequence, they all deem it sounder policy to investigate the ways in which existing regimes can be improved than to count on bringing about all of the conditions necessary for a truly just regime. Their general accord about these matters can be traced to a common judgment about the character of the universe. Although not one of them would claim that this world is perfect, each is confident that he can discern an order in it. Whether that order is grounded in nature or in divine providence, each sees it as providing standards for human life. They all consider that order to be complete in itself and to be the highest object of human understanding. And whether it is identified with nature or with God, none of these authors perceives it as something to be conquered or as something that becomes complete only when it is subjected to human desires.

This is the core of the disagreement between Machiavelli, Hobbes, Locke, and Rousseau, on the one hand, and Plato and Aristotle, on the other. All four modern Western authors deny that nature or God provides any standards for human conduct. Far from holding that the order of things in the universe is the highest object of understanding, each maintains that it is something to be overcome or subjected to human control for greater contentment. As a result, they try to overcome the difficulty of achieving political rule, whose soundness is vouchsafed because of its conformity to this natural or divine order, by lowering the expectations we might have of political association. At first self-preservation and then comfortable self-preservation come to replace virtue and happiness as the end of political life. Each of these thinkers tries to reduce the problems of government to the problem of providing for the proper play of self-interest. And according to Rousseau, both Machiavelli and Locke saw as clearly as he the importance of making the freedom of the citizens a central feature of political teaching. Whether Rousseau's assessment of Machiavelli is correct, it is clear that Rousseau and Locke elevated popular freedom to precisely the level of importance blamed so severely by Plato and Aristotle as well as by Alfarabi, Averroes, and Nizām al-Mulk.

In many respects, Marx's teaching is a radicalization of Rousseau's. And after Marx, the whole tradition of Western thinking underwent a fundamental transformation. It was, however, a transformation in procedure rather than in substance. Whether we look at the new approach to political analysis ushered in by Mosca, Pareto, and Michels or concentrate on the way Comte, Durkheim, and Weber identified the subject to be investigated, we must admit that their premises are very similar to those of Machiavelli and his successors. The difference is that those premises now give rise to different questions. At the risk of over-simplifying a very complex issue, it might be said that concern with politics has now been replaced by concern with economics, society, and history.

If the foregoing analysis has any merit, it must be that it portrays how these new questions or concerns developed from a way of thinking quite similar to that followed by the peoples whose regimes we now study and how these questions or concerns developed insofar as our intellectual predecessors broke away from or rejected that line of thinking. In presenting us with such a portrait, this analysis may also very well be said to force us to consider whether that break was either necessary or inevitable. However, this last remark sounds too much like advice and suggests that it would now be appropriate for me to heed Kai Ka'ūs's advice about the proportion to be observed with wine and speech. The wise, he said, likened speech to wine, for with both it was important to consider quantity and quality; used correctly, speech, like wine, could lead to intoxication and mirth; used to excess either one would lead to headaches (Ka'ūs 1951, p. 6.23).

3

POWER AND
THE STUDY OF ELITES

Iliya Harik

INTRODUCTION

The study of elites is often divorced from the concept of politics as a process that occurs in the context of a field of action. Even most community power studies had for their ultimate goal identification of political elites and their characteristics. Many factors, doubtless, have contributed to this tendency: the visibility of leaders, the attractiveness of the subject and easy operationalization. A no less important reason for this trend has been the theory of political power enunciated by prominent political scientists such as Harold Lasswell. Lasswell's view tends to be representative of academic opinion when he defines power in interpersonal terms. Social definitions of power have not received much attention even when made by noted sociologists such as Talcott Parsons. The view raised by Max Weber and Robert Michels regarding the bureaucratic context of power has been more heeded in organization theory than in political studies of power. Political scientists have been more attracted by Weber's legalistic definition of power and the elitist aspect of Michels' theory.

Studies of political elites in the Middle East have not followed a course of their own, but stem primarily from the Lasswellian tradition.* However, to the extent that many of them are also original works, they reflect Lasswell's thought rather than follow a constrictive and narrow path.

Since Lasswell's theory of political power has guided students to focus on personal and background attributes of elites, an account of his perspective is in

---

*Recent books on elites in the Middle East have followed the same tradition of background analysis. See Lenczowski (1975), Tachau (1975), and Dekmejian (1975).

order. The impact of the Lasswellian outlook on major studies of leadership in selected Middle Eastern countries will then be examined. The chapter will conclude with a statement on political power, merely to emphasize the need for a reorientation rather than to delve deeply into theory formation.

The Personalistic Theory of Power

Lasswell has been a prolific writer and no cursory discussion such as this one would do him justice. Our purpose is rather to underline the thrust of his view on political power and its relation to elite studies rather than to develop an exposition of his thought. Lasswell's interest in psychoanalytic theory goes back to the 1930s and is reflected in several of his works (Lasswell 1930, 1935, 1948). Basically, he conceives power in psychological terms as a deference value since "it is an interpersonal relation" (Lasswell 1950, p. 74). Power behavior is a manifestation of an ego that craves deference for reasons often related to childhood experiences and as a compensation for personal shortcomings. Consequently, he concludes that the power seeker is a personality type, a view to which he devotes most of his book, *Power and Personality*.

The second main proposition of the interpersonal theory of power is the principle of compliance induced by the threat of severe sanctions. The concept of severe deprivation is a basic component of Lasswell's theory of power and is pervasive in almost all his writings on the subject. In *Power and Personality* (p. 12), he uses the concept of power "to designate relations in which severe deprivations are expected to follow the breach of a pattern of conduct." Again, in *Power and Society* (p. 75), where he conceives of power in more positive terms as "participation in the making of decisions . . . ," he holds firmly to the deprivation thesis by defining a decision as "a policy involving severe sanctions" (p. 74). Lasswell is aware that to view sanctions as the main component of the concept of power is to associate closely with "the legal tradition" (Lasswell 1948, p. 13). Thus he is ready to "recognize as power whatever relationships involve the expectations of severe deprivations" (Ibid.), regardless of the kind of institution that exercises them.

The third main principle of Lasswell's theory is the concept that power takes the form of dyadic relations where one party applies sanctions and another suffers them. To conceive of a person who exercises power is to recognize someone who is subject to it. As he puts it, "Power is participation in the making of decisions: G has power over H with respect to the values of K if G participates in the making of decisions affecting the K-policies of H" (Lasswell 1950, p. 75). Despite some qualifications (Lasswell 1950, p. 76), Lasswell's definition of power is conceived in dichotomous terms of agent and patient. He adheres to the dyadic distinction throughout his writings, sometimes using terms such as the elect and the reject of elites and mass (Lasswell 1950, p. 62; 1936a, p. 13). Thus, it may be observed that as an interpersonal relation, the Lasswellian concept of power takes a qualitative form, not subject to an interval scale of measurement. This is, of course, a shortcoming.

In brief, the political system in Lasswell's view is clearly divided into the elites who command and the masses who comply. The elite are all-powerful by virtue of their monopoly of coercive means, material resources, skills, and psychological predispositions. To the European theories of the ruling class, Lasswell has added a psychological dimension.

Lasswell has introduced many ideas and propositions regarding power and the powerful, not all of which are consistent with his theoretical perspective as previously summarized. By delineating his formal theory of power, we do not do justice to his several contributions, but rather underline the basis for his emphasis on the study of elite characteristics. Although in his view every society consists of elite and mass, Lasswell has chosen to focus attention on the elite because they reflect the dominant values in society and because their personal and background characteristics explain why they are powerful (Lasswell 1936a, p. 134).

> Political science, then, is the study of influence and the influential. Influence is determined on the basis of shares in the values which are chosen for purposes of the analysis. Representative values are deference, safety, and income. . . . Whatever the measures utilized, attention is centered upon the *characteristics of the influential* [italics added] which may be described in selected terms, like class, skill, personality, and attitude.

In addition to his essay on *Politics*, Lasswell (1952) and collaborators developed a manual for researchers to follow in studying elites, in which they elaborate on "representative values." Almost all the authors to be considered here have used Lasswell's works, and he has written forwarding statements for the works of Frey (1965) and Quandt (1969).

THE M.I.T. SCHOOL OF ELITE STUDIES

Frederick Frey's influence on the development of elite studies of Middle Eastern societies should be carefully noted here. His book was the first in the series followed by three others written by his former students while at the Massachusetts Institute of Technology (M.I.T.), all of which are of profound scholarly importance. When he wrote his book, *The Turkish Political Elite*, Frey believed that the study of elite characteristics would make an important contribution and hinted in his concluding chapter that more works of the kind were to follow (Frey 1965, p. 393).

Social background research will become truly fruitful only when a series of strategically placed, carefully accomplished studies has been achieved. The present work purports merely to be one early element in such a series.

As he promised, a series of studies did follow his own within a relatively short period of time. Not only have these works informed us on personal and social characteristics of elites in some Middle Eastern countries, but they have also made their own contributions to the strategy of elite studies.

Frey started his study on Turkey in 1956 and published *The Turkish Political Elite* in 1965. His view of political power in Turkish society is made clear at the outset: the Turkish political system consists of elite and mass separated by a very wide gap (pp. 29-30).

He carefully demonstrates the elite-mass gap by underlining the differences in the characteristics of the elite with those of the average Turk. The set of facts he presents is very striking. More than 60 percent of the Turkish elite (1920-1957) had training at the university level, while 60 percent of the male population could not read or write (p. 43). Two-thirds of the male population over fourteen years of age were engaged in agriculture, whereas only 10 percent of the elite had agricultural occupations. Professionals and officials were represented in elite positions by ten to twenty times their "weight in the male population."

When Turkish political elites are compared to their urban environment, the gap persists with minor changes. Professionals and officials constituted 13 percent of urban employed men in 1945, whereas 64 percent of deputies in the period 1920-1957 were professionals and officials. This is accentuated further by the revelation that power ranking of the elite puts officials first, professionals second, and economic groups third in importance (p. 85). In terms of a deputy's birth, officials who were most ubiquitous in parliament were the least likely to be born in their constituencies (48 percent), followed in descending order by professionals (57 percent) (p. 93). In effect, the topmost elite in Turkey were the least representative of the population in terms of their characteristics.

The changes in elite characteristics that occurred during the thirty-seven-year period examined by Frey affected the elite-mass gap, though not dramatically. The most meaningful changes occurred when Turkey moved from a single-party regime to a multiparty system in 1946. The educationally preponderant elite characteristic remained stable, whereas occupational distribution shifted in favor of lawyers and merchant groups at the expense of bureaucrats and soldiers (pp. 180-84, 195). Professionals also moved ahead of officials in top elite positions (p. 267). To a certain extent, this development narrowed the gap by increasing the representation of economic groups, but it hardly made legislators of the 1950s similar to their constituents in characteristics. For one thing, lawyers and other professionals continued to dominate (57 percent of all deputies in the 1954 Assembly).

A change in elite responsiveness occurred during this later period and their ties to their constituencies had been strengthened. The percentage of deputies born in their constituencies rose from less than 50 percent in 1943 to 66 percent by 1958 (p. 188). Free political competition also affected elite stability as can be seen from the turnover rates among legislators. While under the single-party system, two-thirds of the deputies were reelected, in the multiparty system period only about half of them returned to parliament (p. 194). When this fact is viewed in conjunction with the rising rate of localism among legislators, it becomes clear that the shift to a multiparty system strengthened constituency-elite relations. It may, however, be judicious to remain reserved in judgment regarding elite responsiveness to constituents since Frey believed that his study did not cover elite behavior adequately. As for narrowing the elite-mass gap, Frey sums it up: "Though at least some local interests were clearly more amply represented in Ankara, it was not the case that the common man had come to parliament" (p. 395).

But should it make any difference had the common man "come to parliament"? Would the event of his arrival bridge the gap between the elite and the mass simply because background factors had changed? Or would the common man act like the distinguished select whom he replaced? Frey does not address himself to these questions nor does he discuss the constraints and pressures that affect elite behavior in office. It is, however, clear that in his opinion, the social background factors of the common man are of major importance. The implication is that the elite-mass dichotomy in Turkish society can be overcome by the rise of a new elite similar in characteristics to the common man.

At any rate, the bearing of Frey's argument is that one elite group in Turkey has lost some ground to another elite group, and the distance separating the elite from ordinary citizens has remained wide. The only amelioration of this situation is the moderate increase in elite responsiveness under the multiparty system. No measure of the responsiveness of deputies is provided, but Frey and other authorities are of the opinion that constituency interests were better served under the competitive system. (See Lerner 1958; Szyliowicz 1966, pp. 142-44, 160).

Finally, it is worth noting that changes in the Turkish political system affected the political behavior of the elite as well as their recruitment patterns. This suggests that different types of political systems tend to generate different types of elites and political behavior. Moreover, factors such as momentous events, changes in the rules of the game, and rank in the hierarchy, to judge from Frey's account, affect elite behavior to a considerable extent. In effect, the major question remains to be answered: is elite behavior contingent upon background characteristics? Some researchers (Edinger and Searing, 1967) have reached a conclusion that minimizes the role of background factors, a point that calls for further empirical verification.

In 1969, the first book in the series promised by Frey was published by William Quandt, followed two years later by two others written by Marvin Zonis on Iran and by Leslie and Noralou Roos on Turkey. In his study of the Algerian political elite, *Revolution and Political Leadership*, Quandt tries to explain intra-elite conflicts during the course of the revolution and immediately after independence. He finds unsatisfactory such explanations as endemic cultural divisiveness of the Algerians, ethnic diversity, and class differences. The Marxist belief "that certain social 'facts,' such as class origin, can predict what interests an individual will have and whether he will behave on the bases of these interests" is viewed as analytically limited (1969, pp. 18–19).

Quandt explains dissension among the elite of Algeria in terms of differences in political socialization during formative years and adult experiences. Socializing agents such as the family, the school, and voluntary organizations as well as occupational and political experiences loom large in explaining the attitudes and behavior of the leaders of the Algerian revolution.

The socialization approach is doubtless a variant of background analysis, and Quandt is quite aware of this (1969, p. 18), but it would be shortsighted to consider the difference insignificant. By turning attention to the socializing agents, Quandt follows a dynamic approach based on the concept of action, rather than on an attribute, as the unit of analysis, and he endeavors throughout the book to unravel the processes through which background factors become operative. Instead of juxtaposing parallel sets, one of background characteristics and another of behavior, he uses social background factors "primarily to indicate types of experiences which in turn tend to produce values and attitudes which then influence behavior" (1969, p. 19). Schematically, he presents his model in the following form, contrasting it with the simple background analysis model. It may be noted in this respect that Zonis' model (Zonis 1971) of elite behavior is similar to Quandt's. Zonis' model is more differentiated; it does not suggest reciprocal relations between variables.

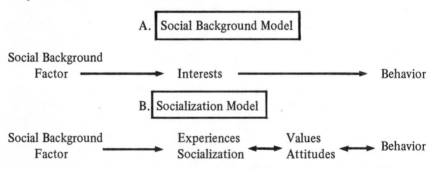

A. Social Background Model

Social Background
Factor ⟶ Interests ⟶ Behavior

B. Socialization Model

Social Background   Experiences   Values
Factor ⟶ Socialization ⟷ Attitudes ⟷ Behavior

Quandt also pays considerable attention to historical events that left a great impact on Algerians in general and their elites in particular. Some of the events specified are the Blum-Violette policies, the 1945 suppression of the mass uprising, and failure to carry out the 1948 elections. The most critical event was the declaration of the Revolution in 1954, a decisive act that galvanized the situation and called for a clear-cut response, for or against the revolution, from the various leaders of the time.

In this analysis, the concept of political system constitutes an implicit variable, in much the same way as is the case with Frey. For instance, the limited accommodative qualities of the French colonial system are shown in the expository part of the book to be a major factor affecting the attitudes and behavior of the Algerians. The momentous events, such as those previously cited, served as a test of the accommodative attributes of the colonial system, and Algerians of different experiences found them lacking.

Independence from France was the single overriding goal about which the Algerian elite were united. Social and ideological cleavages did not detract them from this common cause, although they produced intense struggle and a high turnover rate in command positions. Generational differences, though relatively narrow, were quite noticeable. Older elites were constrained by their earlier concerns and commitments while the new generation broke away from obsolete positions and sought radical solutions. The principle that different political experiences generate political discontinuities, in Quandt's account, explains more effectively elite cleavages than would cultural or ethnic differences.

A typology of political elites, based primarily on different political experiences, is drawn up by Quandt and comprises five categories: the Liberals, the Radicals, the Revolutionaries, the Military, and the Intellectuals. Members of the first three categories participated in political activities before they joined the Revolution while the latter two acquired elite status as a result of the Revolution.

The five elite types are primarily historical attitude groups in that each is identifiable in terms of reactions to a political situation in history. Such attitudes seem to correspond to generational differences, although other dimensions are clearly relevant, such as different social origins and skills. In terms of social class background, there were the relatively privileged and the less privileged. Among the privileged may be listed the Liberals, the Radicals, and the Intellectuals, who also enjoyed professional skills derived from university education. The Revolutionaries and the Military were the less privileged socially and economically and their skills were fairly limited to techniques of violence and warfare. They were also the group that failed to advance politically and economically under the French colonial regime—hence their rejection of the system in toto. In contrast, the former group believed that there were opportunities for them to work within the system, make progress, and, by constitutional means, make the colonial regime respond to Algerian demands.

Quandt does not find ideology to be an important factor in explaining the behavior of Algerian elites since it "did not deeply affect most of them" (1969, p. 124). Instead, he finds explanations in terms of "personality clashes" more convincing (1969, p. 226). On the whole, this is the more difficult and obscure aspect of Quandt's approach. Why does the Algerian not operate on a level consistent with ideology? Why is ideology not a major product of the socialization process and political experiences? How does ideology differ from political culture, which Quandt stresses later in a chapter, "Themes in Algerian Political Culture"? When the burden of explanation is placed on cultural traits such as honor, distrust, and equality in the general value system of the Algerians, earlier emphasis on acquired political attitudes during adult experience is pushed backstage. In other words, the argument shifts from experiences acquired under a certain type of political system to cultural explanations, which were earlier rejected. Moreover, the emphasis on the complexity of the Algerian personality and its uniqueness underlines once again the Lasswellian explanation of politics in terms of personality types.

Views of political culture notwithstanding, Quandt stresses the impact of system characteristics on the individual actors. An actor's behavior occurs in the context of a political structure that places constraints and offers opportunities. As problems become resolved in a manner that reflects the map of political forces, an actor tends to orient himself toward the exigencies of the organized political environment. This point could have been stressed more in the explanation of the behavior of the National Liberation Front leaders and the instability of their political careers and their conflicts, for there is reason to believe that this tendency was due to the nature of the political field of action, that is, the political system of the Revolution. The revolutionary conditions that separated the leaders from the popular base throughout the war period accentuated personality differences and facilitated shifting coalitions and instability. When independence was achieved, leaders of the Revolution were more like national symbols than heads of mass organizations. Without a stable political base, leadership stability could not be expected.

It is instructive to note in connection with this observation that the only elite group that endured after independence was the military, because it had an organized base established before it returned to Algeria. Intellectuals became subservient to the military and acquired increasingly technocratic qualities. Quandt himself refers to this separation of the Revolutionary leaders from their political base and how this made personalism assume a dominant role (1969, p. 15).

The network of power relations in a system, as may be suggested by this observation, deserves more attention than political culture and personality types. The elite-mass dilemma in Algeria takes the form of a missing organizational link with the people, caused by an oppressive colonial situation and guerrilla war conditions in the hills and across the borders. Evidence provided in the book throws doubt on the contention that the Algerian elite were lacking in cultural affinity with the people; the missing linkage was rather organizational.

While subscribing to Frey's emphasis on differences between elite and mass, Quandt offers an explanation of political behavior in terms of personality differences among Algerian leaders. It may be noted in this connection that, in terms of their background characteristics, Algerian elites were more similar to one another than to the general population, an observation true in most political systems. Yet, despite their similarities, Algerian elite have proven to be disunited and quarrelsome, a point consistent with the often overlooked fact that political competition and rivalry occurs among political actors who are most like each other. The military elite who have dominated politics in the region are of very similar training and social background, yet they are the most dangerous rivals of each other. Even in Turkey and Lebanon (see Harik 1975), where political competition occurs freely, there is more similarity between incumbents and challengers than with the rest of the population. When leaders neither owe their power to a constituency nor are accountable to it, personality differences grow out of proportion and generate dissension and instability. Obviously, there is no single or simple explanation for elite conflict and instability, though linkages within a network of social forces cannot be ignored if we are to understand politics in the Middle East just as in any other place.

In *The Political Elite of Iran*, Zonis offers novel treatment of a complex and instructive nature that goes beyond analysis of background and personal characteristics of the elite to issues pertaining to power and personality. Lasswell's keen interest in the relations of early childhood experience and the question of the insecure personality of the power seeker is explored in the Iranian case by using the Maslow Security-Insecurity Index and by taking into account adult experiences that generate insecurity among the elite. Interestingly enough, Zonis confirms Lasswell's position that the powerful are also the insecure, although he does not explain this phenomenon in terms of compensation for personal shortcomings as Lasswell does. Zonis finds elite insecurity imbedded in career uncertainties and political futures in a political system subject to the vagaries of autocratic rule.

Authoritarian governments in the Middle East readily confirm elite theory whose fundamental principle is the prevalence of a ruling class bound together by strong interpersonal relations. Political institutions appear less relevant and, in Iran, Zonis reports that they are "not paramount." Therefore, he turns to the examination of power holders whose relations he finds highly personal and manipulative. Zonis readily discovers that "where individuals in their interactions constitute the essence of the political process, the souls of men, or their personalities ... are of primary importance" (p. 10). An examination of the "souls of men" has revealed marked tendencies of cynicism, insecurity, and exploitation, which "underlie political behavior" in Iran (p. 11).

In Zonis' work one finds the M.I.T. elite study tradition developed to encompass the psychological dimension more fully, yet using a conceptual framework whose essential elements are similar to Quandt's. Both authors view background factors as relevant to the explanation of attitudes and behavior, but not in a simple and direct way; intervening variables are carefully noted.

In both cases, however, the personality typology is psychologically, not ideologically, defined. Like Quandt, Zonis concludes that the "role of ideology is minimized and politics, as enacted at the elite level in Iran, consists of the adjustment of personal differences within an elite perspective" (p. 248). Perhaps the most important contribution made by Quandt and Zonis lies in the fact that both have moved one step further from background analysis and followed a dynamic approach that focuses on the socialization process and character orientation in explaining political attitudes and behavior.

Again, elitism was not difficult to document in Iran, and Zonis describes the elite as the wealthy who enjoy high social status and who are the most educated. The majority are also urban by birth and/or residence, with an overwhelming proportion of the urban group coming from the primate city of Tehran. Occupationally, the majority of the elites have held official positions in the imperial court, cabinet, and civil or military bureaucracies, and parliament, while a smaller group of 20 percent are in private business or self-employment. Multiple occupations of elite members tend to be quite high in Iran; a member of the elite holds about 1.8 occupations on the average (p. 189; for Lebanon, 1.6, Harik 1972b, p. 33). In terms of elite circulation, Zonis has observed some new trends: (1) "political power has begun to pass from the elders of the elite to younger men" and (2) "while the elite as a whole were born of families who claim disproportionately high social status and are extremely well educated, younger men of lower social status but with equally high education have found their way into elite ranks" (p. 198).

As has been observed earlier, character types in Iran are classified by Zonis into the insecure, the cynical, the mistrustful, the exploitative, and the zenophobic. As the more basic and important characterological types, the insecure and cynical receive the greatest amount of attention. Zonis observes that, generally, these are transitive qualities in the sense that members of one group overlap in membership with other groups. Obscured by this generalization, however, are the distinctions revealed by the data between the insecure and the cynical. It has not been clearly or sufficiently brought out that the insecure and the cynical are two different groups, not only two different personality types. Those who "demonstrate the highest levels of manifest insecurity" are the "older elite with lower educations and greater parliamentary experience" (p. 233), members of high social status groups (p. 243), and those who are active in voluntary organizations of a social and political nature (p. 236). In other words, the insecure consist basically of the old-time elite of Iran, such as landlords, merchants, senators, and ranking official families, who tend to have political resources of their own and are more political in career.

In contrast to the insecure, the cynical are the newly rising official technocrats who have higher education, lower social status, and less involvement in social and political activities (p. 267). The Iranian elite who are "characterized by the social background factor most frequently associated with cynicism, i.e., relatively low status, low activity level, and high direct exposure to foreign influences, tend to be the younger, the better educated, up-and-coming members of the elite" (p. 266). In other words, the cynical are the secure technocrats coopted by the Shah to high administrative posts and, especially, to the cabinet. Their careers in public life tend to be "official" in contrast to the older elite whose careers have been basically "political." Zonis tells us that "the vast majority of the more active are the older elite," who are insecure but not cynical; "the higher the activity level, the less the cynicism" (p. 266 ff). The reading of this observation is not the least ambiguous. The most politically involved in the system are not the more cynical; an alternative explanation for cynicism seems to be called for. Insecurity, on the other hand, seems clearly associated with threats coming from a competing elite that enjoyed official favor.

The personality and attitude types developed by Quandt and Zonis gradually become cultural patterns of elite behavior, thus betraying affinity between the psychological and political culture approaches. Excursions into history have enforced this tendency to consider psychological traits, such as mistrust, cynicism, insecurity, and exploitation, as cultural features of Iranians inherited from remote ancestors. While this is not the thrust of either of the two works under consideration, falling back on political culture interpretations does not seem justified.

Generalizations about elite background in all three works on Turkey, Algeria, and Iran are very well substantiated, but the relationship of background characteristics to elite behavior is sketchy and marginal. The authors are aware of this and have referred to difficulties of studying national elite behavior in the Middle East. Nevertheless, the claims they have made regarding the relation of background factors to behavior remain in the realm of opinion rather than fact. Quandt and Zonis go a long way in demonstrating direct relationship between socialization experience and attitude of elite, and this, in fact, may turn out to be their major contribution. They have also contributed toward tempering unqualified claims that background factors explain political behavior.

In *Managers of Modernization*, Leslie and Noralou Roos add a new dimension to the background and psychological approaches of the M.I.T. school. Their interest lies mainly in an actor's attitudes and behavior in the context of his organizational environment, not so much in his background and personal characteristics. "Much of modern Turkish politics," they maintain, "seems to revolve around the relative standing of different organizations" (p. 56). As defined by the Rooses, this approach has three dimensions: the individual, the formal organization, and the political system. It is assumed that an individual actor behaves not in isolation nor with reference to a generalized model of class structure or society, but in response to his immediate environment—the formal organization.

In *Managers of Modernization*, the Turkish civil servant is viewed essentially within the organizational framework in which he operates. Basically, the Rooses focus on the prestige standing of each of the different organizations and the career opportunities available to their members. Interorganizational relations and structures are examined, but in a relatively marginal way. The administrator's attitudes toward politicians and business managers, his job satisfaction, and his career mobility are related to organizational characteristics. The data are drawn from two surveys of Turkish civil servants undertaken in 1956 and 1965, a fact which enables the Rooses to examine their subject in longitudinal perspective. Inavailability of data comparable to the surveys of 1956 and 1965, however, makes the historical venture into the single party period before 1946 no more than a reference point of marginal importance to the Rooses' study.

There are two reasons why the Rooses' work does not adequately integrate the political system variable in the tripartite model. First, the lack of data pertaining to the single-party system makes comparisons of the impacts of the two different systems on the civil servants out of the question. Second, the Turkish political system in 1956 and in 1965 was practically the same—multiparty and parliamentary—and, therefore, does not offer significant contrast for analysis of system effect on behavior.

Although systemic differences are not fully developed, the impact of organizational memberships on elite attitude is. The Rooses discover that the administrators' attitudes differ relative to the organization in which they work. Particular contrasts are noted with regard to the Ministry of the Interior, other central ministries, and state organization enterprises.

It is noted, first, that members of the Interior Ministry are less remunerated, less mobile, and least satisfied with their careers. Moreover, in terms of prestige, the Interior Ministry, though still influential, has lost some ground to the Ministries of Finance and Foreign Affairs during the period under study. Individuals working for the latter two ministries show more job satisfaction, are better paid, and enjoy more skills and mobility than those in the Interior. Aside from Foreign Affairs, managers of state enterprises rank highest in terms of job satisfaction, remuneration, and skills. The differences in the standings of these organizations affect recruitment patterns as well. The Interior Ministry, for instance, attracts low income and low level school achievers as compared with other organizations.

Longitudinal analysis of attitudes, however, reveals significant variations that should not remain overlooked. When members' attitudes in the different official organizations are viewed in historical perspective, the picture changes markedly from the one drawn up by the Rooses. A comparison of job satisfaction among the 241 panel respondents of 1956 and 1965 reveals that attitudes have improved most in the central ministries, especially the Ministry of the Interior (p. 89). (Average percentage improvement for the central ministries is 7.3 while for other it is 0.2 percentage point.) This observation suggests that competitive parliamentary politics contributed to the improvement of relations between politicians and civil servants. Another point that deserves to be underlined is that those who are more critical of politicians are the highly educated and remunerated managers of the prestigious organizations, rather than members of the central ministries (pp. 174, 176). This observation bears a striking similarity to Zonis' finding in Iran that the elite who were more educated and secure in their careers were the more critical and cynical respondents.

An interesting observation in *Managers of Modernization* is that adult socialization has had an uncertain and perhaps indifferent effect on attitudes (p. 171). This is at variance with the positions held by Zonis and Quandt, but since the research instruments in these studies are not equivalent, attitude comparison is not likely to be precise. The Rooses consider recruitment an important factor in explaining an administrator's attitudes and, by implication, experiences prior to joining the bureaucracy deserve special attention (p. 175). Finally, the Rooses tend to agree with Quandt and Zonis that background factors are less directly relevant to understanding attitudes and behavior.

In what it establishes, *Managers of Modernization* stands on its own, like the other studies of the M.I.T. school, and needs no apologies or defense. Conceptual frameworks such as the ones we have encountered in these studies are organizing principles not hypotheses, and, therefore, remain suggestive and helpful in broadening our conceptual perspectives. I personally find myself in agreement with the Rooses' theoretical framework, even though it is only partially fulfilled. Operationally, the impact of bureaucratic environment on the subject of decision making is overlooked in favor of psychological variables such as motivations and satisfaction. The outcome is to minimize the importance of behavioral considerations. As was mentioned earlier, the system variable is to a large extent obscured when it is linked to the concept of "ruralizing elections," which forced the authors to compare the single party and multiparty regimes without have the data basis for such an undertaking. The point that party competition in 1946, inter alia, led to ruralizing elections is neither clear nor is its impact revealed except for occasional references to pressures on members of the Ministry of the Interior. Borrowing the concept from Huntington, the Rooses state that ruralizing elections "are characterized by the defeat of an urban-based modernizing elite, the mobilization of new rural voters, and the coming to power of a non-cosmopolitan local elite" (p. 2). No one would question the fact that, after 1946, new voters were mobilized, but there is considerable doubt that the leaders of the Democrat Party who replaced the Republicans were less modernizing in orientation or less urban. Frey shows them to be just as urban, educated, and professional as the previous elite. Election studies also show that the Democrat Party stronghold was the urban region of Marmara and Izmir, while, curiously enough, the Peoples' Republican Party had some of its strongest electoral bases in the rural east.

It may finally be remarked that the link between alleged "ruralizing elections" and the overthrow of the parliamentary regime of Adnan Menderes is quite speculative. Moreover, downward mobility of civil servants as it is discussed in *Managers of Modernization* does not mean material or moral losses, but simply a difficulty in attaining more prestigious political jobs. As for the military who actually overthrew the Menderes regime, we are told practically nothing. Particular historic events, such as those that brought about the downfall of the Menderes government, have been overlooked, despite the fact that very few would dispute the point that the coup was mainly caused by the imposition of majority dictatorship in the context of a parliamentary system. This is obviously a violation of the rules of the game and of the basic democratic principle that guarantees the political rights of a minority.

More recently, Leonard Binder, in a volume on Egypt (1978), has come out with another contribution to elite studies in the Middle East, not related conceptually to the M.I.T. school, but rather to Mosca, Marx, Barrington Moore, and Deutsch.* Binder finds the synthesis of all four approaches necessary because he is concerned with explaining the Egyptian Revolution of 1952, not with elites as an end product. The assumption is that if we understand the leaders upon whom the regime relies in governing, we understand the type of system and its orientation. From a political science point of view, Binder's assumption is that elite study is crucial for understanding politics and political systems. Elites shape society according to their òwn interests and orientation, provided they are strategically located.

But who are the elites? Binder's approach is to focus on the second stratum, that is, middle-level elites through whom central authorities rule. Unlike central elites, middle-level elites are very large in numbers and spread out in society. By virtue of their position in the middle, they are strongly linked to society below and national elites at the top. The elite–mass dichotomy thus is no longer as sharp as it is represented in the M.I.T. school. An intermediary force is introduced and is seen as permeating power relationships.

Social science theories of the nineteenth century and more contemporary ones make it possible to reconcile elite theory to social analysis. From Mosca, Binder learns the significance of the political role of the middle-level elites, the second stratum. However, the second stratum concept fails to explain the revolutionary character of the Egyptian regime. Marx's concept of partial revolution fills the gap. It is a political revolution in which a segment or class emancipates itself and society, with which it shares common grounds sufficiently strong to make it possible for the revolution to assume the role of representing society as a whole. A partial revolution is thus not a radical revolution that achieves a universal human emancipation. Partial revolutions produce regimes that underplay class struggle and emphasize national unity. They try to forge a national coalition of various forces on a broad basis and under the leadership of the revolution.

---

*I. William Zartman is another writer who does not belong to this school and has concerned himself with elites in his various writings on politics in North Africa.

In Egypt, the rural middle class was able to capture the support of the masses, produce its intellectual segment, and take on some of the tasks of the second stratum. It thus represents the core of the broad coalition upon which the regime's power is based. Marx, however, did not view the rural bourgeoisie as a revolutionary segment or strategically located to transform society. Barrington Moore adds that dimension by bringing into relief the role of rural society in the development of nations. The Egyptian countryside, moreover, was mobilized in both Deutsch's and Apter's senses of the term. The rural middle class or notables, as Binder often refers to them, were quite mobilized at the time of the revolution and joined its course. The strong connection between the rural bourgeoisie and the military bureaucratic apparatus of the state made such an alliance natural.

Having defined the nature of the revolution, one expects that the study will focus on linkages between leaders of the revolution and the second stratum, since a network approach is implied by the interpretation of the revolution. This Binder does not do. He lets it be understood that the linkage between the military bureaucratic apparatus of the state and the second stratum is given. One also has to assume that national elites are themselves the intellectual segment of the rural middle class. Accordingly, Binder proceeds to demonstrate the continued strength of the rural middle class as it is manifested in the prominent role it plays in the regime's official movement in the various stages of its metamorphosis. Most of the empirical study, thirteen out of fifteen chapters, is devoted to demonstrating the strong presence of the rural notables in the leadership of the regime's popular movement at various levels, their political roots in the ancient regime, their strong kinship base, their occupations, and regional differentiations.

Binder examines the officers of the regime's National Union and its successor, the Arab Socialist Union, and finds that the rural middle class is overrepresented at the expense of the urban population. The second major finding is that about half of these middle-level elites come from strong rural families that were politically prominent before the revolution. In this Binder sees not only continuity with the old regime, but also the importance of primary groups such as the family. The attention given family-set elites is understandable in view of their persistence despite radical change. Yet it may also be argued that the new subnational elites, who were just as numerous, reflect transition and individualism that are not less deserving of attention. Binder's stress on the former is perhaps due to his observation that elites from family sets have shown stronger survival qualities than some of the newcomers.

Another interesting finding is the strong link Binder observes between the rural middle class and the new members of the professional, technical, and intellectual groups. Empirically, he finds that the most prominent segments of the rural middle class are the mobilized individuals in the Deutsch sense of the term, namely the urban in outlook. This strong link of affinity leads Binder to conclude that the new professional, technical, and intellectual groups are part of the second stratum. In what may seem to some as a shift in the argument, he points out in the last chapter that the Nasser regime "ruled through the urbanized and educated kin of the rural middle class." In my studies on Egypt, I have found that the mediating elites have been subnational party leaders, bureaucrats, and national intellectuals who used the ubiquitous mass media in the service of the regime. Thus, I find myself in agreement with Binder's broadening of the definition of the second stratum.

Another serious question Binder addresses is the role of the rural middle class. Are its members compliant servants of the regime or are they serving their own interests? Binder finds that they help the regime check the participation of hostile elements and at the same time protect their own local interests. He notes, however, that tension could be detected between the regime and the rural middle class despite their collaboration.

This study focuses on background characteristics of the elites, despite the different intellectual route it had taken. The attraction of identifying the personal and social characteristics of elites is understandable, especially when it is made to serve an informative purpose as in Binder's study. However, in a work such as this in which elite relations, in particular between the second stratum and the occupants of military–bureaucratic apparatus of the state, are of central importance, background analysis can serve as no more than an introduction. Moreover, since Binder does not consider the regime's official movement politically effective at any time, studying its leaders' backgrounds does not tell us very much about their influence. It may, moreover, create the impression that rural notables were a political pillar of the Nasser regime.

In addition to the subnational leaders of the official movement, the Nasser regime ruled through collaboration of the police, the army, the bureaucracy, and the intellectual community who masterminded the all-powerful mass media of the regime. Naturally, we need to know the social identity of all these secondary actors and the manner in which they came to occupy their positions. The second, more important, question is how are they related to one another at various levels and to the different groups in society. Are second-level elites related to one another and do they cooperate along horizontal lines or are they connected vertically and separately to national leadership? The impressive presence of rural notables in the regime's official party does not serve their overall interests, and they are economically the major losers subsequent to land reforms and state control of the domestic market in agriculture. They are, however, performing a holding operation, using their party positions to maintain and strengthen their ties with the provincial bureaucracy from whom they draw a variety of benefits.

METHODOLOGY OF ELITE RESEARCH
AND OVERVIEW

The methods followed for identifying and analyzing elites differ from one writer to another. Frey, Quandt, and Binder used a positional method: in Turkey, parliamentary and cabinet members; in Algeria, leaders of the Revolution; and in Egypt, leaders of the official party. To a limited extent, Frey and Quandt made use of unstructured interviews for obtaining data on some of the elite in addition to documentary material.

The reputational method, used by Zonis, is not limited to holders of formal office but includes other leaders in various sectors of society such as business, professions, and religion. Of the 3,100 names obtained in this way, a panel of informants identified the top-ranking ten percent, a little more than half of whom were actually interviewed. In the case of the Rooses, they relied mainly on two surveys of civil servants conducted nine years apart, but they, like the rest, resorted to documentary and historical data in addition, to expand the range of their generalizations beyond the survey results proper.

This is not the context to examine or question the positional or the reputational methods of studying elites; a great deal has been written about the subject (see Rose 1967, Polsby 1963). Suffice it to say that a more conscious effort by the authors to discuss the limitations of these methods and to specify the kind of results they yield would have been helpful.

Identifying national elites and attributing degrees of influence to them is an undertaking fraught with methodological problems and pitfalls, but this should not discourage us from dealing with the subject. It would be necessary, however, for an author to discuss the methodological dimension carefully and limit his undertaking to its bounds. The studies examined in this chapter shed light on various high-ranking elite groups, but in no case can one say with confidence that all the top leaders of the communities under examination were included. Conspicuously absent are military elites, whose importance in the Middle East cannot be underestimated. Moreover, the question of ranking elites is even more difficult, and in no way could we continue to rely on a single method for this purpose, such as the reputational method, which is most commonly used. Survey methods, decision-making analysis, participant observation, sociogramic analysis, and leaders' records are necessary if we are to place more confidence in conclusions reached by elite studies. Reliance on a single method is misleading, especially since different methods are suited to different situations and tend to elicit different kinds of data (see Harik 1974).

The reputational method, in particular, may be a more adequate instrument for the study of elites in small communities—villages, city quarters, and provincial towns—than national systems. Curiously, even where it has been applied to subnational communities, the method has led to conclusions similar to those obtained in national systems, namely the prevalence of a power elite. As reputational techniques elicit leaders' names in the order of attributed influence, inevitably a group of leaders surfaces on the top as the most influential. I have applied this method to a small community of 6,000 inhabitants and obtained a name list of top leaders, just as in every other study that followed this route (Harik 1974). However, sociogramic analysis demonstrated that those top leaders were divided into separate blocs, were stratified on each bloc level, and maintained varying degrees of contacts across bloc lines. Moreover, decision-making analysis underlined the difference between social status and power standing as well as the question of specialization of influence.

Elite studies represent three different strains or basic assumptions, not necessarily consistent nor adhered to in toto by all elite students. Elite studies, though, reflect one or the other of these assumptions, often depending on the writer's predilections. These are (1) that leaders' behavior is explained by their background characteristics or early socialization experiences, (2) elites are so distinctive that it is doubtful they represent (except themselves and their cohorts), and (3) that elites represent the social class or group with which they share characteristics and interests. Research methods followed in elite studies, however, do not seem adequate for eliciting information relevant to demonstrating such generalizations. In the second place, analysis of elites as surveyed here does not even seek to demonstrate these propositions, but tends to assume their truth.

In view of this, let us not dwell longer on methodology, but comment briefly on some major findings of elite research.

First, the empirical finding that political elites tend to come from a socially more advanced class and to be more educated does not necessarily imply their inability to represent other groups, unless one assumes that elites are immune from the influence of social forces. But since forces govern interactions among actors, it follows that the relations or links between leaders and ordinary people are important features of the political process. Linkage analysis underlines the network of relations among holders of power and between them and social forces in a society.

Second, the tendency of political elites to succeed themselves, especially in democracies, does not necessarily demonstrate that such systems are dominated by oligarchies. In a politically competitive system, reelection often indicates an ability on the part of the representative to be responsive to his constituency (Sullivan and O'Conner 1974, Harik 1972) and consolidate his resources. Elite responsiveness to constituents may be a more important indicator of democracy than elite mobility.

Third, when compared with the average citizen, political leaders—it cannot be denied—have more education, skill, wealth, status, and the like. However, it remains to be demonstrated that homogeneous characteristics and background create unity of purpose among elites and that the elite represent the narrow interests of those who resemble them in characteristics. Interelite relations are more complex than is usually suggested.

Fourth, political elites may be more educated, wealthy, and enjoy a higher social status, but they are not necessarily the most distinguished in these qualities. The most successful physicians, lawyers, and business managers do not generally move to political careers, and one rarely finds them among government officials. Whatever their other qualities may be, elites are political professionals, often in the narrow sense of the term. A leader cannot make a career in politics without acquiring the political craft necessary for success. When viewed in terms of their background characteristics, political elites stand above the average citizen but below the top level of the social and intellectual orders. This is not as regrettable as it sometimes appears to be, for it is by no means certain that the best interest of a political community is served by the most talented and successful of its members. It is often observed that those who have achieved distinction in their firlds of specialization tend to be independent in judgment, distant, and less trustful of the principles of representation, social consensus, and compromise. In short, the more distinguished may be more authoritarian in attitude than is ordinarily the case with professional politicians.

Fifth, when described in terms of background characteristics, political leaders appear more cohesive than they usually are. Common characteristics are not necessarily indicators of political cohesion. It is no doubt possible, especially in small towns, for a political elite to establish unity and hegemony (Vidich and Bensman 1958), but this has to be viewed in perspective of social conditions and the vicissitudes of time. We may be reminded of how few are the political "machines" that have survived in the cities of the United States. The number of reported cases in which an autonomous elite prevails is small, and empirical evidence still does not justify generalizations across the board. Moreover, community studies are not unanimous in affirming the existence of a power elite nor homogeneity in background when such an elite is identified (Dahl 1960 and Harik 1974).

Sixth, the very idea of "recruiting" elites, a term current in the literature, literally selecting them, is out of tune with reality and is charged with ideological overtones. The wide currency the term has received in political science reflects consciously or unconsciously the classical theory of elites whereby those in power determine the selection of their successors. Political science needs a descriptive and accurate term to refer to the process by which elites enter and exit the political arena. Resort to the term cooptation as an alternate reflects the same bias. For the sake of clarity, use of the term elite circulation is more appropriate. It is free from theoretical and ideological bias and is descriptively accurate.

FIELD THEORY OF POWER

Power is a variant form of influence, and influence is a social force. Social forces are aggregates, and actions are their component parts. Human actors who experience a desire for security, for example, and act to achieve that objective are subject to forces driving them in specific directions. The forces that drive human actors are as numerous as human interests, desires, and aspirations. Influence is the resultant of the interactions among various actors driven by the same or different forces.

Influence thus is a dynamic phenomenon, and its study requires the techniques that relate quantity to motion. Hence, an action may be analyzed in terms of its basic components: strengths and direction. For example, a protest march against racial discrimination is a directed activity, a motion from point one to point two. As a directed activity, it also has magnitude or weight (quantity); it could be a strong or a weak protest. A protest demonstration in which 10,000 persons march is stronger than one in which only a few participate. The strength of an action is defined as the degree of its persistence in its own course (the same direction). Direction is the orientation of the activity. The study of influence calls for relating varying strengths and directions of interacting forces.

As a process of interaction, influence is the resultant of the encounter of forces of varying magnitudes and directions. In order to measure power interactions, it is necessary to use techniques in which quantities can be related to directions. A scalar quantity can be measured by means of a unit and a number, as is the case with an object in a store. Simple addition would suffice to determine the total result. An activity, however, is not a scalar quantity and cannot be measured by simple addition.

Influence is a vector quantity; it has magnitude and direction. Magnitude taken alone is a scalar quantity and refers to the strength of the force in play. It reflects the strength of commitment an actor has to a set of attitudes or behavior and/or the resources committed to support them. Direction is a definition of the course of action or motion in relation to a specific point. The point toward which an object moves or an actor is oriented defines the direction of a force. In social science terms, direction refers to the bearing of behavior or attitudes.

An influence attempt generates and/or redirects another social force in the object acted upon. The influence attempt and the response to it are both vectors. The combined effects of two or more vectors is called a resultant. Hence, influence is a process of interacting forces the outcome of which is measured by vector addition. Some political scientists object to quantification on the basis that influence is an activity and an activity is not additive since it cannot be represented by a number and a unit. Understandably, we cannot use simple addition to gauge the impact of an action such as an influence attempt, but we can use vector addition, which does represent actions and their impact. Vector addition is different from arithmatic addition because it takes into consideration directions, not only magnitudes.

A vector may be represented graphically by an arrow, the head pointing to the direction of the force while the arrow length is drawn in proportion to the force magnitude. Thus interaction may be represented graphically, especially when it involves the simple combination of a few forces. Complex analysis, however, would be more easily conducted through algebraic use of vectors. Mathematically, a vector is defined as an ordered collection of numbers written in row or column forms. Algebraically, a vector is written $(x_1, y_1, . .)$ and a second vector as $(x_2, y_2, . .)$ and so forth. This is not the context in which to elaborate on techniques of vector analysis, and we shall assume an awareness of this simple mathematical technique on the part of the reader.* Suffice it to say that vector analysis lends itself to consideration of more than two actors and forces. Influence as the resultant of interacting forces may thus be expressed as the sum of all vectors.

$$(x_1, y_1, z_1, . .) + (x_2, y_2, z_2, . .) + (x_3, y_3, z_3, . .) . . .$$

In other words, when an influence attempt occurs, several forces that involve two or more actors are activated, the outcome of which is registered as the resultant of the combined vectors. The forces released in the attempt often run in diverse directions and have different strengths. The resultant of an influence interaction is relative to the components of all the involved forces. Not only does this formula relate quantity to direction, but it also leads to a broader outlook that encompasses patterns of behavior such as support and convergence.

The view of influence as the sum of all vectors provides a perspective in which influence is viewed as aggregative and integrative rather than as a residual outcome. In all but a few of influence interactions, the process leads to reinforcement of position, the binding together of people, and the accumulation of power. Influence is a force that accounts for social cohesion and effectiveness.

The theory of power based on the dichotomy of ruler and ruled, elite and mass, narrows down the phenomenon to the overcoming of resistance. It is a theory of dominance in which power is the residue of what remains of the encounter. It fails to include the phenomenon of support and convergence of forces as essential aspects of the influence process. In contrast, the vector formula of influence expresses possibilities of convergence as well as of overcoming of resistance. It, moreover, underlines the fact that most influence interaction involves values of convergence and resistance.

Further consideration of the process of power generation reveals, once more, the limitations of the two-tier structure of power and the principle of severe sanctions. For instance, forces susceptible to reorientation and activation are often found in a competitive system. A political actor encounters forces in the field that are favorable, resistant, or uncommitted. Work coordination aimed

---

*Vector analysis is the subject of an extensive inquiry into the theory of power undertaken by the author of this chapter.

at the consolidation of forces that are inclined to move in the actor's direction are convergent, not dichotomous, forces. The concept of convergence throws doubt on the two-tier concept of power in terms of superordinate-subordinate relationship. A voter whose ideals or interests coincide with those of a candidate and who votes for him is himself exercising power, in a small unit value, no doubt, but exercising it nevertheless in such a way as to add to the power sum of one candidate. It can be observed in this case that the dichotomous structure of power disappears as it is no longer possible to classify the two parties in the interaction as agent and patient. Is the voter superordinate or subordinate in this case? Is the candidate superordinate or subordinate? Is it not, rather, true that both the voter and the candidate are generating power at the same time by playing different roles? Are they not both involved in seeking to achieve a common objective, rather than becoming involved in acts of subordination?

The two-tier conception of power gives rise to problems again when one looks at a compromise case. When a compromise decision occurs, one party complies with another party's wishes in as much as the second party is made to comply with the wishes of the first. Under such conditions, each one of the actors can be considered as agent and patient at one and the same time. The dichotomy in the two-tier theory should give way to a concept in which influence relations are viewed as continuous and interactive. In effect, conceiving of power in terms of continuous and interactive relations opens up the range of analysis beyond the elite-mass dichotomy, toward analysis of power aggregation, networks, and generation. Furthermore, the interactive and continuous pattern of power better explains the growth aspect in the volume of power in addition to the zero-sum possibility to which the two-tier theory is limited.

The dominance theory, or what we shall refer to here occasionally as the residual model, applies to one type of social interaction only: when the interacting forces are diametrically opposed to each other. In such a case, direction is held constant and the resultant of the interaction can be expressed by a plain subtraction formula applicable to scalar quantities. The shortcomings of such a model are clear. First, it describes a limited part of the influence phenomenon. Second, it stresses the dissipation of forces and overlooks their generation. For forces that encounter only resistance diminish successively as they use up resources to overcome more resistance. If influence is such a phenomenon and occurs only among diametrically opposed forces, it would lead to debilitation of actors and to social disintegration. A theory of influence that is limited to the loss of resources and ignores the aggregation and integration of forces cannot be very useful.

The integrative view of influence underlines the fact that many interacting forces have converging directions to a greater or lesser degree and that objectives sought are not always exclusive. Unlike the dominant theory, which underlines the characteristics of a ruling class as the focus of the political process, the integrative theory of influence stresses social cohesion, collective action, and network analysis. It shifts the emphasis from looking at individual actors and their social characteristics to social forces. Second, it represents reality as an organized set of relationships or networks in which linkages are of central importance.

It has been necessary to make this formal statement in order to provide the theoretical basis for the criticism made of the elite approach and to integrate the question of power generation into the power theory. On this latter question, the literature follows two separate and discrete courses. Theories of power have been presented in terms of ability of one actor to dominate another, change of attitude, causal sequences, and as an exchange of benefits. None, except exchange theory, to a limited extent, provides a basis for taking integrative activity into account. Empirical literature on the political process, in contrast, is full of relevant information on the generation and organization of power: alliances, coalitions, campaigning, communications, socialization, formations of associations and political parties, mobilization, and other themes. It can readily be seen that the issue of harnessing political resources and support constitutes a major focus of the empirical literature. Yet, hardly any of these relevant empirical data can be explained or better understood in terms of the prevailing power theories. Political analysis of community studies have tried to integrate power theory with empirical examination of social structure and with the integrative political processes, yet such studies have also been seriously limited by the dominance theory and showed a preoccupation with elites and their identification.

Viewing power as a matter of interacting forces that may be of converging or divergent directions makes it possible to study the political process fruitfully and consistently with the theory of power. In short, field theory offers broader scope for analysis of the political phenomenon.

At this point, we may suggest, in regard to the political process, that the question is not the social characteristics of a holder of power, but the identification of social forces, their linkages, organization, and interactions. For, if the objective is to understand the behavior of power holders and the interests they serve, the forces that enable them to take action and place limits on their behavior should be explored.

A political person acts in the context of a field of action and in relation to the forces in the field. A field of action is an analytical concept that helps identify the social unit under study. It is not a label for a fixed object. It could be any social unit: a business firm, a village or town, a tribe, a political party, a nation state, a regional organization, and so on. It is for the student to determine what the unit is and why. Social units are isolated only for study; in reality they are all subject to external influences. To the extent that external influences impinge on the field of action, they become part of it. A student usually notes the source of the external influence factor and focuses on its effects on the field of action under study, without going into its study as a whole. Or, one may, on the guidance of empirical findings, decide to expand or redefine the field of action under study. It should be noted here that the question of boundaries, which preoccupied students of the political system in the 1960s, becomes secondary in the light of this approach.

To elaborate on the study of power in the light of field theory, we may refer to the *Political Mobilization of Peasants*, which offers the advantage of a textual reference. There, a village community in Egypt was examined as a field of action in view of the struggles that occurred among different social forces for influence over its affairs and resources. The political field was made up of male actors only, most of whom were peasant cultivators, workers, and people engaged in off-farm activities. Some 44 individuals were roughly identified as political leaders. In background characteristics, they included poor and rich peasants, government officials, business people, and laborers. They were also possible to rank in importance, but again, the top-ranking leaders were diversified in social background. It was not possible to understand the behavior of these leaders and the interests they served by means of identification of their social characteristics. Many of them shared similar characteristics, yet were engaged in competition on different sides, and alliances were inclusive of leaders of diverse social background. Nor would it have been possible to say how much power and influence they enjoyed by means of defining their social characteristics. For in one system there may be less government than in another, and leaders enjoy far less influence in one system than in another.

The field theory approach directs attention to the actual forces in play: the clusters they form, the linkages among the different clusters, the cohesiveness of each cluster, and the resources available or committed. In Shubra el-Gedida, the Egyptian village under study, several forces were identified and shown to have different degrees of organization and effectiveness.

The forces identified follow. First is the force emanating from the mobilization drive coming from the national government. It found support locally among officials in coalition with young males whose driving force was socialist national ideology nurtured over the years by the national regime. It was also supported by poorer peasants who found political leverage in the national government presence in the community and by individuals with vested interest in cooperation with the government. This was a coalition with a strong core group, but not great cohesion, and therefore it allowed its members the freedom of linkages with other political clusters.

The second main force was organized around the welfare and political status of formerly landless peasants who became owners as a result of agrarian reform and had a sectional interest to promote and defend against other forces in the community. A third force revolved around traditional interests and loyalties represented in the headman, his family, friends, and clients. This served the interests of privilege and status and was on the defensive from the new forces that had emerged as a result of political changes, nationally and locally. A fourth force represented the interests and status of well-to-do peasants headed by two brothers who were politically skilled, ambitious, and wealthy. They coalesced with middle level peasants who shared similar outlooks and interests. In addition, this group was given support by clients such as laborers or individuals who benefited from the largesse of the wealthy peasants. Their access to provincial and national government won them the support of villagers who needed to count on an intermediary with the bureaucracy. The fifth force was agricultural laborers who were struggling to organize and build their forces in the community, to raise their economic status and improve their welfare against peasants, small and large.

The social nature of power was manifested in the fact that all these forces organized or sought to organize in one form or another. An actor who kept his independence usually built links with one or another of these clusters or established links with some individuals who gave support for what he stood for in terms of general community welfare or local values he embodied. However, by focusing on networks we learned about the organization of social power, linkages that developed in the community, effectivness of certain forces, and interests served. The official mobilization force organized its supporters around the official party branch in the community. The beneficiaries of land reform organized their forces around the cooperative society and used the functional organization to serve political purposes. The traditional group of the headman sought to capture the official party branch and the cooperative society to use as instruments of decision making. The rich farmer coalition organized its forces around the official party and municipal council. The landless agricultural laborers tried to harness their forces within a labor trade union. Of these organizations, two were sectional, that is, limited in membership to a special group (laborers and beneficiaries of agrarian reform). Two other organizations were general, that is, of village-wide relevance (the party branch and the village council).

Political forces in this field of action were characterized by mobility and interpenetration. All the different groups sought to have presence or influence in the village-wide organizations of the village council and the party branch. Most tried to penetrate the sectional organizations, the labor union and the cooperative, even when not entitled to membership. Moreover, all the groups had linkages, weak or strong, with one another. In some cases, this meant political cooperation on a number of issues, and, in other cases, it meant that communications lines remained open between the various forces even in times of tension. The proliferation of forces that were organized in this field of action meant that no single force or interest would be served exclusively. Leaders had to act in a restrained way and to seek the support of groups other than their own to be able to make decisions. Therefore, alliances and actors sought to maintain their links with different alliances and to try to minimize differences when possible. Efforts to establish hegemony proved a frustrating experience, and leaders had to take others into account in practically everything that was done in the community. It was tempting to try, however, in view of the limited number of people with entrenched attachments, thus leaving most individuals susceptible to efforts aimed at changing their positions.

The question of cohesion of political clusters was related to the issue of effectiveness of politics. Political actors in the community gave partial commitment to the cluster or force that served their interests, especially because they often saw their interests as possible to serve by different rival groups. Thus members of the community were able to find, in this limited and diversified support they lent to groups, a special political benefit. Thus no single group was able to achieve a strong degree of cohesion, to exclude others completely, or to act independently. Not only were resource commitments on the part of actors diversified, but also very limited. Most village actors, officials included, had very limited resources in time, skill, incentive, contacts, and money to commit to political ends. The least resourceful in this respect was the union of landless laborers.

Thus, in effect, the extent to which the community could mobilize or achieve ends or resolve issues by political means remained limited, though not defective. That way individuals reserved a degree of autonomy and freedom from political interference.

It is generally the case that when linkages of leaders to constituents are weak, leaders enjoy great ability to make decisions freely from considering the public. It may be thought that this was the case in Shubra. The fact, however, is that linkages seemed weak because they were distributed over a number of leadership clusters, but, in fact, villagers did not lack commitment; they simply spread it widely. Any leader who acted in disregard of his constituents stood a great chance of losing his support to other leaders. Moreover, the pluralism of the forces in play meant that different forces checked one another and prevented a hegemony by one representative of a social force. Thus the Shubra situation was not characterized by weak linkages, but by their being extensive and inclusive. When linkages are extensive and inclusive, decisions are made after much consultation and adjustment to the wishes of various forces in order to make their implementation effective and to prevent loss of political support.

In short, the political behavior of actors in this field of action was a function of the distribution of power networks, the linkages established, and the limited resource commitments on the part of political actors. The behavior of leaders in other fields of action with different networks and resource commitments would naturally be different.

It may be interjected that, in this community, freedom for local politics has contributed to the expression and organization of social forces, while in most Middle Eastern countries, national politics is dominated by authoritarian governments which have obtained power by means of violence or have inherited office with despotic powers. It may be noted that eight governments in the Middle East came to power or stayed there by means of military intervention in politics. This suggests that power is highly concentrated at the national level and that those who occupy top positions are extremely powerful. Social forces are pushed underground or are decimated anyway. The conclusion is that focusing on top power holders is more telling than another approach.

This is a credible and meaningful observation, not to be ignored by students of authoritarian regimes in the Middle East. In the light of the outlook enunciated here, however, one looks at the structure of top power to identify its components and see on what they rest. Authoritarianism does not suggest the absence of structure but a different structure, not the absence of contests but different contests. Usually, an authoritarian regime, as we have come to know it in the Middle East, is constituted of a complex network of ties among individuals who are strategically located in the coercive machinery of the state. These are usually the military officers, the police, intelligence agencies, and popular militias. Preservation of such forces, in balance in support of the regime, is a constant job of intensive behind-the-scenes activity. At this stage such regimes depend entirely on coercion, that is, on the overcoming of resistance. Thus they tend to be fragile, despite all their authoritarianism. They are fragile in internal structure, because actors who depend entirely on control of coercive machinery do not constitute a stable force nor do they have a stable policy. thus they tend to be undependable and may threaten the coalition from within. They are weak, moreover, because they depend on intimidation and coercion of others to implement their decisions, rather than on positive forces of support in society. Without positive public support, decisions are very difficult and costly to implement, for those who are supposed to implement and those who are affected by decisions have countless ways of withholding cooperation and subverting policy implementation. Hence, authoritarian regimes tend to have the capacity to make decisions, but not to make them stick.

However, with the passage of time, many authoritarian regimes in the Middle East have developed more sophisticated ways to supplement their coercive forces with collaboration of segments of the public. The more sophisticated and enduring regimes have combined a high degree of coercive power with skill in holding their leadership cohesively and have shown an ability to develop support within society. That is, they combine coercive means to overcome resistance with the harnessing of forces to converge with their own direction of policy.

The pattern developed by these authoritarian regimes to build their social base has one thing in common: undermine and weaken autonomous political and social forces, modern and traditional, then pick up the pieces and construct them anew. Regardless of whether they are hereditary rulers or revolutionaries, authoritarian regimes tend to be levellers. That is, they try to destroy or weaken any social or political hierarchy, even when not hostile to them. They prefer to deal with weakened organizations subservient to them and to prevent the development of new organizations that express the views and interests of modern forces emerging in society. Thus neither the revolutionaries nor the hereditary rulers are actually political modernizers.

Authoritarian regimes constitute a different type of network, not its absence. Let us look at one successful case, Nasser's regime, to highlight the broad outlines of the networks he had developed to sustain his regime.

Nasser came to power at the head of the Free Officers group in the military by an act of violence. Through his control of the means of coercion, he dispersed organized political forces represented in political parties and the institution of the monarchy. Then he used both coercion and political means to undermine the powers of social segments of the population such as landowners, business groups, trade unions, and professional associations. He appealed, over the heads of all these forces, for the support of the masses and mobilized the public against them. He used direct appeal and established linkages with the intellectuals in the mass media to drum up support for his regime. After ten years, a strong populist and authoritarian regime was firmly in the saddle under him and his cohorts.

This authoritarian and populist regime had a complex structure that could not be understood by studying the men on top only. At the top, it was made up of various clusters of holders of sensitive positions in the government and military machineries. These constituted networks that cooperated, competed, and watched each other. In their relations to the rest of society, they depended on two major instruments: first, Nasser's popular appeal to establish strong popular following and second, pervasive administrative and intelligence bureaucracies. All autonomous bodies had been taken over or destroyed. Having weakened if not completely displaced solidarity groups, the regime established links with loyal and collaborative actors—individuals who happened to have skill and/or social position. They were put in or assisted in occupying key positions in the various organizations in society that had lost their autonomy, such as trade unions, professional organizations, boards of the press, and nationalized business, and in the official party movement. Individual actors, in associations and the official party, were heterogeneous and were allowed to compete so long as they abided by the broad lines of commitment set by the regime. Their backgrounds did not matter much so long as they had influence in their immediate circles and were willing to collaborate with the regime. Thus he tapped a large and widespread army of political collaborators who staffed all the existing channels or structures of influence in society and tied them directly to the regime's command. They were given freedom to make local decisions, compete for subnational positions, and interact with the official bureaucracy. They were not allowed to establish any horizontal solidarity ties or to rise to national power by means of individual effort through the official party channels. Selection to national power positions was in the hands of the top command structure of the regime. The official party movement was not the only collaborative organization lacking autonomy and power in national affairs; so did trade unions and associations (Harik 1973). All these organizations proved to be collaborative movements that provided support for the regime on its own terms, in return for being protected and favored. They helped the regime in implementing policy and organizing its political support. Nasser's mass appeal and the popularity of his ideological stance helped to cement these collaborative organizations and to give them more character than as being just a collection of agents in the service of the national government.

In short, the Nasser regime levelled social and political hierarchies and appealed directly for mass support, using individual agents-actors in political or administrative positions to organize its forces and make it possible to put a large retinue of people in its service, especially at the implemenation of power policy levels. Nasser was able to mobilize mass support through collaborators who assisted in winning the cooperation of the people in implementing most policy decisions domestically and in preventing opposition to his foreign policies. His policies, moreover, had a wide basis of support on their own merit. This was a complex system whose pattern illustrates how using coercion to overcome resistance can be combined with harnessing converging forces for generation of effective power by an authoritarian regime.

Other authoritarian regimes in the area developed systems of power relations that have some similarity and major differences. Such relations may be revealed by focusing attention on the linkages among leaders and the type of relations they establish with the rest of society. The stronger and more sophisticated of them were those that were able to establish linkages with the public for the provision of support for their positions and the effective implementation of policy.

Conceptual Framework for Analysis

Having discussed the theoretical basis of field approach and how it concretely relates to the study of politics, we turn now to define the conceptual terms for its operationalism in research.

The field theoretical outlook suggests a change in research orientation and emphasis. First, it suggests greater emphasis on study of action as a function of a collectivity, a social complex, rather than individuals. Let us look at bureaucracies, not only bureaucrats; cabinets, not only ministers; parties, not only party leaders. Individual actors are not to be overlooked; they should rather be viewed as an integral part of interacting collectivities within a field of action. By viewing power in terms of interacting forces rather than interacting persons, it is understood that power is defined in social terms. Second, it underlines the importance of looking at social phenomenon as a dynamic reality, for action is motion; it is change. This means less emphasis on static variables, such as class characteristics of leaders or their social attributes, and more emphasis on changing relations and networks. Third, since politics is an activity oriented toward harnessing social forces for the effective performance of public policy, it behooves us to show more interest in the process and dynamics of power generation, maintenance, and use. More should be done on the study of organization, support, and social cohesion in a way that relates findings to theory. It is time to stop thinking of coerciveness as the distinctive and dominant aspect of power, for the fruitful study of power lies in exploring convergence of forces and the dynamics that govern them.

How does one go about studying social reality to detect the interplay of influence and political dynamics? The following conceptual framework based on field theory offers general guidelines for political analysis.

The first step in studying a complex social order is to determine the formal and informal social structures. This is basically a static and descriptive stage in the analysis process. It is necessary, however, because structures represent the patterns of action formally defined as normative rules. Normative rules map out functions, jurisdictions, and procedures. In addition to providing legitimacy for decisions and imposing constraints on actors performing roles, political action is oriented toward them as the legitimate instruments for public policy.

The second category of political analysis is social forces. Social forces are not defined in normative terms; they represent the actual flow of influence. Social forces are the resultant of people's attitudes, desires, beliefs, interests, cohesiveness, organization, resources under their command, and the extent to which they are prepared to commit them. One looks, therefore, at what constitutes social forces in a particular system, their weight, direction of orientation, and distribution. Power distribution most often is laid out in patterns that develop over time, which makes it necessary to identify networks, cleavages, coalitions, alliances, and rank ordering of actors. How are actors related to other actors within their own group; in more complex networks, this is a question pertaining to power structure, to be determined by empirical means. The overlap between normative rules and social forces as well as the impact they have on each other should be carefully noted and analyzed.

The third category in terms of which political reality is to be examined is strategy and tactics. Strategy is long range plan action and is akin to, but different from, tactics in that tactics are measures taken to achieve short term objectives, not necessarily always consistent with strategy. At this stage, dynamic interaction is the main concern of analysis and is one of the most lively fields of study. When actors are clearly identified in terms of their positions in the normative organization of the social unit and in relation to the social forces in that unit, the question is how do they play their cards. It would be an oversimplification to think that action can be predicted in terms of normative rules and social forces, for these determine the structures within which action takes place and leave the arithmetic of interactions to the skill and circumstances of the situation. Issues become of central importance in the analysis of tactics and strategy, for issues affect the lineup of forces and spur actors to mobilize their forces and commit them for action.

While the empirical study of tactics and strategy is the least developed in the social sciences, it nevertheless has ancient roots going back to Machiavelli and the "reale politick" approach. Yet, this has not developed into a science and is the subject par excellence of journalism in free societies. Some political anthropologists have paid serious attention to questions of tactics and have made a valuable contribution toward developing such science (Bailey 1969).

Formal analysis, as exemplified by game theory, has made a valuable contribution to the study of strategy and tactics in ideal type situations, and its contribution to theory building should not be overlooked. However, this thrust has not led to greater empirical analysis of strategy and tactics or toward the development of empirical theory in this field. The limitations of game theory are appreciated by most scholars in the field and pertain to assumption of perfect rationality of behavior, open information flow, and unchanging structure (rules of the game) in which action unfolds. However, in real life, actors do not always act rationally; they are not in possession of perfect information, and the normative rules and structures of social forces are not always stable, but shifting and diverse. What game theory contributes should not be shunned, but it should not serve as a substitute for the development of an empirical science of political interaction. Particularly significant in this respect is the frequency with which actors in their tactics change sides and alliances and adopt new ones, thus changing the whole lineup of the forces in the contest. The body of empirical generalizations on political contests is extremely limited but needs not remain so.

In the study of strategy and tactics, the concepts of issue and lineup of forces are basic. Political interaction revolves around the generation of an issue or determining its outcome. Once an issue is raised, it evokes reactions, and the forces involved line up in a certain order vis-a-vis the issue at hand. The lineup of forces may or may not fall into the stable or existing pattern of force distribution, but may take a different form in which actors call on their complex networks and draw up new lines of battle. Thus, each conflict requires special attention to determine how the forces line up or change as the contest unfolds. Issues thus have the effect of reshuffling the cards and rearranging positions, especially in an open and pluralist system. Where social cleavages are deep, issues hardly ever affect the lineup of forces.

In Shubra el-Gedida, for instance, the lineup of forces varied considerably according to the issue at hand. In a nearby village, there were two main groups who were little affected in their lineup by the nature of the issue. By examining the social structure and political resource commitments, it became clear that the cleavages in Subra were not deep and the resource commitments of actors limited. In the second community, social cleavages were very deep and political resources commitments very strong. Thus, every time one group took sides on an issue, the other took the opposite side, regardless of the merit of the case. These situations suggest hypotheses that may be possible to test in other cases. The first is that, in a social setting with several political groups and limited social cleavages, issues have the effect of reshuffling the political lineup. In a system of deep social cleavages and strong political commitments, issues do not affect the political lineup. Thus studying change does not mean dealing with discrete orderless situations. The approach is relevant to the study of strongly institutionalized as well as weakly institutionalized or even noninstitutionalized social orders. There is order in action, and we need not seek security in structures because they give the semblance of stability and order.

As an illustration of how strategy, tactics, and lineups are interrelated, let us consider a political actor who decides to run for an office of a larger constituency than the one he represents. His campaign strategy may change radically here and leads to new and different alliances and positions. First, he may find it necessary to underplay his commitment to the interests and views of his basic constituency and stress those in line with the interests and views of the larger constituency. In the process, he may find it necessary to seek new alliances and drop some with which he originally was linked in his basic constituency. Moreover, he will have to spread his time and resources more widely, giving his original constituency less attention than before. Should he continue the same strategy as before vis-a-vis his basic constituency, he might well find that his actions are not productive or reach their marginal returns very quickly.

The manner in which the three levels of analysis go together may be illustrated further. Under an authoritarian regime, it may be observed that linkages of leaders to leaders is of the utmost importance in understanding why they can or cannot act and how they go about doing it. In open systems, with free competition, linkages of leaders to nonleaders may prove to be of equally greater, if not greater, explanatory value. An officer in charge of welfare may find himself taking the sides of his clients in an open system in which competition for national resources in various government departments is free and performance is given high marks. This may occur even when the actor had a different attitude previously and without strong pressure applied by clients. In a system in which distribution of influence is skewed and political patronage is the basis of holding office, the same welfare officer may find himself shortchanging his clients to satisfy his patron. Similarly, when office is subject to keen political pressure but not necessarily to domination through patronage, a welfare officer may find himself favoring some clients over others in response to unequal pressure from different sides.

Research Possibilities and Problems

Political literature on the Western industrialized world, it should be noted, has dealt to a far greater extent with political phenomena in the light of the preceding outlook than has political literature on the Middle East or Third World countries. It is often remarked that the study of political linkages in developing, mostly authoritarian, Third World countries is not feasible. The problem of penetrating the political organization and linkages among national leaders is not an easy task anywhere, but the real problem, it seems, lies in not trying and in approaching the subject with other conceptual perspectives. If one asks how many have tried and failed, one realizes how little effort has been made. Moreover, political scientists rarely try methods of research that yield results on networks and action patterns such as participant observation. In the case of the Middle East, moreover, scholarly orientation is generally less theoretical, unlike the works examined in this chapter.

Some aspects of the field theoretical approach are admittedly more difficult to get at empirically than others, though none of these difficulties are empirically not operational. The problem is one of access, not design. Most difficult to penetrate are such sensitive organizations as the military and the linkages between national leaders' covert supporters. However, this is a question of limited accessibility, not outright closed doors. Even in the case of the military, we can see that when spurred by the increasing involvement of the military in politics, scholars managed to assemble a reasonably informative body of knowledge on the subject.

A number of observations may be made in this regard. First, scholars have first to be interested and willing to do research in the light of this outlook. Second, they have to be versatile and resourceful. One does not always obtain what one wants by direct means. Third, not all the aspects of the field conceptual framework are difficult to gather information about. The most difficult are usually certain aspects of behind-the-counter dealings among leaders. Fourth, political reality is not limited to top national politics. There are numerous aspects in the political society that can be reached and studied without the difficulties one sometimes encounters in the study of national institutions. Fifth, the scholarly process of information gathering and theory development is cumulative, and, as more work is done on action analysis, the task becomes less difficult to others. More methods and techniques become developed for a variety of situations and countries. Students of Middle Eastern politics who wish to embark on such a course may learn a great deal from studies of political anthropology and political sociology, especially those that have been done in the United States. We do not wish to enter into the polemics of applications of what is usually referred to as the Western approaches to developing countries. We stand by the principle that the scholarly quest is indivisible and not culture bound. Sound application of scientific procedures may, moreover, steer us away from explanations of one society, by principles that were found explanatory of another. The literature on political sociology in the United States is recommended because it is far more developed than anywhere else and should provide analysis skills helpful in developing methods and techniques for study in other settings. It is not recommended, however, that the theories developed to explain these societies be carried over to explain Middle Eastern societies. For comparative purposes, one seeks the confirmation or rejection of hypotheses developed in one setting in another. This is legitimate research procedure and to be recommended as well. The explanation of one social order in terms of theories developed in another, on the other hand, is not recommended, nor is it likely to advance our knowledge of the rich variety of social reality.

CONCLUSION

The study of political elites calls for a theoretical reorientation whereby power behavior is viewed positively as a productive action in a field subject to change and growth. This view of power as a societal product guides us to the study of the principles that govern its generation and use and toward networks analysis implied in the interactive and continuous pattern of power relationships. Focus on the repressive aspect of subordination is wrapped up in the whole issue of human values and takes us a very short way in trying to understand the complex nature of political power.

Power-oriented activities are transactions pertaining to the production of political effects within a social order consisting of changeable units of production and capital resources. Since the resources are, as a rule, scarce and the productive activity arduous and costly, the field of power interaction is both exclusive and cooperative. Actors in effect seek to exclude others by containing their ability to act freely, but, at the same time, they seek to generate new resources. The two-tier view of power is predicated on the postulate of fixed resources and prohibitive action. Those who fail to capture a resource become subject to those who do. Two major features of the political process are thus overlooked: that competition occurs in a field in which power is subject to growth in volume and to change in distribution, and that the product of competitive activity does not occur under winner-take-all conditions; it rather consists of continuous transactions in which shares are distributed in greater or smaller volume. The main thing to remember here is that the smaller shares continue to constitute a constraint on the freedom of action by the major holders of power. In other words, it is rare that those who end up with the greater share of power can annul the effect of the holders of smaller shares. That would presuppose the physical destruction of contenders. The fact is that units of power tend to continue to flow in smaller and larger shares within a system of transactions. The mobility in the transaction flow, which redefines the actors and the distribution pattern, can be determined empirically.

It may be objected that what this chapter calls for is an abandonment of elite analysis in favor of analysis of networks and dynamics of power within a specified field of action and that it suggests an alternate course rather than the development of the one under consideration. The answer is a qualified yes insofar as elite study is inextricable from the question of power. Elite studies, even in their present form, are very useful to students in politics, and what has been done here is to point to some of their limitations and offer some suggestions for the future. On the negative side, this chapter questions the extent to which background analysis predicts political behavior, the dichotomy of political society into elite and mass, the extremely limited attention paid to forces that are not in ruling positions and their consideration at times as part of a passive mass, the lack of limited concern with collectivities as power actors, that is, as units of analysis, and, finally, the limited concern with the emergence process of elites, what has been referred to here as the making or generation of power.

On the positive side, this chapter offers theoretical perspectives as the basis for the study of power relations. It, moreover, calls attention to the importance of supplementing current elite studies with analysis of elite behavior in the context of a field of action, linkages among elites and between them and the social forces of which the field is made up, stratification of leaders, abandonment of the term "recruitment" and substitution by the term "elite circulation" as a part of the process of power generation, and broadening our perspective on the concept of power in such a way as to account for its aggressive and integrative aspects.

4

TOWARD A THEORY OF
ELITE CIRCULATION

I. William Zartman

Political systems involve people who use power to make policy in response to group needs and demands. The relation between who such people are and what they do therefore becomes an important subject of analysis. The effects of elites on policy and policy on elites are the two dimensions necessary to under-standing—and eventually to explaining theoretically—the dynamics of a political system in terms of elite circulation. The notion of "new social forces" of Mosca (1939, pp. 65 f et passim), who also introduced the concept of "elite circula-tion," appears to be of particular relevance in discussing developing countries, in which the course of politics is often shaped by the differing rates of moderniza-tion within a society. The basic question of this study was also suggested by Bottomore (1964, pp. 61, 63) and, in commenting on Bottomore, by Rustow (1966, p. 716).

The purpose of this chapter is to establish a framework for analysis of elite circulation in order to permit an explanation of associated events, both those that constitute regular patterns of activity in particular types of political systems and those that stand as exceptions to such regularities. Beyond some simple fascination with the dynamics of "who's on top," this study also aspires to clear up some conceptual inadequacies that have been troubling political analyses.

I am grateful to the Office of Research Analysis of the Department of State for helping me start on this study, to the Center for International Studies of New York Univer-sity for enabling me to pursue it, and to the Joint Committee on the Near and Middle East of the Social Science Research Council and American Council of Learned Societies for pro-viding a continuing context for it.

One concerns the need for a more explicit and more accurate way of framing whole-system analyses of polities, which clearly do not deal equally with everybody in a political system but only with people in relation to the amount of power they exercise. By identifying the objects of study explicitly in these terms, the analyst can pursue his study more clearly than with his sight troubled by extraneous labels. Another problem arises with the notion of class, which is more often asserted than studied. Other things than Marx's class act as Weber's party, and yet a clear conceptualization to deal with this reality still remains to be invented. The third inadequacy in current conceptualization concerns the notion of circulation itself. The term connotes something dynamic, interrelated, circular, and yet, thus far, it is translated only by recruiment, in an unrealistically linear concept. These needs, then, create some of the self-imposed challenges to this study.

DEFINING ELITES

Any study that aspires to explain something about those who exercise power must first indicate explicitly the assumptions and terms of that explanation, beginning with the nature of an elite itself. Not all people use the same degree of power in a polity. Whatever the particular type of system, democracy, dictatorship, or something in between, people exercise more or less power than their share on a strictly proportional basis, the number of people having more power varying according to the type of political system. The degree of disproportion (the shape of the disproportion curve) will also vary according to the political system. In some polities, there is a real gap between those who exercise power and those who do not, while in others the transition between powerful and powerless is gradual; in some there is equality among the powerful, whereas in others there are disparities even among those who exercise power. Furthermore, in most but perhaps not all polities, those who exercise power on one issue may well not be the ones involved in decisions on another, so that differences in the scope of power can also be used to distinguish political systems. These three characteristics—numbers, degree, scope—are useful for describing different types of political systems, but they make it impossible to determine a precise boundary for elites.* One might well come to a point where the next person on the list

---

*This discussion begs the boundary question, without feeling vulnerable about it. Most political phenomena are conceptually clear but operationally without boundary. It also begs the question of the amount of power elites really wield (the unity versus pluralism debate), a question to which an intuitive answer is adequate to allow us to get on with our job for the moment. Lasswell (1966, p. 8) agrees.

Another way of dealing with the boundary problem is found in Chapter 6, in which a boundary-in-depth or mediating layer is treated.

could be said to exercise no power or no more than his share in a given system, but such a point is hard to locate precisely and is often too far down the list to be a boundary for the elite. Operationally, the only viable way out of the problem is to assign an intuitive floor to the list of people who exercise most power by defining them in other terms—position, reputation, family, and so on— and then examining their characteristics—attitudes, behavior, but above all power— to ascertain whether anyone has been left out.

Another problem troubling elite studies, which can be best handled by additional assumptions, concerns kinds of elites. By the division of labor necessary in a complex system, there are specialists (people who expend their primary energies) in politics as there are in the economic and in the social sectors, even though every individual is inevitably involved in the polity, economy, and society. In other words, everyone can be ranked somewhere on scales of power, wealth, and status. One might think of these sectors as pyramids, since generally there are fewer people with a high degree of the scaled value than with a lower degree. (The level on the pyramid indicates the position or accumulated degree.) There may or may not be any relation between an individual's position in one sector and in another. In some societies, power confers wealth and status; in some the reverse is true; and, in still others, there is no connection or a connection is viewed as a thing to be avoided or eliminated. In this study, the problem of dominance is resolved definitionally—the political elite is always dominant in politics—but the relationship between sectors is an empirical question. For the three sectors are not exclusive or impermeable piles of bodies. They are functional or role categories of activities that include individuals and groups more than once, according to their activity. Thus, another way of describing different types of political systems, in addition to the three already suggested, is to indicate their relationship with economic and social hierarchies.

But such indications can be no more static than politics itself. Relationships change over time and in directions that can be hypothesized in regard to particular pressures. It can be assumed that more people will be attracted to political activity at some times than at others, and, in fact, that they will shift their primary energies from economy or society to polity only when they feel a need to do so. Changes of fortunes in other sectors will propel individuals into political activity, first to pose demands to be handled, and then to get into the demand-handling business themselves if the incumbents are not doing it to their satisfaction. (The same individual may not necessarily follow the two-step pattern described; he may become alienated and withdraw in between or adopt a number of other psychological reactions, but the social movement goes on, with another individual picking up the second step.) In the first case, they bring demands that become part of the internal relations of the authoritative political elite. In the second, they themselves seek to become part of that elite, complementing or replacing others to form a coalition that then becomes the new incumbent elite. (Note that the aspirant acts as a spokesman for his client group more than does the incumbent who, by his incumbency, becomes subject to a larger number of demands from groups, and that concentration of authority positions in a limited number of families over a number of generations is more important for those it keeps out than those it keeps in [Bottomore 1964, p. 43].) The process continues. The two activities can be called the responsive and representative functions of elites (Huntington 1968, pp. 142 f).*

A further set of categories to be used in the following analysis concerns these demands. Political actors define themselves as bearers of demands along four major dimensions that may be called ideopolitical, evipolitical, sociopolitical, and geopolitical—or in other words, referring to the terms of Lasswell's definition of politics, as "who gets what, when, how," plus "where."† The four are intuitive dimensions, for which a theoretical grounding has not as yet been elaborated.‡ A justification for each could be lengthy, but will be made only briefly here.** People may define themselves into camps according to their choice (or rejection) of issues, values, and worldviews, and may formulate demands to effect these goals. They may also picture themselves in terms of age, cohort, or other generational criteria, and shape their demands by the experiential image that their life has thus far afforded them. They can also associate according to the way in which they earn their living, which provides them with

---

*On the dangers of substantive politics degenerating into procedural (position) politics, see Scott (1967, p. 119). On elite cooption of group representations who are defined in terms of group dimensions, see Gehlen and McBridge (1968), for another country's examples.

†Evipolitical is from Latin *oevum* (time of life, age) and political, an unavoidable neologism since all current English words use age in the sense of growing old, not simply growing older.

‡These dimensions have often been mentioned individually and sometimes combined, but never systematically. When Christina Harris (1964, pp. 136 f) divides Egyptian interwar political groups into three ideological groups plus "young secular intellectuals," she adds a geopolitical and perhaps a sociopolitical dimension as a reinforcing cleavage with ideological secularism in the fourth group. Peter C. Lloyd (1966, pp. 15 f et seq.) talks of three types of African elite conflict, ethnic, generational, and functional (sociopolitical). When S.E. Finer (1961, p. 40) talks of military intervention for the defense of region, personal status, class, and military institutional status, he is talking of geopolitical, evipolitical, sociopolitical, and organizational dimensions. See Lasswell (1936), Rustow (1966), Fleuron (1977), and Mayhew (1975). This is an attempt to get beyond triangular relations of class, estate, and party, and the notion that political dynamics derive from the lack of concordance among the three dimensions; see Runciman (1969, pp. 78, 136–142).

**On evipolitics, see Mead (1970), Eisenstadt (1965), Feuer (1968), Mannheim (1952), Riley, Johnson, and Foner (1972), Cutler (1975), Erikson (1968), Sears (1975), Stewart (1977), Palmore (1975), and Beck et al. (1973).

On ideopolitics, see Mosca (1939, pp. 70 ff; Higley, Field, and Grøholt (1977), Nagle (1977, esp. chap. 11).

On geopolitics, see Ronen (1976).

socioeconomic interests. Finally, they may identify with their spatial antecedents, their place of origin or their present location, recalling both the physical and human components of the geography. Policy wishes based on such issues,
images, interests, and identities can be grouped together under the name of
demands.

Since people act—both individually and collectively—to express demands,
they will band together for that purpose as well, either because their individual
action is insufficient or because their demand is for a collective good shared with
others. It is this element of group formation—collective consciousness leading to
collective organization to overcome the inadequacies of individual action—that
links social forces to politics. (This point is more generally related to the whole
social contract literature, such as Thomas Hobbes, *The Leviathan* [1968], and
Ernest Barker, ed., *Social Contract* [Locke, Hume, Rousseau] [1961]. Not all
common demands are for collective or public goods, of course; some are for
competitive goods, with a falling out over the distribution of the spoils after-
wards. See Raiffa [1953]. Also, not all individuals benefiting from collective
goods will cohere because of the free-rider problem. See Olson [1968].) There
are many potential groups that generally do not coalesce around a demand based
on their common characteristic—redheads, firstfloor dwellers, retired people,
parliamentarians, uncles, and so on—because they are not threatened or excluded
per se.* Only when they become the subject of specific blockages do potential
groups organize and express themselves to become *demand-bearing groups*, with
a role to play in politics. (To say that certain analytical categories should coalesce to further their true interests makes for interesting normative exhortation
but poor analysis.) Collective political actors, of which sociopolitical class is only
one, are thus demand-bearing groups, and their demands can be categorized
along the four dimensions previously mentioned.

Because of the nature of these groups as a coalescing collectivity, however,
there is an additional type of demand that must also be considered, the procedural or organizational, relating to the politics of position rather than of
purpose. This type of demand concerns the strength and structure of the
organized group or of the authority structure itself, as its fortunes and positions
change. Some groups become permanent organizations or formal institutions;
one of their demands then becomes the defense of their continued existence, but
the content of their other demands—and hence their ability to attract members,
be relevant, keep up with the competition, and so on—changes in substance
and intensity with the times. But new demand-bearing groups also arise, also
with the times, as others disappear, victims of their defeat or of their victory.

---

*For a time when one of these—retired people—coalesced as a political force, see
Holtzman (1963) and Putnam (1970).

Such changes with the times, which give rise to new demand-bearing groups and cause the realignment of demands by established groups, can be related directly to changes and inequalities in development, for developmental changes are merely a more specific type of the same effect.

The other approach that could be used for the study of elites treats them as political beings impelled by internal or personality-related drives. This approach is not necessarily contradictory with the study of external sources of political action, but it will not be pursued here, although some, such as Greenstein (1969, esp. p. 35), argue that it should be.

Of course, demands and their groups do not operate along any one dimension in a vacuum. Dimensions cut across each other, and many writings on pluralist politics have shown how crosscutting ties work to hold society together (Simmel 1955, Coser 1956, p. 80; Lipset 1960; Dahrendorf 1959; Rae and Taylor 1970, pp. 85 et seq.; Shepsle 1971). It might therefore be supposed that coincidence would provide a measure of intensity when several types of demands and demand-bearing groups are operating together in a political system. But coincidence of cleavages is so rare as to be unlikely. Rather, intensity is more frequently related to polarization along any dimension and the existence of a gap or unmediated distance between extremes. Intensity of political conflict arises not when a demand-bearing group on one dimension adds additional demands on other dimensions, since each new demand tends to reduce its following on the previous dimension; it arises when incumbent elites are faced by aspirant elites who diverge widely on particular demands with no mediating groups inbetween and who are then able to subsume or to aggregate, but not crosscut, other divergent demands on other dimensions. Thus, the challenge of young radical poor Northerners in a given polity is not likely to be as serious as the challenge of the young plus the radicals plus the poor plus the Northerners, when the old reactionaries, the rich, and the Southerners are facing them or the challenge of, say, the young who can make other people forget their demands along other dimensions and join them, or, more rarely, the challenge posed when the young are the same as the radicals, the poor, and the Northerners. These various effects can be called reinforcing changes.

Coincidence is not the only way of bringing together demand-bearing groups in common action. The other way is through group alliances effected by elites on the basis of group demands. An alliance is merely a conscious means of overcoming the absence of natural reinforcement or coincidence, although, even as a deliberate policy, alliance does best when perceived demands complement or otherwise reinforce each other. There has been much general mention in literature on social problems to elite or class alliances, but little or no attempt to relate such ad hoc assertions to the theoretical material on coalitions and alliances, on one hand, or to empirical data establishing interests in alliance. Size (minimum winning versus great coalitions), interests (compromise versus continuity), power (augmentation versus diffusion), and sources (complementarity versus competition) are all important considerations in the formation of alliances among elites and their supporting groups (Axelrod 1970, Riker 1962, Seller 1965). A full discussion of the theoretical aspects beyond these concepts would involve a separate chapter; here it is necessary only to emphasize the relevance of this work as the final aspect in understanding the relations among demand-bearing groups and their elites.

ELITE CIRCULATION

In a utopian polity, one might expect to find perfect mobility, even with the assumption of disproportionate exercise of power. In other words, there would still be an elite stratum, but access to it would be open and unhindered to anyone who wanted to get in (Michels 1962; Dahl 1960, p. 90; Dahl 1970, pp. 37–39; Putnam 1971, p. 651). In reality, all elite circulation deviates from the ideal of perfect mobility for a number of reasons. The incumbent elite already has a particular composition, for whatever reason, and hence no polity starts out with a clean slate. In addition, the incumbent elite may well admit certain types of people to its midst and exclude others, whether this action is conscious and directly related to the nature of the groups admitted and excluded or not. Furthermore, the nature of the development process, broadly characterized, is such that certain types of people will be produced as candidates and others will not.

Probably because of the first reason, the second may well not coincide with the third, turning quantitative deviation from perfect mobility into a qualitative one; the intake may well not coincide with the input. As a result, combination of these three sources of deviation from the ideal may result in the appearance of new groups of candidates who feel blocked and neglected and who, in those two elements of commonality, find reason to band together to "get in."* Thus, in addition to an incumbent elite of a particular composition (in whatever terms), a polity also contains aspirant elite groups created by developmental changes and/or by specific blockages. Both of these causes are at least in part, and often totally, the result of the policies and actions of the incumbent elite, just as much as conscious attempts by the incumbent elite to train and prepare its successors are acts of policy. Thus, through various processes, the new elite is a policy-outcome of its predecessors.

---

*"Where a leadership has been accustomed to the assumption that its constituents respond to it as individuals, there may be a rude awakening when organization of those constituents creates nuclei of strength which are able to effectively demand a sharing of power" (Selznick 1966, p. 15).

Although this idea is simple and may even be implicit in works on politics, it has not usually been used to organize the study of elite circulation. The most common way of discussing elite circulation is to assume a continuity of elites from one time to the next by merely speaking of those in power and not analyzing their composition or relation to each other. Too often this absence of analysis is assumed to portray a meaningful fact, continuity is taken for granted,

$$E \longrightarrow E' \longrightarrow E'' \longrightarrow \qquad (1)$$

and a ruling class (intergenerational transmission of power) is portrayed. Ruling classes can exist, of course, but they must be shown, not assumed. The first refinement (2) on this depiction is found in the notion of elite circulation as recruitment, which recognizes that the elite at a later time is never the same as its predecessor in some terms, but rather results from the intake of new members

$$E \longrightarrow E' \longrightarrow E'' \longrightarrow \qquad (2)$$
$$e \qquad e' \qquad e''$$

who were growing up under these predecessors. But it is only with the second refinement (3), which recognizes elites as a policy outcome, that the basic relations linking all three components are in place for an analysis of elite circulation.

$$E \longrightarrow E' \longrightarrow E'' \longrightarrow \qquad (3)$$
$$e \qquad e' \qquad e''$$

Yet even here, the relations are not complete. For not only is the aspirant elite (e) prepared by the incumbent elite (E) by the creation of specific development measures, but parts of this aspirant category are admitted to elite status by the incumbents while other parts are blocked (4). Up till this point, there is no

$$E \longrightarrow E' \longrightarrow E'' \longrightarrow \qquad (4)$$
$$e \qquad e' \qquad e''$$

conflict in the model and hence no politics. It is this disjuncture in the absorption of aspirants into the new incumbent elite, leading to the conflict for scarce values—in this case positions and other bases of power—that is a (if not *the*) major element of politics (Friedman 1972).

The sawtoothed nature of the diagram is partially a graphic artifact and partially a depiction of reality. The previous discussion has suggested that, rather than a smooth cycle of circulation, the process is likely to be doubly bumpy: absorption is mixed with blockage, and generation of aspirants is tempered by bunching. It is the second phenomenon that now needs discussion.

INCUMBENTS AND NEW ELITES

The absorptive model of dynamic stability is essentially a self-stabilizing process in which incumbent elites react to new demand bearing groups generated through differential development. They do so by coopting and controlling group members and by handling their demands. Specific demands can be anticipated from the development process as it is currently occurring, based on generational alienation, regional differences in modernization, ideological issues of equality and distribution, and socioeconomic interests—in other words, based on differentiated access to development along each of the four dimensions. Thus specific age, regional, social, and ideological groups benefit more from development than do others. Yet there is much significance in this simple summary, for it points to the uneven nature of the process of dynamic stability.

The mechanism of this type of critical realignment, sometimes associated with competitive (electoral) systems, has recently been the subject of a good deal of attention relevant to the study of clustered challenges in a cooptive system (Burnham 1970, Sundquist 1973).*

> In its "ideal-typical" form, . . . critical alignment is characteristically associated with short-lived but very intensive disruptions of traditional patterns of voting behavior. Majority parties become minorities; politics which was once competitive becomes non-competitive or, alternatively, hitherto one-party areas now become arenas of intense partisan competition; and large blocks of the active electorate— . . . —shift their partisan allegiance. . . .
>
> Ordinarily accepted "rules of the game" are flouted; the party's processes, instead of performing their usual integrative functions, themselves contribute to polarization. . . . Issue distance between the parties are markedly increased, and elections tend to involve highly salient issue-clusters, often with strongly emotional and symbolic overtones, . . . (E)stablished leadership . . . become(s) more rigid and dogmatic, which itself contributes greatly to the explosive "bursting

---

*See also Key 1955 for the original definition involving high electoral involvement, readjustments in power relations, and new durable electoral regroupings. (I am grateful to my colleague Rita W. Cooley for bringing this literature to my attention.) See also Lowi 1963.

stress" of realignment. . . . The rise in intensity is also normally to be found in abnormally heavy voter participation for the time. . . .

[M]ajor third-party campaigns are often associated with realignments. . . . One type is the major-party bolt, which, organizationally and at the mass base, detaches the most acutely dissatisfied parts of a major party's coalition. . . . The other variety may be described more accurately as a protest movement which may for a time have broad appeal, which is usually staffed by cadres not prominent in . . . major-party establishment(s), and which draws mass support cutting across pre-existing party lines. . . . (P)rotoalignment parties . . . constituted attacks by groups who felt that they were outsiders against an elite whom they frequently viewed in conspiratorial terms. These attacks were made in the name of democratic-humanistic universals against an established political structure which was perceived to be corrupt, undemocratic, and manipulated by insiders for their and their supporters' benefit. . . . Moreover, they all "telegraphed," as it were, the basic issue-clusters which would dominate politics in the next electoral era. . . . So evident is this pattern that one is led to suspect that the truly "normal" structure of . . . politics at the mass base is precisely this dynamic, even dialectal polarization between long-term inertia and concentrated bursts of change in this open system of action. It may well be that . . . political institutions, including the major political parties, are so organized that they have a chronic, cumulative tendency toward underproduction of other than currently "normal" policy outputs. They may tend persistently to ignore, and hence not to aggregate, emergent political demand of a mass character until a boiling point of some kind is reached. . . .

To recapitulate, then, eras of critical realignment are marked short, sharp reorganizations of the mass conditional bases of the major parties which occur at periodic intervals on the national level; are often preceded by major third-party revolts which reveal the incapacity of "politics as usual" to integrate, much less aggregate, emergent political demand; are closely associated with abnormal stress in the socioeconomic system; are marked by ideological polarizations and issue-distances between the major parties which are exceptionally large by normal standards; and have durable consequences as constituent acts which determine the outer boundaries of policy in general, though not necessarily of politics in detail (Burnham 1970, pp. 6-8, 27-39, 10).

This is a partially unfair use of a quotation, since some of the elided material contains specific references to American political systems. Nevertheless, Burnham's summary of critical elections or national realignments is couched in terms that show the current concern for the subject in the study of American

politics to be surprisingly relevant to elite circulation in developing countries.*
A competitive system provides regularly-spaced electoral occasions for changing
elites, fixing blames, renewing hopes, and redirecting aspirations; other types of
regimes must provide successive, if irregular, occasions for incorporating new
demand-bearing group representatives, and demoting or defeating others, and
for handling new types of demands. Periodic buildup and bunching of elites
and demands, with normal stretches in between, are a likely characteristic of
any political system.

It is not merely the fact of periodic realignments, but the reasons for
them, to which less than complete attention has been given, that interests the
present analysis. As the nature of groups making up society changes, three
things can happen. The incumbent coalition can absorb new groups and change
the nature of the coalition gradually, although usually there will be a noticeable
date or event when the major shift is registered and the fact of a different
successor becomes evident nonetheless. Or some of the component groups in
the coalition can join with others outside and reconstitute a new coalition
that replaces the incumbents. Or, finally, new groups can arise that cannot be
made to feel at home in the incumbent coalition without alienating its current
supporters; as the latter lose their power base, they are replaced by the new
coalition.

Change may occur for the simple demographic reasons of change in the
society's socioeconomic composition. Or it may occur because the incumbent
elite loses its responsiveness to the constant problems of the society, either
because it becomes ingrown as a ruling class preoccupied with its own procedural
demands or because it is simply incapable of handling its original demands and
their consequences. Hatschek's rule of British party evolution is apposite.

> First, a party with a distinct and coherent program comes into
> power. This program gradually loses its appeal in the course of
> the party's efforts to realize it. Some parts turn out to be impossible
> of achievement. Others arouse the antagonism of some of the party's
> own following when the practical implications become apparent.
> The party then breaks into divisions. This disintegration offers to
> another party, irrespective of whether it has evolved a distinct and
> realizable program or not, the chance of concentrating and unifying
> its forces (Friedrich 1950, p. 417).†

---

*Burnham himself gives an excuse, however, by suggesting that the United States
might be a new nation in terms of its horizontal cleavages (1970, p. 31).

†The general phenomenon of realignment, which involves new issues as well as
reaggregation around old issues rearranged, is different from the left-right alternance on the
basis of acquisiton and conservation, or of acquiring and digesting, as described by Schlesinger (1939 and 1949); Aron (1951, chap. 14); Dahl (1971, chap. 6); Lipset (1966 and 1970,

Or again elite change may occur because the nature of the problems has changed. In this case, the elites and the combined position of the incumbent coalition will probably have provided a general option or orientation on the dominant problem or cluster of problems at the beginning of the period; thereafter, further policy debates are likely to concern smaller and smaller details and matters of implementation regarding this major option. In the end, people get tired of debates over minutia when there are new and bigger problems emerging on the horizon, and they look for a new coalition whose demands are geared to the new dominant problem or cluster and whose decision-making capabilities are not exhausted by the previous debates. The difference in this third scenario from Hatchek's rule is that, in this case, the problems remained the same and wore out the incumbents, whereas, in the third case, there is a regular change in the nature of the problems, according to a specific pattern.

Thus, the bunching of elites for reasons of issue realignment appears to be a regular and universal phenomenon, although its reflection in the course of political decision making in any particular polity may vary. Whether a dominant issue is decisively and appropriately handled at a given time or not, issues will change and new elites will come to power at a later time. But this shift of elites will occur in very different ways. If the issue (or cluster of problems) is not appropriately handled and resolved, it will hang around to prevent the maturation of succeeding issues and elites, and eventually the effective operation of the political system may collapse. The inability of the French IV Republic to handle the colonial issue(s) and the inability of Faruq's Egypt to handle the independence issue provide examples of systemic breakdown and dramatic elite succession.

But matters of blockage and bunching are not the causes of only cataclysmic effects, such as revolution. They are operative in greater or lesser intensity no matter what the mechanism of elite circulation. If issue realignments and policy outputs produce a new wave of elite aspirants who find no means of access into institutional positions, a revolutionary situation is in the making. But even the most open and permeable system will undergo a noticeable change in the composition of its elite as a result of the cyclical effects of issues and policies. Elections, hiring, institutional change, party splits or takeovers, changes in legal qualifications, and changes in training programs are all ways of producing as important shifts in elites as coups, wars, and revolutions (although the latter's effects may be more dramatic). Revolution is indeed a story of blockage, but all political change—and all politics is change—is a matter of strategies of accession and strategies of absorption.

_____

chap. 8). The two ideas are not incompatible, and the alternance can well be subsumed within the realignment effect, even though the latter includes much more.

Developing societies are anything but constant. Their independence was won by new groups who came together in opposition to the incumbent colonial regime, and it is to be expected that these groups, in turn, face new challenges as issues change. Indeed, the dominant issue centered about independence and the shape of the new political system is usually resolved by an elite coalition who stays in power for a time and then is challenged by a new elite group on the basis of a new issue. Studies of critical elections in the United States have shown the periodic interval to be two to three decades; a study of the effect of the development process in generating new demand-bearing groups in new nations would help establish the period for elite turnover in these polities. Since there is not the same wealth of regular longterm data or longterm history for new nations as for the United States, the following discussion will turn to an examination of the nature of the first cluster of challenges and the establishment of dynamic stability, and then to the building up of the second cluster, which is stretching the limits of available data and inspiration.

The clearest case of elites as a policy output with subsequent problems of blockage and bunching occurs under colonization. Independence in many developing countries was won by a great coalition of political groups centered about new social forces that arose as a result of the colonial impact. Their demands initially grew out of frustrated attempts to overcome the disjuncture between their ascriptive inferiority (native status) and their achievement equality or superiority (évolué status).* The nationalist protest evolved through several political stages. When individual imitation of the colonial conquerors' Western ways proved insufficient to secure equal treatment for members of the small modernizing elite, they joined together in reform groups along the ideopolitical dimension (the first stage). These associations militated for equal treatment for their populations, but particularly for its modernized members, since the reformist elites identified and posed their demands above all in terms of new skills and ideas that came with Western education. Persuasion was the type of power they used, and, as their power base was weak, they frequently appealed to a sense of obligation they hoped to find as members of the modern community. If independence was achieved at this stage, it was granted rather than siezed, usually in the hope (on both sides) of continued privileged relations.

But if the modernized elite saw that their efforts were not achieving equality but were only separating them from their own national compatriots and

---

*A good deal has been written about the following model, much of it in connection with empirical analysis in North Africa and elsewhere in Africa and the Middle East. See Gibb (1932, pp. 320–23); Coleman (1955); Hodgkin (1962, esp. chap. 8); Sharabi (1962, chap. 20); Zartman (1964, chap. 7, and 1973, chap. 23); Micaud, Brown, and Moore (1964, esp. chap. 1), Moore (1965); Kerstiens (1966), Oualoulou (1975); Huntington (1968, pp. 412–420). On relative deprivation and the nationalist revolt, see Gurr (1970, p. 142 et seq.).

national culture, they turned back to the mass as a source of both power and identity and formed a nationalist movement along the geopolitical dimension (the second stage). The nationalist movement no longer recognized the legitimacy of the colonial system, which had proven incapable of accomplishing assimilation, but sought to set up its own system of national sovereignty. In the process of creating a mass-type movement, however, the modernized elites were obliged to dilute their modernism and to include traditional leaders whose shared characteristic was nationality, not modernity. The form of power was persuasion mixed with coercion, with the sources of power greatly augmented by the instrumental mass. All issues and groups were subsumed under a single national demand for independence, the issue that underlay the blockage and bunching of the aspirant elites.

In most cases, independence was achieved by this point; in some cases, however, the nationalist movement was also unsuccessful, and it was necessary to invoke the ultimate form of power, violence. The result was a revolutionary force recruited along sociopolitical lines (the third stage). Here the mass was no longer in an instrumental stage as before but provided its own leadership, and hence its own demands. Independence was not enough, social change was also deemed necessary.

The winning form of the nationalist protest has had much to do with the form of political organization after independence. When reform groups win independence, a system of competitive pluralistic patron-parties generally evolves. When nationalist movements win independence, a cooptive single-party system tends to occur. When revolutionary forces win independence, a controlled technocratic no-party system usually arises.* This discussion will focus on the nationalist movement and single-party cooptive system, and, when necessary, on the reform group and competitive patron-parties system, since these are the most common.† It should be noted, however, that neither single parties nor patron-

---

*Another typology, used by Hopkins (1971, pp. 242–244), labels similar types of political systems bargaining, containment, and coercion, respectively.

On the first alternative, see Hodgkin (1962) and Morgenthau (1964). On the second, in addition to the preceding, see Moore (1965) and Micaud, Brown, and Moore (1964). On the third, Roos and Roos (1971).

†A cooptive system is one in which a given elite brings or accepts new individuals into its membership without their replacing the original elite. In a competitive system, in contrast, one elite replaces another by peaceful means, and there is no constant and overriding group that carries over from one elite to the next and performs the succession. On cooption as a mechanism of stability, see Selznick (1966, esp. pp. 13–16, 259–61); Gehlen and McBridge (1968, p. 1,241). Cooptive system is preferred here to single-party or mobilization system; the term focuses on the mechanism of elite circulation, which is the topic under consideration, and the mechanism can operate whether the party is alive and mobilizing or not (albeit differently). It can even operate in a multiparty system when there is a comfortably incumbent major party.

parties have necessarily any guarantee on life. Their possible evolution and subsequent replacement by other types of systems will be among the topics discussed here.

The winning coalition included liberal professionals, petits bureaucrats, landed aristocrats, and small business managers, to which independence soon added party functionaries, civil servants, and technicians. Geographically, they tended to come from the major city built up by the colonial ruler. Generationally, they tended to be in their 30s and 40s. Ideologically, they were the product of the funnel phase of the nationalist protest, in which all issues become subordinate to the goal of independence. Only after the achievement of independence—in its strict sense of political sovereignty—and often after a period of disarray, did the new goal of development appear—often in the equally strict sense of the construction of a modern economic sector, as the term was also understood during colonial rule.

NEW CHALLENGES

Dynamic stability is not a smooth process in which the challenges of demand-bearing groups arise from potential sources at random, evenly spaced across time. It has been noted that the independence movement developed as a logjam, with blocked promotions and aspirations, mounting tactics, age aggregation, and numerical support all building up behind the single independence issue. It has also been noted that the breakup of the logjam at independence set up a certain specific pattern of elite activity that was bunched as a result of the previous blockage. Major positions were occupied by a definable age-experience cohort. Specific regional groups tended to be on top because they were ahead of others in the developmental process. Some social groups predominated at the expense of others because of available needs and chances at given times. Even certain issues and attitudes outweighed others because of contextual exigencies and opportunities. In other words, specific cohort, regional, social, and ideological groups benefit more from development *and* independence than do others.* As a result, a particular cluster of challenges occurs after independence. If it is successfully handled, there is likely to be a stretch of dynamic stability—punctuated at most by incidents that sound worse than they really are because a strong base has not yet built up—until a new, specifically definable cluster of challenges can build up and a new realignment of the political elite take place.

---

*"The multiplication of these groups, which constitute the more important nuclei of all these revolutionary movements, has been symptomatic of the uneven development of the various spheres of society" (Eisenstadt 1965, p. 314).

New challenges can arise by various mechanisms, not all of them applicable to all dimensions. They may arise dialectically as a reaction (a move in an opposite direction) to current characteristics, or as a result of a new group born of the development process without previous antecedents, or from splits within a previously cohesive group, or as a continuation of a trend in which the current group is only a partial stage, or as a result of old forces bypassed earlier and now renascent. It should be noted that there is no claim here that in every country cleavages will take place in all dimensions in each way indicated; all that is proposed is an indication of the way and place in which cleavages are likely to take place—in other words, a guide to where to look for potentialities and explanations, hopefully useful in identifying both typical and exceptional cases.

Geographically, colonial rule tended to be an alliance of the colonist with new urban and traditional rural elites, until the new urban elite broke away. It has already been noted that the new elites tended to identify with the country's major city. This is understandable since it was the major city that felt the greatest colonially-induced change, promotion, and blockage, although it is also conceivable for similar reasons that the new leadership come from the second largest city, rival of the capital. Only as the nationalist elite moves toward the revolutionary force stage does it tend to change its locus from the major city to smaller towns, as it reaches further down the social pyramid for its leadership. With the passage of time after independence, the elite concentration in the major city is most likely to increase. The new political elite replacing the colonial rulers move into the major city as carpetbaggers, and both the new and the old inhabitants of the largest city become the leading claimants on positions of authority. It is only after urban hypercephalism has set in and the incumbent coalition has become concentrated in the major city for a time long enough to give it a narrow identity that some sort of rural revolt, ruralizing election, or Green Uprising can take place (Huntington 1968, pp. 72–78; Roos and Roos 1971; Kearns 1963).

A subcase of the geographical dimension is the ethnic factor. Although it may seem curious to call ethnic identity geographical, the basis of identification is quite similar in the two cases and tribes do have a generally definable geographic location. Like cities, tribes can be expected to attain political awareness and importance at different times, among other things according to the amount of contact they have had with modernization. Two types of reactions to tribally-identified elements in the incumbent coalition can occur. One is intertribal: if the incumbent coalition is dominated by a particular ethnic, a reaction from secondary or newcomer tribe(s) can be expected as they learn or discover modern skills and needs. The other possible reaction is extratribal and ties together ethnic and urban geopolitics: if identifiably tribal elements of any size dominate the incumbent coalition, challenges from detribalized and antitribalized urban elements can be expected. Independent reasons for a choice between these possible reactions are not evident, but, again, the coincidence of cleavages along other dimensions with tribal or detribalized elements can affect the reaction.

Generationally, the native allies of the colonial rulers were already old at the end of the colonial period. Indeed, the nationalist crisis was the result of the colonial rulers' inability to replace the old elite with a new one that they had been able to generate but not integrate. Of course, the nationalist crisis was not simply a crisis of evipolitics, but a good example of the reinforcing nature of several dimensions. However, the generational homogeneity of the challenging elites at the time of independence has meant that the positions created and then vacated by the colonial rulers were immediately occupied by the ready, blocked cohort of the nationalist elite. Thereafter, the society's new annual production of elite candidates could only be absorbed by two means: new attrition and position vacancies. The first, however, has been rare, since the nationalist generation was still young at the time it came to power. In the government sector, it has been relatively easy to create new positions to swell the civil service, but states have soon discovered their budgetary limits. In other sectors—party, business, labor, and so on—the creation of new positions has depended on economic development, which tends to be slow in absolute terms and nil-to-negative in relation to population growth. Thus, the generational backlog that society knew before independence has tended to repeat itself. Moreover, it has been aggravated by the tremendous expansion of education strongly demanded by newly independent societies, which adds a qualitative element to the quantitative backlog and increases frustration. In other words, evipolitically, elite succession in newly independent societies appears to be naturally (or unnaturally) cyclical and bunched (LeVine 1967, pp. 80ff; Zartman 1978, pp. 97–102, and 1979, pp. 85–91; Shapiro 1979; Nagle 1977).

The notion of bunching suggests a reexamination of the notion of generation. Actually, generation should be conceived of as an age-experience cohort, formed of people who went through it together; their ages will cluster, but need not all be the same. Products of the same type of socializing experience, such cohorts tend to have similar expectations about political actions and political outcomes, among other things. As in years themselves, cutoff points are artificial, and yet such abstractions as the Vietnam Generation or the Class of '48, the Nationalist Generation or Prison Graduates, are meaningful realities. There have been too few studies comparing the attitudes of those who grew up together fighting for independence and were still young enough upon its attainment to fill the positions of power thereafter, with the attitudes of those (to mention only their immediate successors) who received their secondary and higher education in a national school system and then climbed up the national ladders of employment and authority (Ashford 1964 excerpted in Zartman 1971; Makarius 1960; Entelis 1974).* Those studies that do exist tend to show the older generation as

---

*An excellent theoretical statement is found in Shapiro (1979). See also LeVine (1967) on Upper Volta, Niger, Dahomey, Senegal, and Central African Republic; Hopkins

politicians who see leadership deficiency as a major domestic problem and who, ironically, have little faith in democracy and the people's voice; they see foreign problems in an East-West, Cold War context and look to gradual regional integration. The younger generation members appear as technicians who see mass underdevelopment as a major political problem but who, also ironically, have faith in democracy and the people and a low authoritarian score; foreign problems are seen in the North-South context and regional unity should be political. This rough combination of scattered studies would need to be verified more thoroughly to be accepted, but it does at least suggest that there are serious differences between the two cohorts, and that, unusually, Middle East elite generations are negatively socialized by growing up under the perceived failures of their elders.

A major effort is needed to overcome the bunching tendency, and even if young leaders are coopted into the incumbent coalition, they may well, by that very fact, become suspect to the larger group of their generation who are outside political circles. They have two possible reactions: to be more establishment than the establishment because they made it, in effect joining the older generation, or to be more radical than the outs because they feel unhappy at being suspect in the eyes of their peers (the latter the reaction of the évolué elites themselves in regard to the masses during the nationalist protest movement) (Brown 1974, pp. 354f; Quandt 1969; Shapiro pending). The choice of reactions depends on at least three factors: the number of peers in the backlog, the intensity of their resentment, and, again, the degree of reinforcement by other dimensional cleavages.

Ideologically, the unanimity on the independence issue that accompanied the nationalist movement generally carried over into equal unanimity over the next issue of development. Not only has this unanimity been characteristic, but there has been remarkably little divergence over the ways of accomplishing it in the newly independent, developing countries. Compared to the many different approaches to development theoretically available, national socialism in slogan, with some accommodating flexibility in practice, seems to have carried the day rather easily. Its accomplishments have been less overwhelming. Out of the frustration of unfulfilled slogans and beliefs, ideological countercurrents begin to appear. The most notable one is a return to the initial issue of independence, to find in its incompleteness an explanation of the failures of development. After colonialism (the political enemy), neocolonialism (the economic enemy) and then dependency (the socioeconomic enemy), become the antagonististic forces (Ruf et al. 1976). Along with a return to the unfinished task of perfecting independence comes a reevaluation of the development issue in terms of distribution instead of, or as well as, expansion. The fact that independence can never be completely won in an interdependent world of unequal states provides a built-in

(1971) on Tanzania; Goodrich (1966) on Costa Rica and Panama; Flis-Zonabend (1968) on Senegal, and the insightful general work of LeVine (1973a and 1973b).

element of frustration, and the source of a future dynamic, just as the unattainable goal of sudden industrialization provided its own frustrations and dynamics. Later, the fact that distribution can never be equal in a society of human beings will cause a different ideological issue and dynamic. It is between the two poles of these two issues—expansion/distribution of development and emulation/isolation of independence—that the ideological shifts occur, propelled by the short-term inability to achieve any of these goals in its extreme. But when the issues are expressed in these dichotomies, it is obvious that what is involved is not a parochial choice of subjects, but, instead, specific cases of a universal spectrum involving the growth and allocation of material and cultural value systems, respectively, or of welfare and solidarity—values, to put it in a different way.*

The timing of the ideological split on these two issues is more complex than it might first appear.† To begin with, it depends on the two factors involved—the degree of success of the development attempts and the degree of completeness of independence (that is, the amount of metropolitan influence remaining after sovereignty is attained). If both are low, the split may be expected to occur soon after independence: yet, in fact, this is not always the case. Furthermore, it is presently unclear how the two factors are to be weighed in combination; if one is high and the other low, which prevails? For the moment, the only apparent answer lies in a return to the notion of reinforcing cleavages.

Socially, as described, the Great Coalition of independence is necessarily heterogeneous and likely to change. Two types of changes are logically predictable: those involving the elimination of uncomfortable partners and those involving the rise of potential new partners. The first, an often neglected subject, is important and generally involves three or more types of elites: revolutionary leaders, whose skills are no longer suitable for the tasks of the political elite; traditional elders, whose values are no longer suitable; and labor leaders, whose demands are no longer suitable (Alibert 1966). If these three groups are not to be physically eliminated from the coalition, they must agree to become subservient members of it, a conversion that generally involves a good deal of political, and even physical, maneuvering. In addition, the original liberal professional

---

*For some very different analyses using these concepts, see Feith (1962), Lloyd (1933-34), Berrea (1962).

†The preferred indicator, the number and size of factions, seems to be very difficult to operationalize—to measure and to combine. Factions can be identified from political commentaries, a soft-data source, but the phenomenon is no more precise than the source. Also, it would be interesting to add a measure of ideological distance, if there is one. Content analysis might provide a better measure, but the generational problems are overwhelming and the conceptual problems unresolved (content analysis of what, at or over what period of time, and so on).

members that started the nationalist protest movement often leave politics, since their aspirations for equality are satisfied with independence and their skills in competitive debate and adversary proceedings are not deemed relevant to the political process. If their predominant place is taken by administrative and technical elite members, they bring a basic change in the nature and interests of the coalition. Rather than being the creature of ascendant social forces, it tends to represent itself and, hence, its own interests rather than constituent interests.

Nevertheless, the governing coalition must also face the challenges of new demand-bearing groups. Their ascendance depends on some degree of development, which was previously noted to be lagging. It is perhaps more accurate to describe development in newly independent countries as partial or disjointed rather than as totally absent, and it is this disjunction that causes new, rising groups to be dissatisfied and, therefore, to become challengers. The strongest challenges, however, come when large or organized groups of the population have undergone a sudden change of fortunes (up as well as down), and, of course, the extreme challenge—the revolutionary situation—occurs when such groups have been twice shaken by improvement followed by sudden decline (the J-curve thesis) (Davies 1962; Gurr 1970, esp. pp. 52–56; Zartman, Paul and Entelis 1971). In sum, social change creates new demand-bearing groups; the more rapid and widespread the change, the greater the challenges to the governing elites.

One such group is the commercial peasantry, brought from the traditional sector into the market economy and subject to the stresses and vagaries of both trade and agriculture. Although the growth of this sector of society and economy through agricultural development programs is likely to bring a new group into the polity, its challenge is increased if there has been merely promotion to precarity (preemption of farm trade by large landowners, unavailability of fair credit, and so on).

Another group is local business, whose numbers and interests rise slowly as metropolitan business moves out, but whose concern for political influence is increased by its economic uncertainty during the early decades of development. Particularly if good fortunes bring growth and concentration of capital ownership, business increases both its power and its vulnerability (Alexander 1960, Wallerstein 1967, Rugh 1973, Dubbar and Nasr 1976, Issawi 1955, Khallaf and Schwayri 1966, Sayigh 1962, Moore 1980).

Still another group is urban labor, with qualifications. Employed and unionized labor was part of the initial nationalist protest movement seeking equality; after independence, as frequently pointed out, it becomes a privileged sector of society, distinct from a growing mass of uprooted shantytown unemployed. But this position of security only obtains as long as organized labor becomes the vanguard of the lumpenproletariat, with a considerable body of troops behind it. Before this occurs, and lest it do, labor leaders have a successful claim on political participation, supported both by the economic importance of their followers in good times and their economic insecurity in bad.

A narrower group is the military, whose organization, power, and sense of mission make it prone to undertake direct political action if it is too heavily or exclusively relied upon, or, on the contrary, if it is humiliated. The military is a special case, however, since it is the only group directly entrusted with the means of overthrowing the government.

Finally, a broader category of a different nature that is conceptually problematic is the intellectual. Intellectuals, in the special sense used here, comprise the large numbers of people on many levels who consider themselves over-educated for present or available jobs. They may be unemployed, either because no job is offered or because no job is acceptable, or they may be employed but dissatisfied; the latter include civil servants and school teachers (Shils 1963; Coleman 1965, p. 562; Hoselitz 1966; Gouldner 1979).

Withough minimizing the value of the preceding breakdown, it is easier to point out the sources of challenge to the incumbent coalition than to identify when challenge will occur. Indeed, students of potential sources of dissatisfaction have often been so convinced by their analysis that they became bandwagon advocates of a supposed wave of the future, missing the fact that it is only conditional.

One condition is that the potentially rising elites do in fact arise. The preceding list indicates where to look for new groups in developing countries, but it does not claim to predict that all will appear, or, more precisely, that the conditions giving rise to any particular group may obtain at a particular time in a particular country. In other words, a second city, a dominant tribe, an over-educated generation, a rural development program, or a Europeanized leader might well be absent, and, thus, the cause for a new challenge disappears. What is implied, however, is that all of these conditions are not likely to be absent.

Another condition is that, as they arise, the new elite aspirants do run into some sort of blockage, rather than being absorbed into the incumbent elite coalition. If they are assimilated by the incumbent coalition as they rise to perform the responsive function of elites and before they ever get to the representative function, they can be socialized into membership in that coalition, and, if the absorptive capacity of the incumbents is great enough, the coalition will be little changed.

The third is that, as they seek entry, the new elites are able to combine the demands of excluded groups along several dimensions at a time, to take advantage of reinforcing cleavages. These are likely to occur, however, only at periods of issue realignment and elite bunching, after longer stretches of incumbency by the same elites. These potentialities for elite challenges can help in the identification of compatibility clusters in a particular country and thus indicate places to look for new political strains. Such an examination can also be useful tactically to the incumbent coalition, which can weaken the strength of the challenge by coopting elements along any of the dimensions.

Stability is fostered by weathering challenges, more so than by never having had any challenges to weather. The first cluster of challenges is essentially intra-elite and comprises leadership struggles for primacy in the victory parade or in the first independent government. There is likely to be an ideological issue, centering about the meaning of independence, and a generational image, based on the time and type of experience in the nationalist struggle, with social interests and geographical identities possibly involved as well. If the new elite shows the skill and will to overcome the challenge, it emerges strengthened, and all the more so if its victory sets in motion the tactics of cooption that will give the regime its dynamic stability. These tactics involve catching the aspirant elites in their responsive phase: separating demands from their bearers, treating the demand, and then reintegrating the bearer. Keeping the bearer quiet while his demand is being handled takes both skill and police powers and probably some other things, but it also means that there be resources to handle the demand itself. Such resources are initially available from the colonial inheritance. When the golden eggs of colonial development are used up, there is always a goose to kill, through nationalization of ownership and of personnel.

Perhaps the closest thing to regular competitive elections is the periodic reorganization or "perpetual renewal of the party and its related organization" to meet current criticisms and incorporate new groups (Moore 1967, p. 111; also Frey 1965, pp. 415 et passim). Although this notion may appear obvious and commonplace, it is important in what it excludes. It suggests that there is no single organizational structure appropriate for dynamic stability. To the contrary, it implies that defense of a given organization is less likely to further its maintenance than is renovative change. It also indicates, positively, that the formula of the moment must involve both the integration of groups and the aggregation of demands, the particular values for the unknowns in the formula to be filled in according to the groups and demands of the moment. Expansion means adding rather than replacing, producing gradual, incremental, cumulative change. In such types of change, a new member is socialized by the incumbents. The fewer the new members, the smaller the chances of their forming strong opposition groups with clear alternative options. All of these considerations, then, suggest that a dynamically stable cooptive system—by the very nature of the processes involved—is likely to maintain its essential characteristics and policies, its gravest challenges coming from within the coalition and being rather minor in their threats to its nature.

On the other hand, there are also inherent consequences of the processes that suggest that a more serious cluster of challenges is likely in the future. Just as the anticolonial protest arose because of a newly modernized minority's blockage from the promotion for which it was achievementally prepared, so a growing anti-establishmentarian protest mounts over the blockage of a much larger wave of modernized people from the jobs to which they have been taught to aspire.

The blockage no longer stems from prior occupation by Europeans, but, because whatever the rate of economic growth and modernization, there is a foreseeable leveling off or saturation point where labor, business, and government employment will stop growing. The population, education, urbanization, and aspiration growth rates all outdistance the economic growth rate.

Just as the modernized reform groups had to regain contact with the traditional mass as they entered the nationalist movement stage of the anti-colonial protest, so the new authoritative elite has to face a populist renewal in the future. No matter how open the recruitment, the new elite tends to become a class, coopting members, compounding position, status, and wealth, and living differently than its mass following. The more accentuated these tendencies, the more serious the likely reaction. It is ironic, but understandable, that it is the overproduction, not underproduction, of elite aspirants that causes the incumbent elite to become defensive, closed, and classlike.

A Jacksonian influx (as is the Turkish ruralizing election) is the smoothest type of renewal, but it is a strain on the very nature of the cooptive system in which a group invites others to join, not replace it (Sherwood 1967, p. 65). Revolutionary overthrow or a Dantonian influx (as in Syria or Iraq) is least smooth, and it does not necessarily imply subsequent societal transformation and development. In between, a military coup (as in Egypt) tends to combine order and progress in varying degrees and to restructure political relations, either by policy or by reaction. The ideological base for these three types of populist renewal is distributive and isolationist; it also has a generational and social dimension, and probably, but perhaps only incidentally, a geopolitical dimension.

ANALYSIS AND REVIEW

The preceding is hardly tight enough as yet to constitute a single theoretical model, but it is enough to provide a guide for the analysis and explanation of events and a review of literature. This will be undertaken in three parts: a survey of the rise of nationalist-modernist protest and the acquisition of sovereignty as a case of elite circulation, a survey of the effects of nationally-controlled modernization and development on elite circulation, and an indication of further research.

The clearest example of elite circulation or of elites as a policy output is the rise of nationalist elites, which appeared as a result of colonial elite policies and as a reaction to colonial elites. Numerous studies have analyzed this process, although most of them carry their analysis only to the point of identifying historical periods, rather than developing analytical categories and theoretical relations among them. The country that went through all the stages of nationalist-modernist protest was Algeria, one of the rare cases of revolution in the third world.* The sequence of events has been aptly captured by one of the best studies of elite circulation in terms similar to the model here presented. But Algeria's stages were somewhat mixed up, largely because the experience of a large number of workers in France created a different set of demands and attitudes that contested the reform groups, bypassed the nationalist movement, and prepared early for the revolutionary force.

Quandt (1969, p. 14) discerns "a discontinuous process of political socialization whereby each political generation was exposed to radically different experiences while at the same time reacting to . . . the failure of the preceding generation. . . . The result . . . meant that there was virtually no recruitment into an ongoing political process in which the 'rules of the game' were relatively well understood and in which the role of the politician was well defined." Liberal and Radical Politicians—pure and mixed types of reformers—were generated by the mixed effects of colonial education and social promotion. The Liberals were involved in reform groups in the interwar period (notably the Federation of Elected Officials), until the shelving of the Blum-Violette Bill showed the futility of their efforts. Both types then turned to sporadic efforts to form a nationalist movement, despite repression by the colonial regime, interruption by the war, and the eventual enactment of reforms like Blum-Violette. The Algerian People's Party (PPA), the Friends of the Manifesto and of Liberty (AML), and the Movement for the Triumph of Democratic Liberties (MTLD) all saw, by 1948, that the ultimate goal of independence could not be achieved by means short of the ultimate power of violence. The revolutionary force began with the Secret Organization (OS) of the MTLD and reached its successful expression in the National Liberation Army (ALN) of the National Liberation Front (FLN), led by the elite groups that Quandt calls Revolutionaries and Military. Yet the exceptional feature of Algeria is the way each stage or group was foreshadowed by a predecessor out of phase: the North African Star of the interwar (reform group) period had goals and attitudes of a nationalist movement, and the Setif revolt organized by its successor Algerian People's Party (PPA) on V-E Day was a premature revolutionary force. In this light, it is

---

*Sudan is one of the rare countries that achieved independence at the reform group stage, the reform groups having buttressed themselves with a traditional following through their alliances with *turuq* but not having reached other more important characteristics of even the traditionalist nationalist movement. A superficial multiparty system that was soon and easily swept away by a military coup was the result. However, no work on Sudan has looked at the country in any kind of conceptual terms. The further history is also amenable to explanation through the use of the ideas introduced here as well. The stability of military rule created new social forces that responded to their blockage by a "mini" or truncated revolution in 1964, a revolution that was soon voted out of power because the revolutionaries believed they had to hold elections to maintain their legitimacy. Half a decade later, a new type of military coup did not make the same mistake. See Bechtold (1976).

perhaps less surprising that the real nationalist movement of Algeria was the FLN in the second half of the war and notably in the demonstration of December 11, 1961—a result, not a predecessor, of the revolutionary force.

It takes little further discussion to show how these groups and stages were produced by positive and negative policies (development and blockage) on the part of the incumbent (colonial) elites and by the needs of the struggle growing out of the failure of the preceding phase. The reform group leaders were essentially those produced, often from Algerian middle class families, by the French educational system and then prevented from achieving the equality for which they had been trained. The reaction of the Radical Politicians was more violent because their lower social position required greater efforts at social promotion and, hence, greater disillusionment at rejection. The economic dislocations of the war produced marginal workers and ex-soldiers who were ready to become Revolutionaries, and the opportunities of military rank and higher education in the postwar period produced Military and Technicians. These three groups made up the revolutionary force, and then dominated the new independent elite (Zartman 1970, 1975, 1979; Chaliand 1977).

It is out of the experiences of Morocco and Tunisia that the notion of stages comes. In Tunisia, the Young Tunisians were a reform group that gave way to the Liberal Constitution (Destour) and Neo-Destour parties, two distinct parts of the nationalist movement, described as such by Brown in Micaund, Brown, and Moore (1964) and by Moore (1965) and, in more sociopsychological terms, by Memmi (1967). Tunisia never reached the revolutionary force as a full stage, the demonstration of coercive value of violence by the *fellaga* in Tunisia and the FLN in Algeria combined with the skillful political action of the Neo-Destour being enough to bring about independence.

Brown and Memmi both write about the imitation stage, the Young Tunisians, but they do not make a careful distinction between initial individual efforts at imitation and subsequent group efforts at reform when imitation is unrequited. Memmi jumps to mass movement and violence, an ecological fallacy that ascribes individual reactions to groups, and Brown, less drastically, simply combines imitation and reform. But then, Memmi's writing tends to refer more to attitudes and actions and Brown's to historic periods; if Memmi's analysis were refined through the notions of critical mass threshold or appropriate power and if Brown's periods were related to groups or roles independent of chronology, fuller theory and better explanation could be developed. Nevertheless, some important comparisons and understandings are already evident from the analysis.

> Ideally, each of the first three stages should come in order and be allowed to mature before being succeeded by the next stage. . . . The whole process of transition is in danger if there is too great a departure from this ideal pattern. Thus, [quiescence] is frustrated, as in

Morocco and Algeria, if there are too many local uprisings and if public security is not quickly and efficiently secured.... [In the imitation-reform stage,] the premature appearance of the Watani Party ... in Egypt forced the moderates into the role of rather ineffective politicians before they could achieve an intellectual reconciliation between alien and indigenous cultures. This ... stage was more nearly ideal in India, Sudan, Tunisia, and perhaps Lebanon and Syria.... In several countries, in the [nationalist movement] stage, ideological debate was postponed in favor of total involvement in the struggle for national independence; among these were Egypt under the Wafd, Morocco under the Istiqlal, and Pakistan.... One might advance here the assertion that Tunisia has come as close as any colonized state to following the ideal path of development from statis to dynamic society, which would explain its present acceptance of commitment to change (Moore 1965, pp. 5f).

The same scenario found its parallels in Morocco, with some instructive differences in detail from Tunisia and, a fortiori, Algeria. The Moroccan Action Bloc of the interwar period was the prime reform group. After World War II, the Independence (Istiqlal) party was the nationalist movement, its urban Resistance and the rural Liberation Army (ALM) foreshadowing a revolutionary force stage just enough to make the political activity of the Istiqlal effective. The idea of stages is used by Halstead (1967, pp. 5, 195f) in his description of the origins and rise of Moroccan nationalism (on suggestion, apparently, from Mehdi ben Barka). He calls his stages reformism and separatism, and never raises the problem of the revolutionary force because he stops in 1944. Halstead distinguishes roles, groups, and organizations only briefly, but he does emphasize the formation of (counter)elites as a policy output and, particularly, negatively as well as positively, as the result of educational programs. Zartman earlier referred to the stages of Moroccan nationalism and then used them as a background for the explanation of the political evolution after independence (1964; 1973, chap. 26).

Although it has been suggested that Morocco's evolution has been less "ideal" than Tunisia's, the right phenomenon may be identified for the wrong reasons. Rather than premature xenophobic resistance or overemphasis on the overriding independence issue, the breakdown of a commitment to progress and change in Morocco may come more from the inability of modernized elites to shake loose the traditionalist elites in the nationalist movement (until too late, in 1959) and from the related impact of a strong source of legitimacy, more traditionalist than modern, in the monarchy. Morocco's traditional elites had undergone a split between collaborationists and reformists; Tunisia's traditionalists were also split, but the reformists were worn out and secularized, whereas Algeria, in between, had a reformist element strong enough to contribute to, but not strong enough to dominate, the nationalist movement (Marais, de Montety, and Vatikiotis in Zartman 1973).

There is no similar treatment of Syria except for a brief summary given by Berque (1957) and picked up by Seale (1965). There, the National Bloc is treated as a nationalist movement whose unity and drive was subsequently worn out by the failure of the 1936 independence treaty, the loss of the Alexandretta sanjaq, the wartime tug-of-war for independence, the rise of regional and personal factions, and, finally, the Palestine War. The rise and fall of successive elites is depicted, but not explained.

The same characteristic is evident in works on the Egyptian reformist and nationalist movements, although some of the most important and insightful works on Middle East thought and politics have been written on this period (Safran 1961, Hourani 1962, Khadduri 1970, Berque 1972). The schools of Muslim reformist thought, the Egyptian reform parties such as Watan and Umma, and the Wafd nationalist movement have frequently been shown to be successive results of the experiences of each preceding phase or school operating within a changing context and reacting to different allies and adversaries. But the relation of such intellectual and political movements to a changing social base of rising groups, demands, and elites has yet to be shown in depth.

The real test of the proposed approach lies in its ability to explain and project events once the independence struggle or its functional equivalent has ended in victory and things have settled down to slower sociopolitical change that results from differential development. The longer the period of analysis, the easier it is to find the necessary events, data, and trends. Thus the most instructive cases can be expected to come from countries whose independence is not of recent date, incuding those that in the past have undergone consolidating revolutions that serve as watersheds in their development and as functional equivalents of independence in the colonial countries.

Turkey is a fitting subject for an examination of elite circulation and has been particularly well treated from that point of view. The Young Turks, which served as a model for many other later reform groups in the Middle East, actually succeeded in coming to power (unlike most other nationalist reformers), but, even in success, gave rise to a stronger reaction, a secular modernizing nationalist movement embodied by the Ataturk and Inönü Eras. Thereafter, the multiparty period and the two military coups suggest a history that readily lends itself to compartmentalization. Payaslioglu sees in this evolution a series of Aristotelian cycles in which power is concentrated and then dispersed (1964, esp. p. 427). His dynamic element lies in the structure of power itself: power-holders, consolidating in order to defend their power, alienate an increasingly large opposition until a minimum winning coalition is in the opposition, which then takes over. But he never identifies the certain groups that demand changes or the one group that captures power, and he makes no distinction between the types and purposes of power concentration that distinguish each of the five cycles he sees in the past century. For such distinctions and a more evolutionary model, one must turn to other works.

Frey has inductively developed a model from this history that focuses on types of elites and power structures (1965, pp. 406-19, esp. p. 415). He breaks up the nationalist period into organizations of nationalist awareness and of nationalist struggle. Thereafter, with independence, comes the breakdown of the funnel phase and the breakup of the nationalist elite into Ardent Nationalists, oriented toward societal restructuring and a concentration of power, and Post-independence Conservatives, oriented toward social and political pluralism. Frey projects only the dominance of the first through the establishment of a tutelary regime thàt, by its policies of transformation, creates new social groups. While Frey indicates these policy areas—army, education, communications, health—he does not relate the next stage, the opening up of the tutelary system, to the resultant demand-bearing groups but rather to the political structure, through the creation of new power linkages and then organization, opportunity, and take-over by the opposition. He does however indicate that rough spots can occur in the passage from a tutelary to a democratic regime, when "the tutelary regime absorb[s] various elements in the expanding elite too slowly" and when there is no agreement on the proper place of potential sources of power, such as peasants and workers. The study shows that blockage not only causes demand-bearing groups to form, but also incites them to vindictiveness when they finally take over, a conclusion so evident as to pass unnoticed in the anticolonial reaction.

The Rooses (1971) carry this model to further refinement through the use of role types, the Bureaucrats and the Politicians (with side discussions of the Military and Businessmen as well). As the increasingly technocratic tutelary regime developed the country, new skills, elite groups, client groups, interests, and policy options arose. Technocrats began to gravitate to semi-autonomous and private enterprises and liberal professions. Eschewing a frozen system of nationalism, authoritarianism, and praetorianism, the elite opened up the tute-lary system, creating a need and opportunity for Politicians. Fusion between party and bureaucracy broke down, and, instead of dominating government, the Bureaucrats were now told by the Politicians how to do things, even at the cost of efficiency and inflation. The Bureaucrats were too well socialized into their old roles to accept the new role change; following the ruralizing election of 1950, they rebelled in common cause with the military technicians in the coup of 1960. The cycle was replayed a decade later. Such an analysis provides a richer interpretation by relating historic periods or stages to elite roles, or, more analytically, to both the supply (developmental output) and demand (develop-mental need or input) of elite skills.

The elite circulation approach has also been well applied by van Dusen (in Tachau 1975b) to Syria, where a long period of postwar instability covered a clearcut shift of elites resulting from demands generated through aspects of development. Elites drawn from old urban families blocked a rising new village middle class, recently arrived from the countryside, from achieving further social promotion through higher education. Yet the older elite, which had become narrow, factious, and defensive about its positions during the protracted struggle for independence and its aftermath, was unable to generate effective successors from its midst. The aspirant elites found the higher education they sought in the only available opportunities: normal and military schools. Then, incited by the blockage and by the failure of the old elites (notably in regard to the Palestine defeat and the parliamentary ineffectiveness), they swept out the incumbents and their political system, using external allies when necessary. The result was a ruralizing series of coups, with highly distributive results achieved by bringing in a larger new elite with a much broader base than before. The potential size of the new elite made its internal relations much more competitive, however. Party and ideology were used to bridge the old fracture lines of geography and culture, but they provided their own fracture lines instead and brought increased intensity to political disputes. Although the 1950s showed the vulnerability of the parliamentary system to military coups, it took the 1960s to destroy the control of the old elites over both army and assembly and to replace them with the new aspirants.

Typically, the elite circulation approach has been used in studying a country during a period of relatively rapid changes. During periods of relative elite stability, as in the two decades of military rule in Egypt, there are enormous changes in group and aspirant structures that are necessary to understanding the coming events of the last quarter of the century, and yet these changes have not been given much attention. The policy of Sadat is only understandable through an analysis of changes in his supporting elites, an analysis that remains to be done.

The final example of elite studies in the Middle East comes from Israel, a country too often regarded as sui generis, to the neglect of extremely enlightening parallels and differences and, doubtless, to the ultimate misunderstanding of a society that is becoming more and more Middle Eastern. Israel has frequently been analyzed as a polity of generational elite circulation—*Founders and Sons* (Elon 1971), but no one has captured the dynamics of this movement as well as Shapiro (1969 pending; see, however, Seligman 1964, Torgovnik in Tachou 1975, Czudnowski 1972, Arian 1977 and 1978, Guttman and Landau 1975). The political system was established by the generational cohort that comprised the second *aliyah*, who were born in Russia toward the end of the century, immigrated in the first decade of the 1900s, and operated in Palestine during the 1920s and 1930s. The success of their political operations and the pervasiveness of their ideology meant that succeeding *aliyot* and *sabras* alike were positively socialized in the political culture of their elders and dominated by them. Instead of crystalizing as independent generational cohorts with an active nucleus, "generational units," they internalized admonishments not to rock the boat and they found their ambition in following rather than leading, notably through obedient integration into existing patterns and institutions. Their rebellious instincts as youths during a formative political age were diverted into military activity against an external enemy well past independence, disciplined under the continued political dominance of the *yishuv* (pre-independence) leadership. When an organizational manifestation of issue realignment occurred, in Rafi party in 1967, typically it took place under the leadership of the leading politician of the established elite turned rebel against his own generation, Ben Gurion, and the movement died for lack of effective younger leadership. Instead, the same younger generation came to power in the Labor government of 1974, now elite followers without their older generation leadership and without direction or cohesion. When the critical election occurred in 1977, the emergence of a number of competing third parties and the shift of voters to an opposition movement—all features associated with critical elections—brought the latter to power, but it was still a party dominated by the older generation, which internal ideology and external beleaguerment had allowed to dominate and to stifle normal generational succession through Israeli history.* The shift in issues and attitudes and the weakness and division of leadership provide for a new generational reaction, but the necessary cohort may not yet be ready, simply not yet old enough, to assert a different pattern in Israeli politics.

CONCLUSION

It would doubtless be possible to find other works that could contribute to an understanding of the process of elite circulation in the Middle East, but enough examples have been mentioned to permit a summary at this point. The first part of this chapter concentrated on a number of salient aspects of the process. The study of elites as a policy output resulting from uneven development measures allows a fuller understanding of the process of circulation. The concept of the demand-bearing group and of situational needs and blockage provides the dynamic for this process. The notion of four dimensions, along with the ideas of reinforcing cleavages, permits an analysis of the threshold when a group turns critical, that is, political. The phenomenon of bunching, and the reasons for it, allows for an explanation of stages or generations that would otherwise only be dates and time periods.

The second part of the chapter has reviewed some of the empirical work already done and inductive models drawn from it. One purpose of this review has been to show that work does exist that has utilized some of the notions mentioned here as associated with elite circulation and has established their correspondence with real events. All four of the major ideas of this presentation—elites as a developmental policy output, coalescence of demand-bearing groups

---

*For the same idea applied to Turkey, see Ozbudun and Tachau (1975).

through blockage, dimensions leading to reinforcing cleavages, and bunching through issue realignment—have cropped up in empirical case studies, even if they have not been combined in any one study or even fully developed as explicit instruments of analysis.

Thus, although the reality of the analytic concepts has been supported, their use for analysis has been limited and indirect. A number of studies have used the device of historical stages, time periods dominated by a particular elite group or role and institution or organization. Few of them, however, have separated period from group and/or role in order to discover relationships and to explain why a particular group or role was dominant in a particular period. Nor has there been much attention to the types of developmental policy that create particular types of elite aspirants, either as skills or as demand-bearing groups. Education is the source of change most frequently used to explain different types of elites in these studies, and culture (traditional versus modern), a related matter, is also cited.* An additional variable is power relationships and attitudes toward political and social structures, but these do not explain why some groups rise rather than others. These tasks are not easy, but for that reason they demand attention. It is not surprising that the first section as well as the second section of this chapter has been less than explicit on the relation between development and the rise of new elite groups and roles. It is there that more work needs to be done.

Yet even after more study of the policies that generate and that block new demands, groups, and elites, it is not likely that the dynamic of elite circulation in independent Middle East polities can be encompassed in a single-issue model such as the one used to analyze the struggle for independence. There are a number of reasons for this. For one, there is no conceivable issue that provides an overwhelming concern like the struggle for independence and for the control of one's own destiny. Revolutionary challenges may provide a serious issue and one whose course is not unlike the nationalist protest model, but the challenge is not universal, as the independence challenge has been.

A major point of the analysis has been that developmental change is country specific, so that a single-issue model would seem unlikely. Yet the purpose of conceptual analysis is to overcome the unique. The cited country studies and others suggest that the unique cases fall into at least three categories: overproduction of technicians who are blocked from access to the bureaucracy and form a demand-bearing group around the private sector; overproduction of

---

*There is a provocative model of stages of educational development in Harbison and Myers (1964, esp. pp. 38f, 57-95), but the dynamics of the passage from one stage to another are not discussed, and the outcome before the millenium of full development is apocalyptic: revolution or dictatorship. The same scenario, with the same outcome, is very well treated by Kautsky (1962 and 1972).

educated individuals who are blocked from positions of authority and form a group in opposition to incumbent elite institutions and culture; overproduction of expectant semiurbanized ex-peasants, blocked from access to their expectations, who form a distributively-oriented group. These categories are related and sometimes overlap, and they indicate political events evoked in a number of developmental studies. The demand-bearing group in formation is a sort of lumpen-bourgeoisie, a residue of the New Middle Class Man of the Middle East thesis (Halpern 1963 and 1969, Sternber-Sarel 1969, Van Nienwenhuijze 1977, Bill and Teiden 1974, chap. 3, and Hussein 1975), and the issue for elite circulation—no matter on which dimension it is viewed by the participants—concerns recurrent cycles of distribution and digestion. The expansion and subsequent problems of absorption of aspirant elites accounts for the issue realignment and bunching. Thus, the problem of uniqueness is a problem of detail and perspective. The particular cause for aspirant overproduction and blockage, in terms of a particular country's differential development, is an empirical matter. It may bear resemblances to the situation in other countries, and will do so—in the terms indicated in this chapter—to a greater extent as the names of the variables become more abstract. The theoretical matter, however, which this chapter has attempted to establish, concerns the fact that, for whatever specific causes in a given country, bunching and blockage, elite production, and demand-bearing groups do occur.

5

APPROACHES TO ELITE RESEARCH

Leslie L. Roos, Jr.

Elite research has made considerable methodological progress since the case studies characterizing the early literature. Research designs considerably more sophisticated than early cross-sectional surveys are becoming more common, and data quality has undoubtedly improved. More advanced analytical techniques are being used, while some truly comparative studies have been successfully undertaken. This chapter selectively deals with some of the newer developments in elite research, focusing upon critical methodological issues. The emphasis is upon treating several issues in depth, rather than upon covering the entire range of research approaches and methodological applications.

Campbell and his collaborators have highlighted many of the problems in interpreting research findings (Campbell and Stanley 1963, Cook and Campbell 1976). Their discussion is particularly germane to elite studies, since at least some of the empirical research on elites has proceeded without careful methodological underpinnings. Cook and Campbell define internal validity as referring to "the validity of any conclusions we can draw about whether a demonstrated statistical relationship implies cause" (1976, p. 23). They then go on to elaborate the different threats to internal validity, the many ways in which research can be rendered uninterpretable. This list of threats to validity is presented in this chapter and later used to emphasize some of the problems with my own research. The threats to validity are important for structuring the arguments presented here because well thought-out designs provide the only way to improve the interpretability of research. Thus, this chapter will emphasize the systematic and careful collection of data according to a plan that permits the clearest possible interpretation of the findings. Such attention to design is invaluable in helping the researcher survive the numerous things that go wrong, the unpleasant surprises that bedevil empirical studies.

Because experiments are seldom possible in such fields as political science and sociology, research design must deal with situations where threats to validity have to be handled without relying upon randomization and intervention at the convenience of the researcher. The subject matter of elite studies requires the academic to take a passive approach towards the data; with a few notable exceptions (such as Kissinger), he is in no position to actively intervene in the process. The quasi-experimental approach to research design uses the logic of experimentation in an effort to systematically eliminate different plausible explanations for a particular finding.

This chapter will also deal with a particular data analysis approach, causal modeling, which stresses powerful econometric approaches. The use of a series of structural equations permits comparing formal models of causal influence with sample data. The approach is primarily statistical, emphasizing not only the elimination of various hypotheses but also the estimation of the magnitude of causal effects. Data analysis approaches such as causal modeling are useful, but cannot substitute for research design. Cook and Campbell (1976) have criticized the tendency to overreliance upon causal modeling in much of the sociological literature, while Blalock has emphasized that ". . . improvements in data-collection procedures will be far more important, in the long run, than the kinds of weak predictions that must be made whenever inadequate attention has been given to measurement problems at the data-collection stage" (Blalock 1974, p. 454).

Data collection and research design are closely related to considerations of data quality. Most elite researchers have assumed that their data were reliable and valid. The use of advanced analytical techniques highlights problems of data quality often ignored in elite analysis. Thus, although available American data on occupational mobility might safely be considered to be of higher quality than most of the data used for comparative elite studies, the causal models generated are very sensitive to assumptions concerning measurement error. Depending upon the assumptions, an individual's early occupational history was seen to be either rather important or relatively unimportant in determining his status several decades later (Kelley 1973). How much more critical such assumptions are likely to be in our comparative elite analyses!

These methodological approaches suggest techniques applicable to several important types of substantive questions.

The reciprocal relationships between such variables as elite composition and such events as elections, revolutions, industrialization, and so on.

Elite movement into and out of various positions and organizations. A number of analysts have emphasized the entry and exit of social groups to and from elite positions as central to understanding political stability (Tilly 1973).

Attitude change as a function of socialization to a particular job, of aging, of historical change, and so forth.

Without an informed approach to research design, data collected with considerable work may be underutilized, wasted, or useless. A knowledge of research methodology may be particularly important for the professional development of the area specialist, since recent research has highlighted the need for area expertise in generating data for use in multivariate models (Welfling 1975). An effort will be made to develop guidelines for the researcher's overall investment in data collection and analysis. Several criteria will be forwarded to aid the researcher's choice of the data-gathering strategy appropriate for his particular problem.

A QUASI-EXPERIMENTAL PERSPECTIVE

This chapter follows Campbell (1970) in emphasizing the importance of forwarding causal statements, then probing such statements by systematic data collection and analysis. Popper's position concerning falsification is germane to the discussion of adequate explanation.

> Popper has advocated . . . a falsifiability criterion, in which a theory becomes scientifically meaningful if it is capable of being falsified by empirical data, and in which a theory becomes the better established the more experimental opportunities for falsification that it has survived and the more exacting these probes (Campbell 1970, p. 81).

One research strategy—that of experimentation and quasi-experimentation—is especially helpful in "probing" theoretical formulations, yet has seldom been applied to elite studies.

When presented in an appropriate fashion, both the reasoning and procedures characterizing the quasi-experimental approach may be usefully applied to a number of situations. Our position is in contrast with Weingartner's emphasis on the difficulties of extending experimental reasoning to such social sciences as history.

> Think of the stuff histories are made of—outbreaks of wars and revolutions, spreads of religions, failures of foreign policies. No simple laws will do as generalizations belonging to the explanation of such events. And finally, there is the problem of truth or confirmation. Even when a law is stated, how likely is it that it can be well confirmed? The historian is in no position to conduct experiments; the number of instances of any generalization he might have wanted to use may forever be insufficient to establish it (Weingartner 1968, p. 351).

Later in this chapter an effort will be made to deal specifically with some of these problems.

One central thrust of this chapter is that an understanding of the various threats to internal validity is basic for better research designs. These threats are rival explanations that, if not taken into account in the design stage, can explain away the results of an investigation (Campbell 1969, pp. 410–11).

History: events, other than the experimental treatment, occurring between pretest and posttest and thus providing alternate explanations of effects.

Maturation: processes within the respondents or observed social units producing changes as a function of the passage of time per se, such as growth, fatigue, secular trends, and so on.

Instability: unreliability of measures, fluctuations in sampling persons or components, autonomous instability of repeated or equivalent measures. (This is the only threat to which statistical tests of significance are relevant.)

Testing: the effect of taking a test upon the scores of a second testing; the effect of publication of a social indicator upon subsequent readings of the indicator.

Instrumentation: in which changes in the calibration of a measuring instrument or changes in the observers or scores used may produce changes in the obtained measurements.

Regression artifacts: pseudoshifts occurring when persons or treatment units have been selected upon the basis of their extreme scores.

Selection: biases resulting from differential recruitment of comparison groups, producing different mean levels on the measure of effects.

Experimental mortality: the differential loss of respondents from comparison groups.

Selection-maturation interaction: selection biases resulting in differential rates of maturation or autonomous change.

To deal with the threats to validity, a research emphasis should be placed upon longitudinal data collection. To justify this point of view, a review of some fundamentals of research design seems appropriate. The starting point for experimental and quasi-experimental designs is the basic pretest-posttest design O_1 X O_2 where O_1 and O_2 are the observations at times 1 and 2, respectively, and X is the experimental intervention—a treatment or event. Even if a strong difference is observed between O_1 and O_2, there are many plausible interpretations of such a difference. In an effort to better determine whether X (the treatment or event) actually caused the observed difference, a number of research strategies have been suggested (Campbell and Stanley 1963):

use of one or more control groups.

use of one or more additional experimental groups. Random assignment to experimental and control groups is a characteristic of true experimentation.

extension of the observations, both before and after the treatment (event) to provide more points in time. Such a series of data points is generally referred to as an interrupted time-series design (Campbell and Stanley 1963; Campbell 1969).

In quasi-experimental research, the emphasis upon randomization and planned intervention is relaxed in an effort to generate needed information without the technical and political difficulties of true experimentation. Developing a strategy for eliminating plausible rival hypotheses under these weakened assumptions is the essence of quasi-experimental design.

The variables of concern to social scientists present many problems. Useful methods for doing research on events must deal with such circumstances as events of interest that may be relatively infrequent, separated by a significant amount of time or space, and the fact that the appropriate level of measurement for many events is difficult to treat in other than dichotomous fashion, either a given event has occurred or it has not.

Quasi-experimental designs have been oriented toward adapting experimental designs to new circumstances; researchers have emphasized the extent to which particular applications deviate from true experiments. In true experiments, the intervention (the event in many quasi-experimental situations) is under the control of the researcher. Thus, in most quasi-experiments, the investigator's focus has been upon the effects of the event upon one or more dependent variables. The determinants of the event are characteristically not considered.

Although such a research strategy is understandable, given the disciplinary background (psychology) of such early advocates of quasi-experimentation as Campbell and Stanley (1963), a concern with the determinants of events is critical for historical and political analysis. Thus, depending upon the interests of the investigator, events can be treated as either dependent or independent variables; both the causes of the event and the effects of the event are legitimate subjects for research.

THE INTERRUPTED TIME-SERIES DESIGN

One quasi-experimental design, the interrupted time-series design, is especially suitable for elite analysis. The design utilizes longitudinal data on at least one dependent variable and information on the timing of at least one event. A particular event or policy is posited as the independent variable; this event is measured in discontinuous terms. Either the event has not taken place (before) or it has (after). Essentially, a burst of variance in a variable, which may be defined at a very macro-level, is considered as the possibly causal factor (Caporaso 1973). The dependent variable(s) are typically measured in interval fashion. This design has been reviewed by Caporaso (1973), Cook and Campbell (1976), and Glass, Willson, and Gottman (1975).

If adequate data were available, this design could be applied to a number of cases illustrating the declining representation of administrators in legislatures over a period of time (Quandt 1970). In order to proceed further, examining the pattern of changes in this dependent background variable is desirable. The first step in probing the hypothesis that the event is causally important in determining the composition of an elite body is to examine the shape of the trend line.

If the trend line is completely linear (and thus can be closely fit with a single regression line), the use of this quasi-experimental design is not appropriate. But if the trend is better conceptualized as two lines, one before and one after the event, that are significantly different from each other, the rival hypothesis of no difference between the before and after segments is rendered less plausible. Figure 5.1 presents several possible patterns of behavior of a time-series variable, illustrating general trend (line A), a cyclic pattern (B), random fluctuation (C), and possible true changes (D–G) (Caporaso 1973). Various statistical models have been proposed for analyzing these lines; more advanced models assume random shocks and a somewhat erratic, rather than linear, pattern.

Quasi-experimental designs presume a sharp cutting point between before and after conditions; a burst of variance in a variable, which may be defined at a very macro-level, is considered as a possible causal factor—the treatment or event. But changes do not occur overnight. Specifying dates of change is full of dangers. In this gray period when the policy change may or may not have occurred, some changes in one or more dependent variables may begin. Since the basic statistical models for quasi-experiments presume an abrupt shift between before and after conditions, gradual changes cannot be easily accommodated. If data were collected frequently enough and the gray period were long enough, the time period might be divided into before, during, and after segments. Obtaining a long enough time-series is the problem here.

When the specific date of the relevant event or policy change is in doubt, frequent data collection is valuable for several other reasons. The more powerful statistical models are based on a large number of measurements (Box and Tiao 1965, Box and Jenkins 1970, Hibbs 1977).

A short interval between collection of the last before and the first after data also helps reduce the plausibility of several other rival hypotheses: that these changes in the dependent variable(s) were a normal pattern to be expected with the passage of time (maturation) regardless of the occurrence or absence of a particular event, and that one or more other events occurring about the same time were responsible (history). When multiple replications involve sites differing in a number of ways, the possibility of other events being regularly linked with the treatment event is greatly diminished.

Comparative research is particularly useful in reducing the plausibility of rival explanations (Duvall and Welfling 1973b). Thus a particular event may be

FIGURE 5.1

Possible Patterns of Behavior of a Time-Series Variable

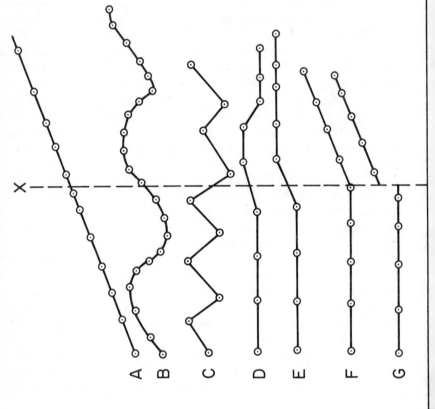

judged to have certain consequences (changes in one or more dependent variables) in a given site (organization, nation, or whatever). By a multiplicity of replications, by what Campbell (1969) has called a "control series," the rival hypotheses of maturation and history may be downgraded.

This mode of analysis can be clarified by reference to an actual case. Turkish data compiled by Frey (1965) and Tachau with Good (1973) permit tracing the percentage of various occupations in the fourteen Parliaments from 1920 to 1973. These studies have suggested that the election of 1950, in which the Democratic Party came to power for the first time, led to a change in the representation of different social groups. In analyzing this proposition through the use of the interrupted time-series design, the data presented in Figure 5.2 can be divided into a before (1950) segment and and after (1950 and later) segment. The slopes and intercepts of these lines differ significantly when appropriate statistical tests are applied (Roos and Roos 1971; for review of these tests, see Caporaso and Roos 1973). But stopping here is not totally adequate. As can be seen in Figure 5.2 and Table 5.1, changes in the representation of social groups appear to have taken place before 1950. This general problem of specifying when and if the critical event (in this case, an election) did take place is noted earlier. Substantive considerations must determine this, although sometimes further statistical analysis is useful.

Looking more closely at the Turkish data on the Parliamentary representation of three different interest groups highlights some of the possible difficulties in interpretation. Table 5.2 shows the effects of systematic variation in the before-after cutting point. Statistics are generated using different cutting points, starting with the before-after cutting point after Parliament III (data from Parliament I-III as before, from IV-XIV as after), then moving the cutting point in increments of one until it is after Parliament IX. Two statistical tests on the differences between pre- and post-event lines are presented. The data generally suggest that for two of the three interest groups the before and after regression lines differ most markedly when the cutting point is after Parliament VIII; the data on the representation of business managers are ambiguous. Since the 1950 election produced Parliament IX, the data are in accord with the interpretation of this election as particularly important.

At a general level, this sort of argument—that a particular event has affected a given dependent variable—is a common one in social science. Specifically with regard to elites, Quandt has suggested that various macro-events during and after the Algerian independence struggle influenced the character of those coming to power. Huntington's concept of the "ruralizing election" incorporates this idea of an event affecting elite composition (1968). After the rural population has been mobilized, a particular election is likely to lead to the ouster of the cosmopolitan elite and the coming to power of a rural-oriented elite. Huntington's approach is nonquantitative, but he notes several other examples that might be said to provide multiple replications of the Turkish case study.

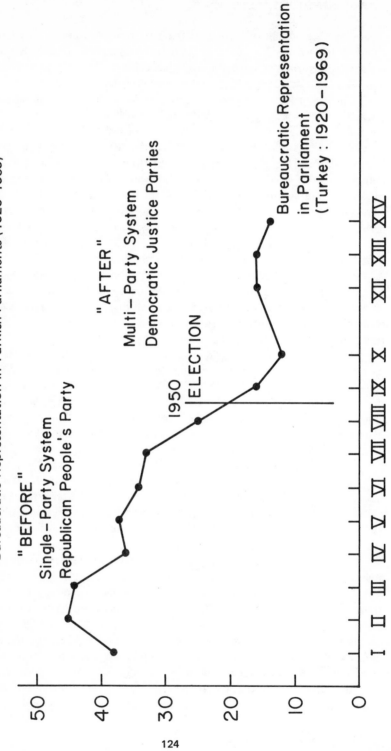

FIGURE 5.2

Bureaucratic Representation in Turkish Parliaments (1920–1969)

"BEFORE"
Single–Party System
Republican People's Party

"AFTER"
Multi–Party System
Democratic Justice Parties

1950
ELECTION

Bureaucratic Representation
in Parliament
(Turkey : 1920–1969)

TABLE 5.1

Changes in Representation of Different Occupations in Turkish Parliament (1920-1973)
(Percentage of Selected Occupations in Turkish Assemblies)

	I 1920–1923	II 1923–1927	III 1927–1931	IV 1931–1935	V 1935–1939	VI 1939–1943
Officials	38	45	44	36	37	34
Professionals	18	20	22	22	24	27
Business Managers	13	8	10	12	11	13

	VII 1943–1946	VIII 1946–1950	IX 1950–1954	X 1954–1961	XI 1961–1965	XII 1965–1969	XIII 1969–1973
Officals	33	25	16	13	16	16	14
Professionals	31	35	45	44	46	45	44
Business Managers	9	15	19	19	20	16	18

Note: Data on Assembly XI were not available.
Source: Information taken from Frey (1965) and Tachau (1973).

The technique proposed here has been used for research on European integration (Caporaso 1973), on organizational efficiency in Turkey (Roos and Roos 1971), and on political change in Black Africa (Duvall and Welfling 1973). The longer time-series available with British economic data has permitted Hibbs (1977) to use better statistical models to analyze the effects of different economic policies. The interrupted time-series design seems appropriate for several Middle Eastern data sets. Figure 5.3 shows suggestive elite data from Lebanon (Hudson 1966 and 1969).

One difficulty with the interrupted time-series design concerns interpretation of the particular event postulated as causal. Elections are obviously causal in producing changes in parliamentary representation, but a deeper explanation is certainly desirable. Many of the changes accompanying social modernization occur more or less simultaneously, thus complicating analysis. Most developing countries have been characterized by ongoing efforts at industrialization, the

TABLE 5.2

Interrupted Time-Series Analysis with Different Cutting Points
(Turkish Elite Data)

Pre-Post Cutting Point After Parliament Number	III 1927– 1931	IV 1931– 1935	V 1935– 1939	VI 1939– 1943	VII 1943– 1946	VIII 1946– 1950	IX 1950– 1954
Interest Group Representation Double-Mood Test-t Value (Walker-Lev Test 3-F Value)							
Officials	1.36 (.02)	.41 (.10)	.80 (.13)	1.23 (1.28)	2.88 (9.29)	3.35* (6.89)	1.35 (.27)
Professionals	.32 (.75)	.37 (.03)	1.13 (.63)	2.01 (4.10)	3.07 (9.30)	6.71* (24.17)*	1.28 (.00)
Business Managers	.64 (.14)	.08 (.28)	.40 (.00)	.23 (.01)	2.71* (8.52)*	2.87* (6.84)*	1.27 (.53)

*Indicates statistically significant at the .05 level, with correction for autocorrelation (Sween and Campbell 1965).

Autocorrelations of observations (lag one) for the detrended total series were .35, .52, and .09 for data for officials, professionals, and business managers, respectively. This information on autocorrelation is important in accounting for the nonindependence of successive observations when applying tests of significance to the data.

Due to the small number of observations and the differing number of pre- and post-observations for each cutting point, comparisons of t and F statistics for various cutting points must be made with great care.

Note: The double-Mood test "involves both a pre-X and a post-X linear fit and a comparison of the predictions by these two estimates of a hypothetical value lying midway between the last pre-X and the first post-X point" (Caporaso 1973, p. 28). Walker-Lev Test 3 "yields an F-Statistic which tests the null hypothesis that a common regression line fits both pre- and post-X distributions."

Source: Frey (1965) and Tachau (1973).

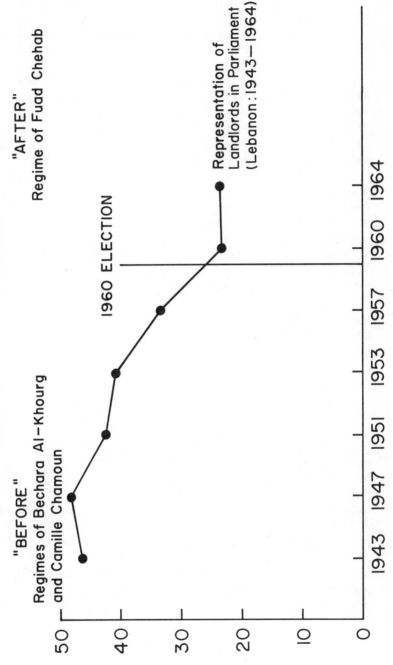

FIGURE 5.3

Landlords' Representation in Lebanese Parliaments (1943–1964)

"BEFORE"
Regimes of Bechara Al-Khourg
and Camille Chamoun

"AFTER"
Regime of Fuad Chehab

1960 ELECTION

Representation of
Landlords in Parliament
(Lebanon:1943–1964)

creation of new public and private organizations, and an expansion of the educational system, coupled with increased demands by various social groups.

In the interrupted time-series design, one variable must be taken to be the event, while another can be considered the dependent variable. In each individual case, criteria for determining that an event did or did not occur must be developed. As is suggested above, this may sometimes be difficult. The nature of the relationship between variables is also important. If an event does affect the dependent variable, but the effect is delayed and/or relatively slight, the statistical tests are unlikely to show any differences between pre- and post-event lines. A different type of conceptual and statistical approach may be appropriate for these problems; some general guidelines are developed later in the chapter.

The problems mentioned here often relate to construct validity, to "the correct labeling of cause and effect in generalizable and theory-relevant terms" (Cook and Campbell 1976, p. 226). Even in true experiments where the researcher controls and initiates the treatment, there are possibilities for misinterpretation. What the experimenter perceives to be causally important may not be the significant part of the treatment. The situation is considerably more complicated in quasi-experiments, where events take place in the real, as compared with the experimental, world. Such events are more likely to be multi-dimensional, incorporating several independent variables of interest. Although multiple experimental and control groups are useful in interpreting quasi-experimental data, developing such relatively complex variations depends upon being able to say which events are equivalent to which other events and the important dimensions along which they differ. Efforts to do so are likely to be both difficult and theoretically rewarding. Comparative politics would benefit from an explicit statement of similarities and differences between particular events, coupled with an analysis of their effects. In this way, a comparative perspective may help isolate the important causal component of the event.

Micro-analysis of the components of an event that might be causally important has been suggested (Coleman 1972). Both the duration of events and their intensity (the amount of an event or policy change) must be scrutinized to help establish equivalence or nonequivalence and to isolate important causal components. Sometimes quantitative criteria can be used; Duvall and Welfling (1973b, p. 118) studied the impact of civil strife on institutionalization in Black Africa, including strife events "only if greater than a certain 'magnitude,' since single demonstrations or strikes in a year are not expected to have any significant or lasting effect on party-system institutionalization." Their criterion appeared to be a combination of two or more riots, strikes, or declarations of emergency in a single year.

If a policy change is the event, a close correspondence between the implementation of a part of a new policy and a shift in the value of the dependent variable may provide clues as to the most important elements of the policy. Such a strategy risks "fudging" of the before-after cutting point; one event rather than another may be forwarded as important on an ex post facto basis. Without good theory to specify the critical part of the change, the data (that is, the dependent variables) may be relentlessly eyeballed in straining for substantive and statistical significance.

In summary, the interrupted time-series design is appropriate to situations in which the independent variable can legitimately be treated as dichotomous. The design provides rules of inference in the form of statistically significant differences between the forms of the lines before and after the event took place. A conservative approach to inference is recommended, given the criticism of available tests (Hibbs 1977). Relying on similar results from several statistical tests is one way to be conservative. More stringent levels of statistical significance (.01 rather than .05) could be used, but the numbers of data points are often insufficient to reach the .01 or .001 levels. If such tests are not significant, the null hypothesis, that the event did not have a causal effect, is accepted. However, if statistically significant differences are found, a number of alternative hypotheses must be rejected before assuming that the event was causally important. The alternative threats of history and maturation have been discussed; some additional hypotheses are treated in the section on data quality.

THE EVENT-CAUSING DESIGN

In the standard interpretation of the interrupted time-series design, an event is seen as affecting a variable; the presence or absence of such an effect is measured statistically. The same longitudinal data used in the interrupted time-series design suggest another design in which a shift in variable "causes" an event. Both causal frameworks rely on time precedence of the independent variable as an aid to causal inference. In the interrupted time-series design: E (event) → V (a change in intercept or slope of a variable). In the event-causing design: V (some characteristic of a variable) → E (event). Although a fair amount of systematic research has been done using the E → V framework, the situation differs with regard to the V → E framework. This latter model underlies much social science and historical research, but has not been approached from a perspective that emphasizes plausible rival hypotheses.

The event-causing design is implicitly used in much historical analysis; for example, what were the causes of World War I? Variables such as inflation, escalating levels of distrust, and so on are typically suggested as causal factors. Taking an example from comparative politics, the ruralizing election is said to occur because modernizing policies of the urban elite lead rural dwellers to vote for a more traditional, locally-oriented party (Huntington 1968). Thus, one or more variables—the policies and backgrounds of the individuals coming to power at the time of independence—led to the event, their being ousted from power by means of an election. The logic behind interrupted time-series analysis is useful for structuring data necessary for hypothesis testing with the event-causing design.

In the V → E formulation, time-series data from several sites (political units, for example) are most desirable. Such data are needed both from sites where the event occurred and from sites where it did not. The concern is no longer with collecting time-series data before and after the event; only the before data are necessary. The focus turns away from interpreting interruptions in a time-series to other types of explanatory factors: levels of variables preceding events, rates of increase in variables, and interrelationships among variables.

Several logically distinct possibilities are based upon the V → E causal formulation. One is that the *level* of the variable led to the event, that is, the extent or total number of programs directed toward modernization might have led to the ruralizing election. At all sites where the event occurred was the level of the independent variable(s) the same, and where it did not occur was the level lower (or higher)? (See A and B in Figure 5.4.) Another possibility is that the *rising (or falling) value* of the variable led to the event, that is, the relative increase in the number of modernizing programs might have led to the ruralizing election. Was a particular rate of increase (or decrease) observed at sites where the event took place and a different rate of increase observed at non-event sites? (See C and D in Figure 5.4.)

The outline of possibilities clearly parallels the interrupted time-series design in terms of the treatment of level (intercept) or rising-falling value (slope) of a variable.

Several points should be made. First of all, the (independent) variable in the V → E sequence might be at a macro-level, several steps removed from the direct cause of the event. Thus, in the example here, the modernizing programs presumably caused disgruntlement among rural voters, which led in turn to their electoral behavior. Secondly, unmeasured intervening variables are often introduced into the analysis; "disgruntlement" might intervene between the variables "number of modernizing programs" and "voting preference."

The situation becomes more obscure when the independent variable either appears to be constant or moves in a counterintuitive direction. In the example forwarded in Figure 5.2, the pre-1950 Parliamentary representation of Turkish administrators declined somewhat in the years before the ruralizing election. Several explanations can be forwarded. The decline in official representation can be seen as a sign that power was building up elsewhere in the society. Perhaps the number of years the bureaucracy enjoyed a relatively high degree of influence was important; such a long period of bureaucratic power led to increased societal tension and/or rural dissatisfaction. Without direct measurement of an intervening variable, such an argument raises the possibility that the *constant value* of the variable led to the event. This argument is weakened by the question,

FIGURE 5.4

Variables as Predictors of Events

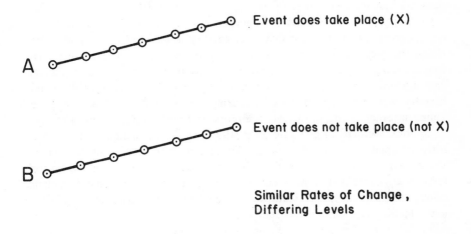

Event does take place (X)

A

Event does not take place (not X)

B

Similar Rates of Change,
Differing Levels

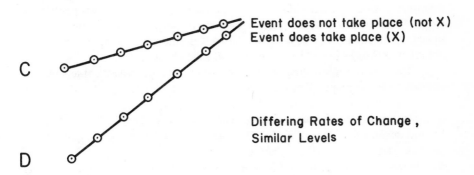

Event does not take place (not X)
Event does take place (X)

C

Differing Rates of Change,
Similar Levels

D

why did the event not take place earlier? Answering this question leads one to refer to an intervening variable, to some explanation such as the tension was not yet great enough. In order to restrict such weak, ex post facto arguments, it is suggested that the constant value explanation not be accepted; measurement of intervening variables is particularly important in this case.

A number of threats to validity of causal interpretations are implicit in the event-causing design. One is the inability to distinguish between *level* of a variable and *rising (or falling) value* of the variable as the predominant causal factor. Even cyclical phenomena might be important. Another threat is that several variables may have been involved in causing the event. Both might have to be present in order to trigger the event. Or, one variable may be able to substitute for another, perhaps in affecting a causally critical intermediate variable. Another, completely unrelated variable may have been responsible for the event. Its association with the measured variable may have been fortuitous; except for its reversal of the E-V sequences, this threat corresponds to what Campbell (1969) has called "history." Maturity may also be a threat. The passage of time might, in due course, have led to the event.

Under some circumstances, the roles of level and slope can be separated. If slope—the rising or falling rate of variable—is proposed as causally important, the question of why the event has not taken place earlier remains relevant. If new data points are relatively close to the slope generated by older data, level and slope cannot be separated. The argument revolves around a slope of a particular magnitude extended over a given length of time; level is obviously affected by these growth rate considerations. Examining the residuals provides clues as to the importance of absolute level, beyond that expected from growth rate. If the last data point is off the slope—markedly higher than a rising slope, for example—then level would seem to be of independent importance.

A multiple replications or control series strategy would seem particularly appropriate—both substantively and methodologically. This suggests replications across different countries or systems of other types in order to consider the possibility of other variables being operative. Only in this way can various competing hypotheses, various threats to internal validity, be treated.

More substantively, this sort of V → E argument is popular in elite studies. Such an argument might be summarized:

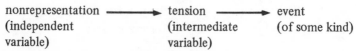

nonrepresentation ————→ tension ————→ event
(independent   (intermediate   (of some kind)
variable)   variable)

But the literature suggests additional possibilities (Huntington 1968, Zartman in this volume). It may not be (only) blockage of the representation of particular groups that is causal. The general complications listed previously are relevant; policies adopted by the ruling group might contribute to tension in a number of ways. Other variables, such as communications level in the country, might be important. Finally, the particular type and intensity of event that takes place may depend on some of the factors previously mentioned. In developmental terms, whether the event is a ruralizing election, a rural revolt, or a Green Uprising may be influenced by the degree of blockage, by the types of policies adopted, or by other variables.

SOME COMMON PROBLEMS

A problem common to both the $E \rightarrow V$ and the $V \rightarrow E$ models is the level at which both events and variables are often conceptualized. The strengths of the formulations are their weaknesses: the "black box" approach to measurement permits linking rather different phenomena, but does not allow the investigator to precisely specify causal linkages. This suggests the desirability of microanalysis to try to probe more deeply into possible causal relationships.

These event-variable approaches raise a number of questions that will have to be discussed more extensively. As noted elsewhere, variables can often be reconceptualized in a way that has implications for both research design and substantive findings (Roos 1973). Alternate reconceptualizations need to be treated and explicitly compared. Any research design has characteristic threats to internal validity, characteristic plausible rival hypotheses suggested by the approach. What additional types of data may be necessary to help substantiate a particular causal formulation?

A partial approach to the problems of feedback might be gained by combining the $V \rightarrow E$ and $E \rightarrow V$ formulations. The Turkish example previously cited is also relevant here. As suggested earlier, V_1 (the before conditions of the variable) influences E (the event); E (the event) then influences V_2 (the after condition of the variable). In qualitative terms, the modernizing program of the Turkish administrative elite (V_1) has influenced the results of the 1950 election (E), which feedback to change the program (V_2). Quantitatively, bureaucratic representation in Parliament might be taken as the V variable, measured before (V_1) and after (V_2) the event.

More substantively, these event-variable models seem highly relevant to formulations emphasizing crises in comparative politics and history (Binder et al. 1971), and in organizational development (Greiner 1972). The overall approach is very compatible with a concern for "time sequences and rates of change" (Nordlinger 1970). Given the state of theory and measurement in social science generally, a focus upon events seems most appropriate (Zartman in this volume). The interrupted time-series design is particularly suitable when longitudinal data on at least a single dependent variable, coupled with information on the timing of at least one event, are available. Besides its relevance for theory-building, the design seems especially useful for policy analysis, output evaluation, and so forth.

As noted earlier, various other sorts of information aid in dealing with different plausible hypotheses threatening the E → V causal interpretation.

More generally, a time-series framework has been utilized by Putnam (1976, p. 437) to study elite transformation in three historical case studies: "(1) the impact of the industrial revolution on West European and American elites during the nineteenth and twentieth centuries; (2) the impact of nationalist and Communist revolutions on elites in this century; and (3) the impact of technology and bureaucratization on contemporary elites . . ." Sometimes his description deals with particular events and the type of rapid changes suitable for analysis using an interrupted time-series design. At other times, gradual changes are portrayed, since industrialization took place over a series of years. This nonstatistical presentation is useful in highlighting the variety of explanations that can be built upon comparative longitudinal data. More explicit considerations of research design can help sharpen the focus of such studies, eliminating plausible hypotheses in a more systematic fashion.

CAUSAL MODELING

Political elites, perhaps more than other social groups, both influence events and are influenced by them. As treated above, theories and methods of elite research should reflect this fact. At the same time, elites age, work in organizations, and have careers. Thus, research in these areas is also relevant for the study of elites.

Several sociological formulations are important to elite research in dealing with concerns like social mobility, careers, and organizational structure. Moreover, a number of methodological innovations such as causal modeling, directly relevant to elite studies, have been used by sociologists.

The data requirements for causal modeling of the type exemplified by sociological studies of careers (Duncan, Featherman, and Duncan 1972, Sewell and Hauser 1975) are somewhat different from those of the quasi-experimental designs previously discussed. Depending upon the assumptions concerning measurement error, time lags, and direction of causation incorporated into the model, cross-sectional data may sometimes be used, although certain threats to validity are likely to present problems. Longitudinal data are almost always preferable.

The path analysis framework is useful in providing a convenient way of summarizing and diagramming causal relationships; a methodology for evaluating possible causal relationships, since the plausibility of causal models that do not provide a reasonably close fit with the data is reduced; an estimate of the magnitude of causal effects; a stress upon the probability of multiple influences upon one or more variables; and a clear presentation of different models to highlight the effects of assumptions of various types.

Much of causal modeling might be seen as an effort to fit available data to a model in which some of the total number of causal possibilities have been eliminated. In causal modeling, it is standard to assume linearity, additivity, and noncollinearity (Heise 1970). Further simplifying assumptions concerning unmeasured variables and measurement error aid in reducing the total possibilities. If unmeasured variables and measurement error are taken into consideration, "the causal models connecting the variables of real interest must be very simple indeed" (Blalock 1970, p. 1,110).

The simplest form of causal modeling, equated here with path analysis, assumes a recursive system of equations. "The basic idea is that variables can be hierarchically arranged in terms of their causal priorities in such a way that it becomes possible to neglect variables that are clearly dependent on a given subset of variables" (Blalock 1971, p. 2). Thus one-way causation is assumed (that is, an individual's occupation may be affected by his social background, not vice-versa). Here the task is to estimate "the paths which may account for a set of observed correlations on the assumption of a particular formal or causal ordering of the variables involved" (Duncan 1966, p. 1). Given the assumption of one-way causation, Duncan (1966) describes how to express the correlation between any two variables in terms of the paths leading from common antecedent variables; Land (1969) also provides a detailed introduction to path analysis. More complicated, sophisticated approaches to causal modeling are presented elsewhere (Duncan 1975). For the purposes of this discussion, the assumptions of one-way causation, of no unmeasured variables, and of only random measurement error are important because they permit estimating causal paths by means of conventional regression analysis.

Various statistical routines such as Statistical Package for the Social Sciences can be used to calculate the standardized regression coefficients (beta coefficients) for the variables predicting each of the dependent variables (Nie et al. 1975). Path coefficients are standardized regression coefficients that are statistically significant using the usual criteria (Duncan 1966). To paraphrase Duncan (1966), path analysis provides a pattern of interpretation, making explicit the rationale for regression analysis.

The rapid adoption of path analysis in sociology, organizational behavior, and political science has been due to its utility in handling different types of data. Path analysis provides a way to specify plausible causal relationships, going beyond earlier techniques of presenting mean scores, cross tabulations, and correlation coefficients. For example, causal modeling could have usefully been incorporated in Harik's (1971) study of opinion leaders and the mass media in rural Egypt to structure the contribution of different variables in predicting knowledge of provincial and international affairs. Szyliowicz's (1971) study of elite recruitment in Turkey could have benefited from path analysis.

In a preliminary way, path analysis has been used to compare the length of cabinet tenure of political elites in Egypt, Lebanon, and Israel (Dekmejian 1974).

The causal sequences and significant variables differed markedly across the three countries. Occupation appeared to have an indirect effect on cabinet tenure in each country, but it acted mainly to affect such country specific variables as Core Cadre (Egypt: membership in Nassr's Free Officers Association) and Za'imism (Lebanon: the relative power of ministers by virtue of their political, economic, and familial connections).

Path analysis is also helpful for combining hypotheses about general occupational stratification with the study of careers. My recent research on Turkish managers uses this framework to relate "parameter values to changes in the institutional environment," helping to link quantitative research on organizational behavior and social stratification with comparative historical inquiry (Goldhamer 1968, p. 437). Treiman (1970, pp. 218, 228) has proposed such hypotheses as:

In more industrialized societies parental status should play a less important role in educational attainment than in less industrialized societies.

The direct influence of father's on son's occupational status should be weaker, the more industrialized the society.

The more industrialized a society, the greater will be the effect of current status on behavior relative to the effect of parental status.

Kahn has discussed the concepts of occupation and role in a way that aids the linkage between elite and social structural formulations and those of organization theory (1972, p. 183).

[Occupation can be regarded] as a role that is defined in terms of certain rewards for its performance. Each occupation comprises a unique cluster of satisfaction-giving and dissatisfaction-imposing activities, and a unique set of extrinsic rewards [and penalties]. When occupations are ordered according to status, we are simply asking people to tell us which occupation-defined sets of activities and rewards are best and which are least attractive.

Rather different approaches to the study of careers have been adopted by sociologists, on the one hand, and psychologists, on the other. The basic model used by sociologists in studies of the socioeconomic life cycle emphasizes the importance of such background variables as family and schooling as determinants of an individual's occupation. Such research characteristically ranks individual occupations without incorporating attitudinal data (for example, Duncan, Featherman, and Duncan 1972). Psychological research on careers has emphasized the influence of job-related variables on job satisfaction, turnover, and the like. The few studies with a longitudinal focus have generally emphasized personality and attitudinal variables, but neglected sociological factors (Schein 1971,

Hall 1976). Psychological and sociological models can be explored using path analysis and several sets of Turkish elite data. Some very basic results and problems of interpretation are presented; a discussion of the analysis of one data set leads into the section on data quality.

The overall design of the Turkish research involved combining biographical and survey information to study changes in career patterns over a relatively long period of time (20 to 30 years). The availability of biographical information on graduates of an elite faculty (the Political Science Faculty) and survey information collected by other investigators (in 1956) permitted the use of sophisticated panel and cohort designs. Such designs are valuable to the student of elites in allowing a partial separation of the effects of maturation, history, and membership in a particular birth cohort (Hyman 1972, Cook and Campbell 1976). Thus, the research design of the Turkish study is considerably stronger than that of a single point in time, cross-sectional study.

The data in Figure 5.5 are more complex than suggested by Treiman's hypotheses. Economic and social changes within Turkey, in combination with the path analyses, suggest that, with the industrialization of the 1950s, the course of study within the Political Science Faculty (somewhat akin to a school of management oriented toward the divil service) became increasingly important as a predictor of later organization of work. By the late 1960s, graduates from different courses of study were changing their career patterns, perhaps taking advantage of family contacts. Overall, it is clear that the relationships among social background, education, and organization of work are complex and can vary markedly in a relatively short time.

A comparison of Figures 5.5a and 5.5b shows substantial differences between the cohorts in 1949 and 1959. Course of study at the Political Science Faculty was a significantly better predictor of recent graduates' organization of work in 1959 than in 1949. One interpretation might be that in 1949 graduates could move into almost any organization; by 1959, they needed specific types of training, such as accounting and finance, to move into many kinds of jobs. This increasing emphasis upon technical training may have resulted from efforts to introduce financial controls, to expand banking, and so forth. Other data indicate that by 1969, graduates of the faculty were moving into new types of organizations, many of them economic organizations founded during the 1960s (Roos and Roos 1971). Figure 5.5c indicates that rather different channels were being used for these career patterns. The longitudinal data do permit making some limited before-after inferences about the effects of different types of modernization programs, but variables other than those postulated (the threat of history) may have been responsible for the observed differences.

Another explanation for the differences is that the measurement domain may have changed over time (Stinchcombe and Wendt 1975). Perhaps applying the same ranking scheme to 1949, 1959, and 1969 data is inappropriate. In 1949, the Ministry of Interior did not have the same political pressures it

FIGURE 5.5

Alternate Path Analyses Across Three Time Periods—
Turkish Elite Data

5a. 1938–1940 Graduates ; 1949 Organization of Work (N=72)

Social Background $\xrightarrow{\text{0.19}}$ Course of Study $\xrightarrow{\text{0.42}}$ Organization of Work Early in Career

5b. 1948–1950 Graduates ; 1959 Organization of Work (N=124)

Social Background $\xrightarrow{\text{0.28}}$ Course of Study $\xrightarrow{\text{0.79}}$ Organization of Work Early in Career

5c. 1958–1960 Graduates ; 1969 Organization of Work (N=97)

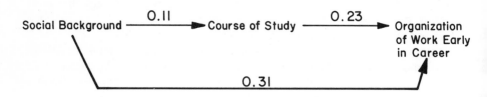

Social Background $\xrightarrow{\text{0.11}}$ Course of Study $\xrightarrow{\text{0.23}}$ Organization of Work Early in Career

0.31

experienced later. Thus, at that time it may well have ranked higher in the organizational stratification scheme.

A number of checks should be incorporated into such analyses. A central question concerning such multivariate procedures as path analysis is their sensitivity to changes in decisions about the assignment of numbers to observations, decisions about coding. For example, the organizations in which the administrators work are relatively easy to rank. Several lines of evidence support the general ranking used in Figure 5.5; Interior was ranked lowest and Foreign Affairs highest. This evidence includes data on salaries, on the employment of university-educated personnel, on individual ranking of careers and organizations, and so forth (Roos and Roose 1971, Mihçioglu 1972).

But going beyond simple ranking to ratio-scale coding raises questions of assigning appropriate numbers. According to Tufte, "the simple linear assignment of numbers [for instance, assigning 1, 2, 3, 4 to four ordered categories] usually won't do" (1969, p. 645). Each of the specific criteria previously mentioned would lead to a different numerical assignment for organization of work, although the order is similar across criteria. Path coefficients may vary significantly according to one's coding choices. With regard to the data used in Figure 5.5, several different coding schemes were tried without altering the results markedly.

Ascertaining the presence or absence of certain causal paths is only a first step in the analysis; the discussion of Figure 5.5 has already addressed "the more general research question (beyond the mere establishment of a zero or nonzero relationship) . . . the determination of the magnitude of the relationship under changing conditions" (Schoenberg 1972, p. 3). Because variances may differ across samples or subsamples, Schoenberg argues persuasively that path coefficients (standardized regression coefficients) should be used "only to compare the effects of independent variables on a single dependent variable in a path analysis computed within a single set of data" (1972, p. 5).

The comparison of unstandardized regression coefficients is recommended, although problems of measurement error remain regardless of the analytical technique used. In the analyses performed in Figure 5.5, the unit of measure of each variable is essentially the same. Comparisons using the unstandardized coefficients led to no differences in interpretation.

Finally, Duncan has noted that "there is always more than one model (even if we are not clever enough to suggest them) that is equally as compatible with the data as is the model under consideration" (1972, p. 63). Path models assume that persisting individual differences, what Pelz and Lew (1970) call "long term" stability, do not obscure the data on the dependent variables. Such tendencies for a dependent variable to persist at the same level through time have been shown to obscure the interpretation of path coefficients. Another problem is due to the biases resulting from single-method data collection. When several variables are measured using the same instrument, they may be correlated because of an underlying "shared method factor" (Cook and Campbell 1976). In both of these situations, a common factor or factors, when measured with error, could be responsible for the interrelationships among observed variables.

This common factor explanation has been proposed as an alternative interpretation of data generally analyzed by causal modeling techniques (Brewer, Campbell, and Crano 1970). For the specific data presented in Figure 5.5, such an explanation seems less relevant. It is, however, a competing interpretation for studies based on the repeated measurement of attitudinal variables. When the author's three wave (1956-1965-1974) panel data from Turkey were analyzed in terms of attitude change (Roos 1978), common factor explanations had to be examined using principal components analysis (Blalock 1960, Nie et al. 1975).

Causal modeling is no panacea, no substitute for research design; problems with the data will emerge as problems in the interpretation. On the other hand, path analysis and related forms of multivariate analysis do illuminate areas where comparisons might otherwise be impossible. These techniques are especially appropriate for using data from several points in time. Hannan and Young (1977) have provided a discussion of when and how information from different time points can be pooled for purposes of data analysis. Other applications of path analysis relevant for elite research include its use in panel studies (Duncan 1972, Wheaton et al. 1977), for analyzing assumptions concerning measurement (Blalock 1971), and so forth. Hannan, Robinson, and Warren (1974) have explicitly treated the methodological problems of using crossnational, longitudinal information in developing causal models of economic and social change. The sensitivity of multivariate procedures to measurement error, plus the particular data collection problems associated with comparative elite studies, highlight the need to systematically consider data quality.

DATA QUALITY

In a carefully designed study, the information is collected so as to eliminate threats to validity as efficiently as possible. Design considerations are important in suggesting ways to check on data quality. Often it is inexpensive to gather extra information, information that might be redundant in a perfect world. Such redundant information is essential for dealing with threats to validity relating to data quality. Such threats as instability, instrumentation, testing, selection, and experimental mortality are particularly likely in research on elite characteristics and attitudes. Imaginative treatment of diverse data sources is a necessity.

Several different sorts of redundancy can be incorporated into research operations to deal with these threats to validity. A common type of redundancy not treated here is item redundancy (including several items in an effort to better measure an underlying variable). This topic is treated in standard works on behavioral science methodology (Blalock 1971, Kerlinger 1973). This section will discuss three types of redundancy: coding, method, and sampling.

In coding redundancy, having multiple coders of the same data helps handle instability by providing one set of estimates of measurement reliability in instrumentation by taking interobserver variation into account.

In method redundancy, using several methods for obtaining information on the same individuals is useful for dealing with instability and instrumentation since relatively high method agreement suggests that measures are reliable and calibrated equivalently. Method redundancy may help treat the testing threat to validity; if relatively unobtrusive measures are used, data will be gathered without disturbing individuals and testing effects will be minimized.

In sampling redundancy, sampling the same larger group several times enables the researcher to handle selection and experimental mortality threats.

TABLE 5.3

Redundant Data Collection Incorporated into Design of Turkish Research

	Biographical information collected from following samples:	Coders	Data quality checks based on:
1.	Systematic sample of graduates of Political Science Faculty, classes of 1938–1940.	Individuals A and B (Differences resolved)	
2.	Systematic sample of graduates of Political Science Faculty, classes of 1948–1950.	Individual A	Coding redundancy (Intercoder agreement for reliability) (A versus B for individuals on both Sample 2 and Sample 3: N = 56.)
3.	Respondents to 1956 survey, graduates of Political Science Faculty, classes of 1948–1950.	Individual B	Method redundancy (intermethod agreement) (Sample 3, Coder B versus 1965 survey information; N = 61.)
4.	Systematic sample of graduates of Political Science Faculty, classes of 1958–1960. (Sample used for sending questionnaires in 1965.)	Individuals A and B (Differences resolved)	Method redundancy (intermethod agreement) (part of Sample 4 versus respondents to 1965 survey; N = 33.)

NOTE: Additional checks on intermethod agreement were made using 1956 survey information for the classes of 1948–1950 (see Table 5.5). Checks on intermethod agreement were also made using Sample 2 (individual A as coder).

Respondents and nonrespondents to the 1956, 1965, and 1974 surveys could also be compared using the biographical data. Samples 2 and 3 provide further sampling redundancy, but this is confounded with coding redundancy.

Source: Compiled by author.

Questions about bias in a given sample are particularly likely to arise in secondary analysis, in which details of the original sample may be unknown, and in longitudinal studies in which experimental mortality because of nonresponse, mobility, and so on is a problem. Drawing a new, redundant sample can help deal with these questions. Sometimes necessary extra information can be gathered unobtrusively, thus disturbing the individuals under study as little as possible (Webb et al. 1966).

A strategy is needed to integrate the researcher's substantive interests with various methodological concerns. The following example from my 1974 Turkish study shows how redundancy can be profitably incorporated into the research design. I wanted to analyze changing patterns of recruitment to the Political Science Faculty and to different organizations over a time period that encompassed a number of political and economic developments. At the same time, I hoped to build in checks relevant to both the data collected in 1974 and to data from 1956 and 1965. Table 5.3 presents the research design for redundant data

TABLE 5.4

Intercoder Agreement with Turkish Biographical Data (1948–1950 Political Science Graduates)

	Number of Disagreements; N=56	Percentage Agreement	Reliability
Variables:			
Father's occupation	6	.89	—*
Place of birth	7	.88	.80
Social background	3	.95	.85
Course of study	2	.96	.91
1959 place of work	9	.84	.86
1969 place of work	5	.91	.81

*Reliability was not calculated for the father's occupation variable since these data were coded into nine nominal categories. Data on place of work were recorded into a form suitable for correlational analysis.

Note: The social background variable is derived from the father's profession and place of birth variables combined to produce a dichotomous variable: privileged or less privileged background (Roos and Roos, 1971).

Reliability is based upon the correlation beween the scores produced by one coder with those produced by the other.

This table refers to the agreement between two coders independently using a biographical source to compile information on the same individuals.

Source: Compiled by author. The biographical source used was Cankaya (1972).

TABLE 5.5

Intermethod Agreement with Turkish Biographical and Survey Data
(1948–50 and 1958–60 Political Science Graduates)

	1948–50 Graduates		1958–60 Graduates	
	Number of Disagreements	Percentage Agreement	Number of Disagreements	Percentage Agreement
Father's occupation	24 (N = 94)	.79	7 (N = 33)	.79
Place of birth	4 (N = 61)	.93	3 (N = 33)	.91
Social background	9 (N = 61)	.85	0 (N = 33)	1.00
Course of study	6 (N = 94)	.94	4 (N = 33)	.88

Note: The percentage agreement ratio was calculated by dividing the number of agreements by the number of cases.

Source: The survey data on father's occupation and course of study for 1948–50 graduates were taken from the 1956 study by Fahir Armaoğlu and Guthrie Birkhead; the other survey data were taken from the 1965 panel followup on the 1956 study. These studies are described in Roos and Roos (1971). Material was compiled by the author.

collection. Coding and method redundancy are highlighted in the table; sampling redundancy is treated in the note.

Coding redundancy and method redundancy can be treated in similar fashion by first presenting simple tables as to the degree of agreement for different variables. Table 5.4 shows that coding problems tended to be fairly evenly distributed across the different types of variables. Difficulties in treating place of work were due to coding decisions concerning several organizations with some characteristics of both ministries and state economic enterprises.

In this study, two different data sources, a biography of Political Science Faculty graduates and the 1965 survey of these graduates, are taken as the different methods. Table 5.5 points up the considerable disagreement between biographical and survey data in assigning father's occupation. Because many individuals had two occupations or practiced their profession in the public sector (for instance, doctor in the Army), the occupation checked off on the closed-end survey was often different from that filled out on the open-ended biographical form. Because several of the occupations most frequently held were included in the "privileged background" category, the recoding to produce the "privileged" and "less privileged" dichotomy substantially reduced the number of disagreements.

The relatively low intermethod agreement as to social background presented more problems than did any of the coding discrepancies. Checks on coding discrepancies were easy to perform, and judgments as to the correct code could

FIGURE 5.6

Comparisons of Biographical and Survey Data

DATA FROM BIOGRAPHICAL SOURCE

6a. Total Sample (N=97)

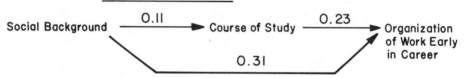

6b. Individuals Responding to 1965 Survey (N=41)

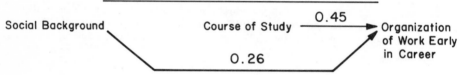

6c. Individuals Not Responding to 1965 Survey (N=56)

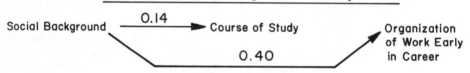

DATA FROM SURVEY SOURCE

6d. Individuals Responding to 1965 Survey (N=41)

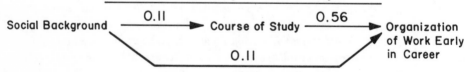

usually be made by the researcher without difficulty. Father's occupation, one of the two items used to make up the social background variable, could not be treated so easily. Arbitrary decision rules could be applied by the researcher when several occupations were noted in the biographical directory, but the two

TABLE 5.6

Multitrait-Multimethod Matrix for Turkish Data
(1948-50 and 1958-60 Graduates)

		Place of birth	Social background	Course of study
	Method I: Biographical Data			
Method I				
Biographical Data	Place of birth	(.80)*	(Monomethod block)	
	Social background	.65	(.85)	
	Course of study	.19	.18	(.91)
Method II				
Survey Data	Place of birth	.88a	.64	.23
	Social background	.71	.75	.17
	Course of study	.22	.23	.91
	Method II: Survey Data			
Method I				
Biographical Data	Place of birth			
	Social background			
	Course of study			
Method II				
Survey Data	Place of birth	(.92)	(Monomethod block)	
	Social background	.72	(.80)	
	Course of study	.23	.14	

Note: Correlations using the father's occupation variable (as in Table 5.5) were not relevant since these data were coded into nine nominal categories.

*Reliability coefficients are in parentheses along the main diagonal of the mono-method matrices. Intercoder agreement for the biographical data was used for the Method I Biographical Data matrix (N ß 56 from biographical samples 2 and 3). Survey information collected and coded independently in 1965 and 1974 was used for the Method II Survey Data monomethod matrix (N ß 186 from 1946-55 and 1958-61 graduates).

aValidity coefficients, correlations between the same information produced by different methods, are italicized on the main diagonal of the heteromethod matrix. These correlations were calculated using the 1965 survey data and the biographical data (with obvious coding errors corrected; N = 94 from 1948-50 and 1958-60 graduates). Similar results were obtained using the 1956 survey data.

bInformation on course of study was not available.

Source: Compiled by author.

methods (survey and biography) often generated different information. Rather than forcing the data, another strategy seemed more appropriate. The important question concerns the effect of method bias upon the substantive results. To examine this, causal models were constructed using the same variables and individuals, but with the information taken from different sources. Figures 5.6b and 5.6d show that the inferences were generally similar, but not identical, when the two different methods were used. Weak relationships, such as that between social background and course of study, may be insignificant (as in 5.6b) or significant (as in 5.6d) depending upon the method used. Figure 5.6 is discussed in more detail later in the chapter.

These data can be treated more formally by means of a multitrait, multimethod matrix (Campbell and Fiske 1959). The overall multitrait, multimethod matrix is made up of monomethod and heteromethod blocks. Correlations among variables measured by the same method make up a monomethod block. Reliability values are the monotrait-monomethod values in parentheses along the diagonal of the monomethod block. Correlations among variables measured by different methods comprise the heteromethod blocks, which also contain two types of entries: the monotrait-heteromethod values, designated as validity values, and the heterotrait-heteromethod values. As illustrated in Table 5.6, the underlined validity values make up a validity diagonal. Method redundancy can also help judging the validity of the data, the degree to which a specific instrument measures what it is designed to measure. Each method of data collection may reflect reality in its own way, but assessing validity is impossible without a common core of agreement. Thus, convergent validity is measured by the relative agreement of independent attempts to measure the same concept using maximally dissimilar indicators (Campbell and Fiske 1959). The validity values provide a measure of convergent validity, although it is difficult to specify when two methods are maximally dissimilar. An inspection of this multitrait, multimethod matrix points up the problem with the social background variable: both its monomethod coefficients and its heteromethod coefficients are relatively low.

Campbell and Fiske advance four criteria for validity (convergent and discriminant) based on the multitrait-multimethod matrix (1959, pp. 82-83).

> Entries in the validity diagonal should be significantly different from zero and sufficiently large to encourage further examination of validity.
>
> A validity value for a variable should be higher than the correlations obtained between that variable and any other variable having neither trait nor method in common.
>
> A third common-sense desideratum is that a variable correlates higher with an independent effort to measure the same trait than with measures designed to get at different traits which happen to employ the same method.
>
> A fourth desideratum is that the same pattern of trait interrelationship be shown in all of the heterotrait triangles of both the monomethod and heteromethod blocks.

The Campbell and Fiske criteria are generally satisfied by the data in Table 5.6. However, a comparison of the biographical data reliability coefficient for place of birth and the validity coefficient for this variable isolated a problem with the coding of place of birth. The validity coefficient, based on two different methods, might logically be expected to be lower than the reliability coefficient for a single method; instead, the validity coefficient is higher. One coder's incorrect understanding of coding rules for several types of locations was found to be the problem here.

The main checks on sampling bias involved comparisons of respondents and nonrespondents to the 1965 survey. As seen in Figures 5.6b and 5.6c, there were major differences between the 1965 respondents and nonrespondents from the classes of 1958–60. These differences would not have been picked up without the deliberate effort to gather biographical data so as to check on the results of the 1965 study. Such differences were unexpected, since similar difficulties were not found for the 1948–50 graduates in the 1965 survey. Because the differences between respondents and nonrespondents led to substantively different results, the problems cannot be brushed aside. The 1965 survey results from the younger respondents must be interpreted with caution.

Sampling redundancy was also incorporated into the research design by drawing both a systematic sample (Sample 2) of 1948–50 graduates from the biographical directory, which was essentially a census, and another sample (Sample 3) based on those 1948–50 graduates answering the 1956 questionnaire. After correcting obvious coding errors, a comparison of substantive path analysis results from the two samples supported the quality of the 1956 sample. Both samples generated similar causal paths and path coefficients.

These results suggest that a major threat to validity in making inferences about causal paths can come from incomplete coverage of the relevant group, particularly when there is the possibility of systematic error. Nonresponse bias in sample surveys provides an excellent example of threats related to selection. Such biases can occur even when the basic frequency distributions or means of a particular sample are close to those derived from an independent estimate of the population mean.

Problems of operationalizing concepts were highlighted. In certain societies it may be rather difficult to appropriately code such variables as father's occupation, due to multiple occupations or overlapping categories (for instance, is a professional working for the government to be classified as a professional or as a government employee). The choices made in writing detailed coding instructions are likely to themselves affect the results of the data analysis. Moreover, individuals contacted at two points in time and for two separate studies might provide honest answers sufficiently different to cause different coding decisions, regardless of coding instructions.

The analysis is more reassuring with regard to several sources of error. If the field operations are relatively well managed, extensive double coding to deal with simple coding error on the order of five percent seems a luxury; few changes in the causal models were noted when data corrected by double coding were compared with uncorrected (single coded) data. In similar fashion, if efforts to enumerate a population result in lists with a high degree of overlap, it may be unnecessary to worry about six to ten percent of the population that may appear on one list but not on another. Important considerations here are the actual degree of overlap and the degree to which systematic bias might be postulated.

Other researchers studying with other societies or other historical periods may have to deal with a different set of data quality problems. But the difficulties highlighted here suggest the need for stringent standards as to what is accepted as evidence. As Campbell (1969) has emphasized, a statistically significant relationship or difference answers only one of many threats to internal validity—that of instability. The many threats to validity involved in doing comparative research across several time periods suggest a conservative approach to causal inference.

Research designs incorporating redundancy have an important role to play; parallel studies through time using different methods or data sources are recommended whenever possible. When results are roughly replicated using different methods, their internal validity is considerably enhanced. On the other hand, comparisons between periods using data gathered by a different method at one period than at another (such as biographic sources before 1974 and a survey in 1974) must be made very cautiously because of the various possibilities for bias. As discussed here, methods may differ both in the extent of their coverage of the relevant population and in the specific information gathered from each individual. Well thought-out designs are the key.

The approach presented here should be compared with the more usual technique of checking all the sources and coming up with the most reasonable judgment (Frey 1965, Dekmejian 1971). One advantage of systematically checking coder agreement and method bias is that the checking process highlights problems inherent in the data. For example, the coding disagreements showed that many members of the Turkish elite have several occupations in the course of their working life (see also Tachau 1975a). Moreover, combining sources and making the appropriate judgment is hazardous in that the researcher may unconsciously introduce systematic biases into his data. Separate analyses that are in general agreement produce increased confidence in the findings. On the other hand, if the analyses do not agree, the researcher can go back and attempt to uncover the reasons for the disagreement.

From a broader viewpoint, the approach presented here differs from other strategies emphasizing purely analytical approaches to data quality. Both textbook approaches to measuring reliability (Kerlinger 1973) and newer works stressing path analysis (Schoenberg 1972) tend to underemphasize the role of design in ensuring high-quality data. The various analytical strategies are obviously important, but they both depend upon access to sophisticated computer facilities and must be applied after the bulk of field data have been gathered.

Incorporating redundancy at the time of data collection is an efficient strategy for treating threats to validity that cannot be handled by the analysis of data collected according to more standard procedures.

CASES AND COMPARISONS

The previous sections have stressed the importance of carefully thought-out data collection, combining strong research designs with triangulation—approaching the subject matter from several points of view to ensure data quality. Triangulation has been defined as using "multiple methods focused on the diagnosis of the same construct from independent points of observation" (Campbell 1975, p. 189). Even within the domains of a single case study, having several observers helps clarify both the data itself (Naroll 1970) and the theoretical constructs being used (Campbell 1975). An explicit concern with making the most efficient use of information highlights the research possibilities. Thus, the longitudinal aspects of Lewis' restudy of a Mexican village, originally studied by Redfield, have been stressed by Hyman (1964) in a chapter on research design, while comparisons between the same two studies have been mentioned by Naroll (1970) in an essay on data quality control.

Comparative research can be approached from a similar perspective. Other justifications for comparative research emphasize the logic of discovery; such research does provide valuable insights into new variables, relationships, and causal patterns. But more systematic approaches are possible. Campbell has suggested that "typical one-observer one-culture study is inherently ambiguous. For any given feature of the report it is equivocal whether or not it is a trait of the observer or a trait of the object observed" (1975, p. 189). Triangulation can be approached by having researchers from two or more cultures (nations) study two or more cultures (nations) systematically, in ways parallel to those treated in our discussion of the multitrait, multimethod matrix.

Such a planned approach differs from the usual focus of comparative research in its concern for the various threats to validity. Comparisons can help eliminate plausible rival hypotheses to the explanation forwarded by the investigator. As has been mentioned earlier in connection with the interrupted time-series design, comparison sites or groups are particularly useful when incorporated into the research design of a longitudinal study. By selecting similar sites where a given event has and has not taken place, various threats to validity (particularly that of history) may be handled. Putnam (1976) uses this logic in his comparative study of elites. Having several comparison sites where the event has occurred in different intensities might prove theoretically fruitful. In such ways, longitudinal and comparative inquiry might be combined.

If research is seen as a procedure for eliminating false propositions (Meckstroth 1975), comparative research may be particularly valuable. Putnam's (1976) discussion of the industrial revolution and elite transformation was strengthened by comparative data from France and Germany showing that particular features of British society (such as its steady constitutional evolution) were not responsible for the findings. Examining different systems helps both in establishing the internal validity and in assessing the generality of relationships observed in a particular site. Having several cases to look at helps identify particular deviant cases, which may be especially useful in understanding the causal mechanisms underlying given findings.

The more ambitious form of comparative research tries to replace the names of social systems with the names of variables of causal significance.

Such a view of comparative research has been discussed by Przeworski and Teune (1970) in terms of the "most similar systems" design. The "most similar systems" design assumes that if the systems (nations or other units for comparison) are appropriately chosen, their characteristics can be used to explain intersystem differences in the relationships between variables. The basic idea of the "most similar systems" design is that research sites very similar along almost all dimensions can be chosen. The one or two dimensions along which the sites differ can then be taken as responsible for differences in relationships between variables across sites. Przeworski and Teune criticize this design on the grounds that systems assumed to be similar probably differ along a number of dimensions. Moreover, variance that cannot be explained at more micro levels is often arbitrarily assigned to "system" ("nation" in the case of crossnational research), thus treating it as a residual variable. Such a practice is a theoretically inadequate way of treating crossnational differences.

Much comparative work suffers from being based on weak designs, crosssectional designs from one point in time. Although advanced analytical techniques may be applied to such data (Verba, Nie, and Kim 1971), the problems with this research design have been emphasized by several authors (for example, Campbell and Stanley 1963).

Longitudinal research, using data from at least two points in time, provides a number of advantages over cross-sectional data collection.

First of all, research designs considerably stronger than the cross-sectional designs characteristic of most cross-national studies can be used. In particular, pretest-posttest and panel approaches are likely to be appropriate for making causal inferences. A number of alternate interpretations of data can be reduced in their plausibility through longitudinal designs.

Secondly, tracing the impact of recent history on a set of individuals can best be done through the use of data from several time points.

And, data from two or more points in time permit switching to weaker designs if this seems called for; data from each time point can be analyzed cross-sectionally. The generality of models used for data from t_1 can be tested with data from t_2. Thus, moving to cross-sectional analysis permits replication, with its power to increase confidence in the findings.

Also, complex dynamic models of the type developed by Brunner and Brewer (1971) are feasible with longitudinal data, although here a number of time points are necessary. These models can be extremely useful for the development of better theory (Simon 1969; Brunner and Liepelt 1972).

Another advantage is that time precedence can be most helpful in approaching questions of causality. If advanced techniques such as structural equation modeling are used in conjunction with time precedence, certain causal paths can be rendered less plausible because of the time lags between the gathering of data at t_1 and subsequent data collection.

And, because many aspects of social systems will be very similar at t_1 and t_2, longitudinal data can help satisfy the shortcomings of "most similar systems" research mentioned by Przeworski and Teune. Developments between t_1 and t_2 may be relatively few and unambiguous enough to permit judging the cause of t_1-t_2 differences; such a situation of few clear differences between systems will generally not be found in cross-national research. This longitudinal variant of "most similar systems" research might be most productive in uncovering causal relationships, even if some sacrifice in generalizability is involved.

Finally, many problems of data quality and measurement can be fruitfully approached by data from at least two points in time. A concern for design would contribute to the effective resolution of several types of measurement questions. Longitudinal data permit combining measurement concerns with substantive questions more powerfully than can be done using cross-sectional information. Since the units studied at t_1, t_2, and so on can be considered as different groups, the methodological techniques used for comparative research can all be applied to longitudinal data.

In addition, three sorts of methodological checks can be made. Nonresponse problems on data collected at t_2 (and subsequently) can be fully treated because of t_1 data on these nonresponding individuals. The reliability of the measures used (and the stability of the variables being studied) can be estimated by causal modeling techniques (see, for example, Wiley and Wiley 1970). Manaster and Havighurst (1972) note that test-retest methods are the preferred way of approaching problems of reliability. Such a stress on test-retest reliability also suggests checking items for which there would be no real change between t_1 and t_2 (for example, father's occupation and, in most cases, formal education).

These concerns might be placed in a broader perspective. One well-known approach to research design (Campbell and Stanley 1963) has concerned measurement instability as one threat to the validity of various designs. Thus, the emphasis has been on the measurement → design linkages. On the other hand, structural equation modeling has stressed the reciprocal linkages between the investigator's assumptions concerning measurement and those concerning substantive causal chains. The more complicated the assumptions regarding possible measurement error, the simpler must be the substantive model (Blalock 1970).

In partial contrast to these two approaches, research design might be emphasized as a tool for systematically analyzing measurement questions. Thus, a researcher would be justified in spending a great deal of effort on questions of design. Effective designs would enable the analyst both to evaluate the reliability and stability of his measures and to study the substantive problems of interest. The earlier discussion of data quality has provided a specific example of such a use of research design.

Better comparative research might rely upon better design and better analysis. Relatively few comparative studies have gone beyond analysis of marginals or, at the most, of correlations. By comparing marginals, some indication of differences is provided, but the data are not explored with any depth. The increased use of structural equation models may be helpful but the cautions noted here and elsewhere (Cook and Campbell 1976) obviously apply. The dangers of all such multivariate techniques must be stressed; the issue is that "of doing tests of multiple hypotheses and then writing up as conclusions those that are 'statistically significant' by a significance test which assumes that one went into the inquiry with only this one hypothesis" (Campbell 1975, p. 187). There are ways to check on these problems, but techniques of cross-validation and jackknifing one's data have been generally unexplored by social scientists (for a good discussion of these approaches, see Mosteller and Tukey 1968).

Such advanced methods are most important in structuring the between-nation and within-nation diversity that Przeworski and Teune recognize as a central problem for theory-building. Some studies of political participation across several countries have produced findings that point toward a high degree of generalizability. Thus, Verba, Nie, and Kim (1971) have reported considerable similarities in terms of relationships and plausible causal models, even when absolute levels of variables differ significantly. But other studies within a single country have pointed up incredible diversity among patterns of organizational behavior, both cross-sectionally and through time (Roos and Roos 1971). Such diversity poses a major challenge to many comparative studies, based as they are on haphazard samples across nations (see many of the managerial studies collected in Webber 1969). Macro-theorizing should also be affected by such findings, given the difficulties of considering the administrative or managerial elite as a whole.

But new combinations of experimental and analytical techniques to help structure different problems are most desirable. In particular, I would stress the need for a discussion of possibly appropriate designs and approaches that emphasized the assumptions underlying each approach.

Questions of design validity, of the extent to which the underlying assumptions of a given approach are met by the data, might profitably be discussed. Longitudinal designs that modify the powerful assumptions of experimental research need to be treated from a design validity perspective. Design validity is important because the usual time sequence of design → data collection → analysis is often reversed in quasi-experimental research. Several quasi-experimental designs may be used to structure one data set. This has been done for both the Turkish elite data (Roos and Roos 1971) and for data on mobilization, institutionalization, and conflict in Black Africa (Duvall and Welfling 1973a and 1973b). Design assumptions may be changed on the basis of preliminary results—an obviously dangerous procedure.

At the same time, by the application of several different perspectives, the same data set can help increase confidence in the reliability and validity of research findings.

No hard and fast rules about the relationship between concept formation, research design, and data collection have been developed. Campbell and Stanley's (1963) checklist of threats to validity is clearly useful, as is Stinchcombe and Wendt's (1975) discussion of the different ways to relate concepts of causality and actual data. More specifically, some of the tradeoffs between comparative and longitudinal data collection have been discussed.

Additional advice for the researcher might include the following. Try to conceptualize and measure variables as if they were both dichotomous and interval variables. This is helpful in suggesting different designs and modes of analysis. Think about the startup and marginal costs in conducting the research project and data collection. How can redundancy be incorporated into gathering the data for the lowest additional cost? Be explicit in defining the data collection procedures and building in checks on data quality. The choice of measures that have been validated in other contexts is useful in helping to avoid many of the difficulties inherent in constructing new instruments.

The task of developing further guidelines for field research is a challenging one; tradeoffs between various threats to validity need to be discussed. By addressing themselves to such questions, scholars will both aid the researcher and help create sounder methodological underpinnings for comparative inquiry.

6

STRUCTURE AND PERFORMANCE OF MEDIATING ELITES

Marvin G. Weinbaum

The function of mediation, broadly conceived, is performed by all political leadership. As Rustow observes, mediation may occur among the conflicting aspirations of politically articulate citizens, or between the traditional foundation of politics and an emerging new order, and even between a nation's aspirations and reality (1971, p. 88). In this chapter, we are concerned with mediation in still another vein—that which occurs between a nation's highest authoritative decision makers and its mass publics. The subjects of our inquiry are familiarly called intermediaries, middlemen, and brokers. Social scientists have coined such terms as "skill and custodial elites" (Lasswell), "strategic middle level elites" (Deutsch), and "the second stratum" (Mosca) to describe prominently located mediators of national policy. Our cast of intermediaries is more extensive and its functions more numerous. It encompasses several levels of elites and a host of actors participating along a network of communications that transmits and effects the commands of a nation's rulers and the demands of the ruled. The mediating elites include such diverse types as administrators, media specialists, party agents, and communal heads. Their interventions may be overt or behind the scenes; their roles can be formalized or follow weakly-defined expectations. Intermediate structures may vary in strength, accounting for a virtual insulation of elites and nonelites, as well as nearly direct penetration of the masses and mass pressures on elites (see Kornhauser 1969, pp. 76–90). Finally, the length of intermediary chains can extend from direct two-step processes to diffused multiple links.

Recognition of intermediary institutions and actors underlines the difficulties in drawing sharp boundaries between elites and nonelites. For analytic convenience, it is useful to distinguish those responsible for shaping basic values and policies from those affected by (or conceivably who effect) elite decisions. Yet the existence of intermediary structures, varying in distance from a society's governors and its governed, emphasizes linkages rather than boundaries. As such, the study of intermediate relations is a necessary corrective to simplistic notions of political influence. By the nature of their location, intermediaries are often in a critical position from which to implement as well as distort policies. They are also well positioned to regulate the access to top decision makers. Understandably, then, intermediary elites figure conspicuously in designs for social and political integration and in the transition from traditional to modern societies.

This chapter is concerned with the structure and performance of mediating elites in the Middle East. As discussed below, the traditional centrality of mediate processes in the region's mass-elite relations is well attested to. A brief examination of traditional roles lays the ground for a classification and description of several mediate functions, all conceived in the context of reciprocal communication flows. Four major systemic influences on intermediary behavior are also identified. In subsequent sections, mediate functions are identified in the activities of a number of elite institutions in the contemporary Middle East. Studies from the literature on leadership, political parties, bureaucracies, and the mass media, among others, provide the materials for an assessment of the substance and style of mediate performance. A final section depicts the linkages among intermediary institutions and compares their performance of the several mediate functions. The discussion also posits the relative growth of particular intermediary activities. It concludes with an overview of the evolving roles of mediating elites as the Middle East moves from communal to various forms of mass society.

TRADITIONAL PRACTICE

The intermediary is hardly an alien figure in traditional Islamic societies. Interpersonal social contacts were normally predicated on the availability of a broker, especially when contacts bridged groups and transcended classes. For while established avenues of mobility, notably through religious education and military service, occasionally punctured social class barriers, social distances could be crossed as a rule only with the assistance of third parties. Use of an intermediary further served the social and psychological needs of petitioners. The ability to engage a reputable go-between was frequently a measure of an individual's own social standing. An agent's successful intervention might reflect on both the petitioner's wisdom in choosing an intermediary as well as on the merit of a claim or request. Conversely, the failure of an intermediary often saved the petitioner the embarrassment of direct rejection and allowed explanation of the failure as a consequence of the go-between's inadequacy or impotence.

Approaches to those of higher social standing typically called for the intercession (or *wasita*) of individuals acknowledged in their community or corporate group for a familiarity with the proper protocols. As in nearly all social relations, mediation incurred an indebtedness that could oblige payment at any time and in a variety of ways (see Rosen 1972, p. 438). Yet any attempt to bypass the services of an intermediary risked inattention or rebuff. Worse still, insufficient deference could be interpreted as a challenge to status and authority.

Approaches to government officialdom conformed to many of the same expectations. Outside the larger towns and the principal trade routes, contacts with government were at most limited to a shaykh nominally accountable to higher authorities. The reality of distant state authority barely touched the lives of people bounded psychologically as well as physically by their clan and tribe. About all that came to be known of outside events were the sketchy reports of occasional travelers. A tribal member was not expected to have an opinion on the external world apart from the authoritative view furnished by his shaykh. Indeed, the notion of a private interest separable from the community's interest was incomprehensible.

Even in regions more accessible to agents of an amir or sultan, the concerns of the state were mainly fixed on the collection of taxes or tribute and the maintenance of public order. Peasants, artisans, or tradesmen confronted government, if at all, through its most immediate manifestations, the local militia and subordinate administrators—often their own natural leaders. Occasional government proclamations were passed down by these communal heads or delivered by town criers (*dallal*). In any case, communications to the masses, as Lerner points out, "were not designed to enlighten or persuade opinion, but to prepare and proscribe" (1958, pp. 113–14). If common people developed any feeling toward government, it was one of distrust and fear. Most officials of the state were viewed as "legitimate robbers," a legitimacy derived from the officials' usually superior social status and the general belief that their activities were ordained by God (Stirling 1965, p. 267).

Wasita was deeply rooted in village life. In theory, any local influential could fill the role of intermediary with the state. Even so, the village headman or shaykh typically assumed the heaviest responsibilities as go-between. Within the confines of his village or area, the headman exercised wide discretionary authority. Ordinarily a clan elder or the choice of the leading local families, the headman customarily collected taxes, publicized official notices, and assisted in settling local disputes. What business government officials and higher notables had with the community was frequently communicated through the headman, who was in regular contact with the villagers. The headman was thus a direct, if sometimes passive, agent of external authority that was simultaneously political, economic, and social. At the same time, the headman was also the principal spokesman for the community and a patron of its interests. If it was necessary to petition higher officials, he was the likely go-between. And when subjects appeared before the authorities, they often did so in his presence. The headman's liaisons both within and outside the community usually brought him gifts from the villagers and coveted economic and status rewards from his superiors. Through higher notables, with their economic power and family reputation, there was also access to provincial officials and influence with authorities of the empire (Hudson 1977, p. 101).

The intimacy of the *ulema* (clergy) with the masses made it an obvious choice for intermediary responsibilities. Clerics who lived and worked among the common people enjoyed their esteem and confidence. Frequently the only literates in a community, the clerics were perceived as repositories of secular as well as religious wisdom. Although not above pursuit of personal gain, clerics were more often cast in the role of protector of the lower classes. Their varied class origins and family connections sometimes gave them unique access to a provincial aristocracy. In the main, however, the ulema acted as a surrogate for the state. Education fell entirely within its domain. And so long as the central bureaucracies and secular codes remained skeletal or nonexistent, clerics were unchallenged in the most sensitive areas of judicial administration. As Avery remarks about the *mullas* in Iran, "They had to validate the most vital acts of man: marriage, divorce, testimonies, deeds of trust and possession, transfers of property, and commercial contracts" (1965, p. 286).

Nearly every agent of the state had a hand in tax collection. According to tradition, the Prophet himself had appointed agents (*ummal*) to collect alms-taxes from those tribes that had fallen to his armies (Levy 1969, p. 355). Ordinarily, a collector retained a portion of his take or gained exemption from certain taxes in exchange for his services. But under the Ottomans, tax farming enabled local elites, usually abetted by local garrison commanders, to acquire enormous personal wealth and power over provincial affairs. By the eighteenth century, the provincial tax farmer had usurped much of the authority of the feeble central administration, assuming the role of feudal lord rather than go-between. Even the heralded nineteenth century reforms designed to end the autonomy of these notables failed to centralize taxation, and powerful tax farmers were left interposed between the citizens and the state treasury (Lewis 1961, p. 385).

The state's usually minimal requirements for information about its subjects were at times filled by systematic intelligence-gathering instruments. Under the Abbassids, a *barid* or postal system flourished, serving the dual purpose of conveying messages between officials scattered across the empire and providing an effective intelligence service. Messengers were expected to keep close watch on local events and to send detailed reports to Baghdad. Later, the *wali*, policing the town and city, was instructed to pass on written reports to the Ottoman sultan (Levy 1969, pp. 299–300). Yet it was to communal and group leadership that higher authorities normally turned for information. With the appearance of guilds in the seventeenth century, an important new connective between urban dwellers and government was added. Organization of the guilds around residential, family, or religious units facilitated the tasks of supervision and intelligence gathering. Although essentially engaged in issuing franchises (*gidils*) in the trades and professions, guild shaykhs kept officials regularly apprised of restiveness among their membership. They also furnished commodity data and, in Egypt and Syria at least, were employed for tax collection (Baer 1970, pp. 33–36). The same guild elders were meanwhile expected to intercede with the authorities when their members' interests were threatened and to keep them informed of government actions that impinged on their livelihood.

Where guilds came under the influence of religious brotherhoods, channels to governing elites were frequently widened. Dervish orders, for example, although essentially popular movements, also attracted adherents well-placed in the Ottoman bureaucracy (Lewis 1961, p. 407). Moore writes that the devout, literate members of religious brotherhoods in Tunisia, by providing the sole links between the tribes and Islamic traditions in settled areas, had helped to mitigate inter-regional antagonisms (1965, p. 12). The interlocking *anjumans* (political societies) of nineteenth century Iran were similarly able to improve communication among tribesmen, clerics, tradesmen and government administrators. As events often demonstrated, however, brotherhoods and societies could be useful in mobilizing the masses against those in authority.

Non-Muslins normally appointed independent emissaries to government and formed parallel intracommunity linkages. The autonomy granted by the Ottoman millet system to minorities in the administration of education, the law, and other community affairs, in practice, turned communal heads into quasi-employees of the state. As liaison to the Ottoman government, the *millet basi* maintained an official residence in Istanbul and accepted the responsibility of keeping his community informed of as well as responsive to imperial demands. The minorities also filled mediating roles outside their communities. Jews farmed taxes for the Turks, especially customs collections (see Wood 1935, p. 214). In Morocco, Berbers gave protection to Jewish merchants who served as intermediaries in dealings with more urban-centered Arabs (Rosen 1972, p. 445). Generally, both Christians and Jews furnished intermediaries in most official transactions with foreign traders and diplomatic missions—roles for which Muslims often felt unprepared or found distasteful.

With rare exception, then, intermediaries in traditional society were neither disinterested messengers nor neutral arbiters. The processes of mediation carried many opportunities for individuals to enhance their private and class interests, even in ways that came at the expense of those they served. Not unexpectedly, those invited by the authorities to transmit and share privileged information were able to strengthen reputations. Wasta, successfully exercised, both testified to and furthered claims to power. Because go-betweens were designated from those already in positions of some influence, mediation in general served to reinforce prevailing social and political hierarchies. In the process of what Bill calls, "balancing tensions," the go-between was often central to the survival of cross-societal contacts, even to the point of at times supplanting officials whose authority had waned (1973, p. 142). Once installed in office, the intermediary naturally enhanced his capacity for wasta through contacts with wider networks of government agents and local influentials. To retain their special status, intermediaries had ordinarily only to avoid offense to higher authorities and to keep the largely inert populations in a state of dependence. And, if as Dawn and others suggest, the masses and notables formed a symbiotic relationship, its success seems predicated on the practices of traditional mediators (1971, p. 24).

A TYPOLOGY OF MEDIATE FUNCTIONS

Both elite and mass stratifications are indicated in the foregoing discussions. So too are the often lengthy intermediary chains within social and political spheres. Adherence to well-established social networks, necessitating face-to-face communications, is also apparent for the plurality of actors and institutions interposed between the ends of society. Characteristically, intermediary roles—assumed mainly by traditional group leaders and other local influentials—were weakly differentiated. Highly specialized go-betweens were atypical, and mediation was for many a secondary though significant activity.

Historical patterns additionally suggest the utility of distinguishing two classes of mediate processes: the descending and ascending. The former describes interventionary behavior that comes as a consequence of communications initiated by primary elites. The latter is prompted by the attitudinal states and petitions of clientele publics. Neither rules out that intermediaries may also make a significant independent contribution to the content and impact of what they transmit.

Several possible mediate functions are encompassed by these essentially vertical processes. The first involves *amplification* and refers simply to the downward dissemination of messages through intermediary activity. The performance of this function may be more manifest and routinized than any other. While amplification is sometimes undertaken by nonelite types (such as the town crier), the function falls in large measure to those who hold the confidence and respect of their audiences and who are versed in the arts and sciences of transmitting information. A second function is that of *interpretation*. Frequently coupled with amplification, it engages intermediaries in the screening and filtering of descending communications and delegates responsibility for the intelligibility and acceptance of messages by those "below." In earlier periods this proverbial "gatekeeping" function was regularly undertaken by tribal shaykhs and other influentials. A third category of mediate functions involves intermediaries engaged in the implementation of values and policies. It includes a broad range of supervisory, enforcement, and adjudicative activities best classified as *control*. These functions encompass many of the most overt and customary activities of a state's governing apparatus. However, the very inclusiveness of control perhaps explains why it often fails to be identified or fully appreciated as a mode of intermediary behavior. Historically, the militia and the tax collector cum administrator were the most visible mediators of control functions.

An equal but asymmetric set of functions is detectable in ascending channels. First, the *monitorial* function describes the intelligence operations of intermediaries, whether solicited or unsolicited by higher elites. It involves transmissions that may disguise as well as reveal mass and communal opinion and behavior. Virtually no traditional intermediary avoided entirely the obligations of reporting and informing. A second ascending function, that of *representation*, involves the intermediary in the articulation of nonelite interests and petitions. These mediations ordinarily take the form of advocacy and promotion, but representation need not provide for accountability and does not rule out possible distortion or misperception of demands or interests. While the representational function was weakly institutionalized in earlier Middle East societies, local elites serving as spokesmen and protectors had frequently performed this function. Finally, the *brokerage* function identifies intermediaries active in the adjustment of the competing interests of citizens and government. As a species of interest aggregation, mediation efforts are typically devoted to moderating claims and discovering mutually agreeable solutions. Although brokerage in social intercourse was commonplace in the region's past, it was never fully legitimized as a form of mediation in mass-government interactions. Where brokerage occurred, it more often involved the compromise of interelite interests.

The scope and nature of mediate functions vary with at least four system parameters. The first of these is readily apparent from the discussion up to this point. Intermediary processes are heavily colored by prevailing cultural norms and the residual strength of historically precedented patterns. In the Middle East, we therefore anticipate intermediary behavior characterized by informality and personalism within modern as well as traditional populations. In much of the region, the veracity of mediated communications is determined less by the length and consistency of channels than by the fiduciary relationships within the networks of information. Control activities by intermediaries standing outside an intimate social fabric are likely to be suspect. The skills necessary for brokerage activities are apparently readily acquired, but the weakness of representational function appears more endemic. Only where the legacies of the past are faint do highly specialized intermediary roles appear. Finally, there is much in the traditional culture that encourages self-serving by intermediaries, regardless of the class of mediate behavior.

A second factor, obviously related to the first, recognizes that mediate functions are associated with political integration. Local elites in weakly cohesive national communities have a nearly exclusive grasp on mediating activity and carry the burden of communications between the center and periphery. In practice, however, these usually well-institutionalized intermediary structures act as insulators for their communities, performing vital but nonetheless minimal levels of mediate activities. In general, mediating functions necessarily expand and activities become more differentiated with the transition to more politically cohesive societies. Indeed, as we explore later, the expansion in scope and intensity of mediation can be a useful index of system change. Meanwhile, these same processes can also stimulate competition among mediating institutions. And the consequences of any breakdown in mediation threatens to be more serious to systems at higher levels of national integration.

A nation's authority structure and supportive ideologies establishes a third set of parameters for mediating behavior. At any level of integration, the more pluralistic the distribution of political power, the more likely that representative and brokerage functions will be both in demand and observable in practice (see Kornhauser 1969, pp. 81–82). Where a regime also legitimizes its policies by reference to democratic ideals, a formalization of representational and brokerage activities and restrictions on monitorial and control activities are predictable. In more hierarchical systems, by contrast, representation and brokerage are essentially latent functions and their scope is limited. Authoritarian ideologies, moreover, create few expectations about the performance of these ascending functions. On the whole, intermediary activity in the hierarchical system is manifest and heavy in descending channels, and the opportunities for autonomous activity by intermediary institutions are highly circumscribed. The paradox is that the means necessary to maintain pyramidal authority frequently call for multiple and efficient mediating structures that can be acquired only by a willingness to share power with secondary elites.

Fourth, political mediation is influenced by the level of technology, modified by the capacity of citizens to absorb changes, particularly in the mass media. By multiplying the channels of communication, media growth makes available alternative sources of information where there were once effective monopolies. To most observers, it has also created more direct linkages between citizens and government. The apparently easy manipulation of media institutions by higher elites promises a means of reducing the distortion in descending communications. Accordingly, most Middle East regimes have invested heavily in the rapid expansion of electronic media, and none has denied itself regular, if not exclusive, access to all the mass media. Along with media growth, however, comes a new class of intermediaries, the media specialists. The dependence of top elites on their know-how in the arts of mass persuasion leaves the extent of the specialists' influence as intermediaries problematic. While it is customary to stress the amplification role of the media specialists, their impact as interpreters and monitors is often underrated. But any generalizations about functional consequences must take cognizance of the media's differential meaning for populations widely separated by education and sense of political efficacy. For some people, the media's transmissions may be no more irresistible than they are intelligible.

The foregoing observations are not all self-evident. In the sections that follow, we are thereby drawn to examine in some detail the principal intermediary institutions in the Middle East, looking for illustrative materials and evidence of the utility of these categories. The analysis focuses on six sets of intermediaries: the local status, party and legislative, associational, bureaucratic, military, and media elites. For each, we explore the circumstances of its emergence as mediators and the forces that have molded its contemporary roles. Various instruments of mediation and the patterns of their use are also identified.

LOCAL STATUS ELITES

The scholarly emphasis on patterns of change in the contemporary Middle East often results in a depreciation of local elites in policy and opinion mediation. The indisputable pervasiveness of new classes, institutions, and beliefs should not obscure how older sources of authority continue to bulk large in competition for the attention and allegiance of the masses. The intermediary activities of local status leaders have persevered, in part, because of the uneven penetration of change in the region. But the survival of traditional structures appears even more to fill the continuing needs of communal clienteles and as a natural supplement of more modern forms of mediation. At times the old and new are so interlaced that a headman, cleric, or other local notable may be an indispensable component in a national network.

This is not to underestimate the strains placed on traditional institutions by the regionwide technological, social, and political changes. As suggested, the challenge to local status elites is nowhere more apparent than from the mass media and, especially, from the ubiquitous transistor radio. The sheer volume of information disseminated, as it were over the heads of traditional leadership, touches all but the most passive and remote populations. Physical and intellectual barriers lowered by the interventions of party, military, and educational cadres have deliberately or unwittingly done their part to discredit many traditionals, particularly in the urban centers. Examples of local leadership transfers from scions of primary families to those of less prominent social origins are found everywhere. Even when status leaders continue to hold the respect of their communities, their narrowed sphere of influence casts doubt on their ability to advocate individual and group causes with higher authorities. Still more, the availability of competitive mediation channels may expose a history of corruption and self-indulgence among the traditionals. Age-old perceptions of legitimate and necessary authority can be easily shattered even before modern ideas and their relevance to nonelites are implanted.

Neither those regimes striving to expand their national authority nor governments committed to mobilize assenting masses can tolerate heavily distorted and parochially slanted interventions by locals. Almost every nation thus has a considerable stake in determining the identity of intermediaries at the periphery. In some cases, the obvious solution has been to make them direct appointees of the state. Clerics and village heads in Turkey and guild leaders in Iran, for example, were easily incorporated into an administrative chain of command. Government intervention in the election of local leadership has often sought to undermine the social bases of patron-client relations. Radical land reform in several countries simply ousted landlords as intermediaries, ending their protection as well as their exploitation of peasants. Some central governments rudely evicted tribal leadership, but chiefs have also voluntarily deserted their communities. Raoof observes how many tribal shaykhs in Saudi Arabia became absentee leaders, agreeing to sacrifice much of their influence with tribesmen in order to live and prosper in the cities (1970, p. 362).

Many local status elites are obliged to adopt new lifestyles and attitudes. Landlords have made perhaps the most painless adaptation. Aside from those in socialized economies, landlords could often readily transfer their capital to the cities for reinvestment in commercial enterprises and real estate. Other village elites have lost much of their insularity, as they are obliged to become leading consumers of the modern media and increase their intimacy with higher government and party officials. The older bases of authority are themselves subject to change. Newer connections may almost entirely overshadow, for example, the influence a cleric draws from his religious role, and the prestige and contacts a shaykh holds outside the community can become important in determining his power within.

Local elites are regularly compelled to foster government programs whose goals may in fact seriously undermine provincial autonomy. However, village leadership has little alternative to normalizing relations with the intruding agents of government and at least not openly impeding their programs. The promises of a better life, made vivid by development projects and government loans, offer strong incentives for accommodations with a central government. Dependence on government for employment and franchises are more characteristic of urban settings in which citizens also must find their way around or through the maze of bureaucracies designed to regulate much of their lives.

In general, the functions of mediation have been increasingly, though by no means entirely, nationalized. This process is likely accelerated by the appearance in the mid-twentieth century of a large upwardly-mobile, educated, and salaried class. As the offspring of industrializing and secularizing societies, this class would appear to have an obvious interest in discarding traditional mores. At the same time, as members of a generation that has both a familiarity with and lingering respect for older allegiances, members of the new middle class are conceivably ideal candidates to mediate between the old and the new. In some cases this no doubt happens. Lerner notes that Lebanese lawyers and politicians can be indispensable in promoting social demands in Beirut and in interpreting a nationally imposed legal system that supersedes custom and informal understanding (1958, pp. 185, 187). He also describes how in villages and towns a moderately educated, indigenous younger elite gains acceptance. "The villager needs a sympathetic personal intermediary to bridge the gap between his traditional communications ... and the heavy new demands of empathy by media that report varied events far beyond the range of village experience" (1958, p. 190). Village leaders among the Israeli Arabs similarly turn to a younger generation of educated and often lower status individuals in a continuing need for go-betweens, fluent in the Hebrew language, to deal with the Jewish authorities (Shamir 1962, p. 99).

There is additional evidence, however, that the new middle classes, notably in the urban centers where the most ambitious and best educated settle, in fact encumber elite communication with the masses. Workers and peasants, less exposed and often resistant to the forces of change, are more easily estranged from the rapid and open embrace of modern lifestyles and values exhibited by the more privileged classes. To compare with the attractions of ideology and universalistic principles for the elites, the masses cling to particularistic loyalties and heterogeneous communal ties (see Harik 1972a, p. 312). Patai sees the divergent cultural experiences arising under the impact of westernization as steadily widening the distance between the top and bottom of society (1965, pp. 123-24). Whereas the ruling classes once shared a cultural frame of reference with the lower classes, the widening gulf now breeds mutual suspicions. Under such conditions, intact village elites and other unassimilated older structures of mediation may retain much of their earlier functionality.

To the illiterate villager and even the more sophisticated urban dweller, the mechanics of government and the motives of its officials are very often confusing. While the notion that everyone has a right to petition government has no doubt gained acceptance, apprehension about administrators and older folkways still keep many people from directly approaching officials (see Stirling 1965, p. 290). The custom of local influentials accompanying individuals in appearances before government officials often perseveres, even among the better educated and more socially emancipated, and despite the recognition that an intermediary may be neither necessary nor useful in seeking jobs or favors. In another vein, the experiences of Iranian literacy and health corpsmen following land reform are also illustrative. The hostility of many in the village hierarchy was anticipated but, as Bill relates, peasants after 1963 remained uneasy in relations with the newer agents of authority. The villagers had much preferred to deal with landlords and their representatives, people who had in the past protected them against arbitrary government and with whom a modus vivendi had already been negotiated (1972a, p. 147).

Surveys of the Turkish countryside indicate that village headmen, particularly those who are locally elected, retain much of their influence, even where a community's insularity has been considerably stripped away (Frey and Roos 1967, pp. 37-41). Headmen are probably the only class of administrators whose orientations run essentially downward. Their first allegiance goes to their fellow villagers, to whom they owe much of their effectiveness. Yet a sympathetic view of the interests of locals does not relieve the headman of heavy demands imposed by bureaucratic superiors. In describing the headman's formal responsibilities, Szyliowicz writes:

> He had to announce, explain, and execute the government's laws and decrees and notify the authorities of suspected criminals, draft-dodgers, deserters ... He had to cooperate with officials of the national administration, aiding in every possible way the tax collectors, gendarmes, and process-servers who came to his village. He was also required to keep a register of vital statistics ... He had to enforce decisions of the Village Councils and supervise the execution of the projects that it approved. He also acted in a judicial capacity, being empowered to hear both sides of a village dispute, and, if he wished, to send the disputants to trial (1966, pp. 45–56).

Except where traditional rules have been brutally suppressed or, as in the case of rural Egypt, overwhelmed by modern actors—some of them outsiders (see Harik 1971, p. 736)—village elites have often found it possible to infiltrate party branches, district councils, and other newer institutions. On occasion, older elites may, in effect, be invited to reassert themselves. Following independence in Algeria, for example, party and government leaders largely withdrew from the countryside, leaving peasants once again under the sway of holy men, village chiefs, and elders (Ottaway and Ottaway 1970, p. 241). While, in general, the traditional go-betweens have lost the exclusivity they once held in some mediate functions, they are called upon to fill obvious gaps in contemporary communication networks. Indeed, rural and urban populations alike may be confronted with the need for more, and not less, assistance through intermediaries.

Intermediaries active at the level of the village or urban quarter are synonymous with the patron in clientele relations found throughout the developing world. Essentially, they are engaged in defending the interests of low-status individuals in return for deference or material rewards. Local patrons are increasingly, however, members of a higher level of patron-client system in which the local influential is a client of a modern, national elite. While the local relationships tend to militate against social and economic change, the intermediary to national urban elites has become a critical actor in political development strategies as well as a two-way channel in communications with the elites (Bertsch, Clark, and Wood 1978, pp. 423-26). Springborg, in examining the Egyptian elite, concludes that clientele ties provide the chains of command through which the nation is ruled (1975, p. 91; also see Dekmejian 1975, pp. 169-84).

Familial and informal groups remain, of course, primary modes of amplification and interpretation. The kinship group offers the most immediate and enduring structure of communications. For all the rivalries of the Middle East family and clan, its solidarity and cohesion, particularly in face of outside challenges and impersonal institutions, makes it a highly trusted and reliable source of information. Yet the extended family's normally limited ability to assure individuals sufficient social and economic advantage in complex societies leaves a wide field for supplementary friendship cliques (see Bill and Leiden 1979, pp. 84–91). Organized along religious, ethnic, as well as familial lines, or built on social, intellectual, or recreational interests, these circles permit both the sharing and forming of political beliefs. Membership in interlocking clubs can also cross social class lines, thereby assuring the swift diffusion of opinion and information (Bill 1972a, p. 49; 1972b, pp. 429–31). Miller identifies the bazaar's *dowrehs* and the extended family as the major components in a system that links every section of the country (1969, p. 164). He also found that no system of oral communications rivals the urban bazaar rumor for the transmission of political information among merchants, clerics, and the lower classes. The same network contributed to the rapid undermining of the Shah's power during 1978. In other contexts, however, oral communications through friendship groups give ruling elites one of their most credible sources for monitoring popular feelings.

The advantages of building modern structures of mediation on traditional patrons and informal groups is well understood by the region's political leaders. Party strategists usually take for granted the convenience and occasional necessity of coming to terms with intact networks of influence. Both Turkey's People's party and later its Democratic party allowed country notables and wealthy landlords to dominate provincial party organizations. Frey notes how politics in Eastern Anatolia is still "frequently a matter of negotiation between great agas and tribal chiefs on one side and the party representatives on the other" (1965, p. 191). The decision on party affiliation by a family head usually committed the family to an allegiance inherited over generations. The rhetoric of Egypt's Revolutionary Command Council following the 1952 coup seldom compromised on the need for a new society. In practice, however, the military vested responsibility for operations of the Liberation Rally with the older rural notables (Binder 1966, p. 229). In Iran, the ruling party, consistent with the tenets of the Shah's White Revolution, had shunned direct ties with the former landed aristocracy. The Iran Novin policy of ignoring traditional village and provincial leadership was. largely disbanded by the late 1960s, however, as it became apparent that their affiliation might help overcome the stubborn local apathy toward the party. At the same time, Iran Novin and its royally-designated successor, the Rastaqhiz party, rarely hesitated to use traditional patterns of personalism and *parti* (influence) in either its rural or urban activities.

The confluence of local status elites and national institutions is most apparent in the politics of pre-1975 Lebanon. Power went to those who had both acquired economic success and preserved older allegiances. Hudson describes how village priests, headmen, and leaders of important families were cultivated by candidates for the parliament. To bring in the vote, candidates were particularly beholden to local political bosses (*zuama*) whose own influence derived from a combination of family ties, wealth, and leadership skills (1968, pp. 22, 126; also Suleiman 1970, pp. 233–34). An urbanized version of the zuama system attracted many more professional types, but as Peretz notes in 1958, these city politicians adopt "confessional ties which resemble the once all-powerful local political network" (p. 332).

The mutuality of older and newer patterns sometimes results in a revival and strengthening of the status elites. This is clearly the case when traditional activities are recognized and formalized in statutes. The intervention of locals may be indispensable in assuring the compliance of government policies by people outside the effective reach of administrative control. A marriage law in prerevolutionary Afghanistan is a good illustration. In effect, it delegated to the nation's mullahs the job of translating the law into terms intelligible to the Afghan public. Without the close cooperation of provincial officials and clerics, neither an awareness nor the enforcement of the law was contemplated outside of the small urban middle class. Village leaders in rural Iran have willingly participated in government programs aimed at transmitting family planning information to their communities. In Morocco, dispersed and discredited rural elites were brought back to life by the introduction of local council elections in 1960 and 1963. According to Waterbury, these older elites were intentionally revived to help spread the responsibility for unpleasant decisions made by local administrators (1970, p. 283). Israeli government officials, much as the British mandate administrations before them, have openly sought to preserve older class leadership as a means of maintaining reliable, pliant contacts within the Arab community. Until faced with the strident nationalism of the 1970s, Jewish authorities largely ignored a more educated and ideological generation in favor of arrangements that brought an exchange of material benefits in the villages for electoral support and loyalty to the state.

The mass media should in theory supplant traditional communication specialists. Instead, they may only heighten the dependence on local intermediaries. The growing tide of information aimed at illiterate populations has seemingly increased the requirements for a two-step process of simplifying and interpreting news. Many observers point out, for example, the difficulty of Arabic-speaking audiences in understanding the formal style heard on radio and television broadcasts. One study in an Iranian province indicates that village leaders have considerably wider exposure to the radio than do peasants and have listening behavior similar to local agricultural agents and health corpsmen (Lieberman, Gillespie, and Loghmani 1973, p. 95). In most populations, the loss of credibility of the more literate rural elites has not gone so far that their mediation of news is no longer in demand. In fact, as the desire to comprehend the news grows among the rural masses, the local status intermediaries, at least those holding some modern credentials, find that the communications revolution has given them a new source of power and respect.

According to Pye, "there tends to be—paradoxically—an increase in reliance upon direct word of mouth communications" in societies where there is simultaneously a growth of mechanical communications, effective organization, and more extensive travel. Communication systems thus have two levels. One is the more familiar structure produced by technological progress and professionalism. The other is a face-to-face process in which opinion leaders link attentive and passive publics. Both are integral parts of a modern, developed communication system (Pye 1963, pp. 25–26). Experiences of local status elites in the Middle East suggest that a two-tier, partially integrated system is an especially apt way to describe communication structures in the region. The older mediation processes cannot be dismissed as anachronisms. Local elites frequently stood in the way of change, but they have also figured significantly in ongoing political and social transformations. While some status elites have evolved and others have been virtually swept away, many still actively ply their trade as intermediaries with large segments of a nation's population. Moreover, the practices and values that are associated with the locals are widely shared in the national sector. As noted, party and administrative elites continue to rely on person-to-person communications and to fall back on traditional loyalties in reaching the masses and in mediating their demands. For additional evidence, one has only to examine the several intermediary institutions that are the pillars of contemporary government.

PARTY AND LEGISLATIVE ELITES

Political parties normally offer peculiarly modern solutions for societies faced with crises of participation, national integration, and legitimacy (see LaPalombara and Weiner 1966, pp. 3–21). No institutions have assumed greater responsibility for mediating the social changes and ideologies cast up by modernizing societies. Nor have any offered a greater potential for narrowing the wide gap that exists, both symbolically and in practice, between national leadership and the masses. As such, parties are the work horses in efforts to link a government's decision makers with its citizenry. Writing about political parties in the Middle East, Halpern argues that "only a party can be in daily contact with the constituency, teach, propagandize, or put pressure upon that constituency to adopt new ideas and patterns of action. Only a party can stimulate involvement in campaigns for literacy and higher production no less than particular political issues, and gather new talents and thus regularize recruitment into the new elite" (1963, p. 283). The region's parties and to a lesser extent its interest groups thereby carry much of the burden of disciplining the masses and mobilizing support for national authority. Though they offer the usually inarticulate publics their best access to national policy forums, parties are more familiarly powerful tools for the implementation of policies formulated at the top.

No one would pretend that all political parties in the Middle East can be viewed analytically as one. On the contrary, we are more often struck by the vast differences among them. The region offers up multiparty, dominant, and exclusionary one-party systems in some countries as well as only incipient party movements in others. Structurally, parties span mass and cadre classifications and include both ideological and pragmatic types. There are parties that demand total allegiance of members and champion a new social consciousness alongside of parties that require minimal commitment and serve primarily constituent and communal needs.

Through all this diversity, however, parties in the Middle East also have much in common. Leaving Israel aside, they are organizational forms for which there are no antecedents in traditional Islamic society. While contemporary parties, as we have observed, often draw sustenance from older institutions and traditional cliques may be disguised in modern forms, neither political parties nor voluntary associations have an organic relationship to the social structure (Halpern 1963, p. 283). As such, they possess a high potential as agents for social change. Yet this same freedom from the past leaves them exposed to the political ideas and appeals that have periodically swept the Middle East. Earlier in the century, parties and voluntary associations were thus almost universally inspired by liberal Western models. More recently, few organizations have eluded entirely the imperatives of pan-Arabic or anti-imperialist themes. Their leadership has additionally confronted common problems in educating and activating supportive publics. For those parties and associations seeking mass followings, there has been a very similar challenge in reaching populations that are indifferent until motivated and difficult to control once mobilized.

Party elites in the Middle East are ordinarily faced with two sets of decisions. One involves the kind of investment they are prepared to make in building an extensive, grass roots organization and in fostering allegiances to the party among the people. The second requires a decision on the extent of their willingness to permit the party structure to mediate popular demands through representation and bargaining with policy elites. Whatever their resolve, parties have not always been successful in following a blueprint. Some organizational goals have proved to be beyond their resources. At times, external pressures have obliged parties to tolerate greater input activities than their leaders had contemplated. As long as parties remained mainly parliamentary cliques and status quo-oriented defenders of class and personal privilege, their posture toward the lower classes was largely settled. Thus, few of Iran's largely ad hoc and personalistic parties of the 1941–53 multiparty era were either capable of or eager to establish strong extraparliamentary bonds. Egypt's prerevolutionary Wafd managed to establish broadly regional organization networks, but necessarily rejected any meaningful participation by peasants, workers, and craftsmen while it served the interest of rural middle classes and higher status urban groups (Binder 1966, p. 225).

Wherever the politics of reform and modernization are a declared policy of government, it usually follows that the mass party is elevated to a national goal. The believed utility of the mass party in the mediate functions of amplification, interpretation, and control have not been accompanied by a similar commitment to construct ascending structures. This absence of reciprocity is well illustrated during the first two decades of the Turkish Republic. While few citizens could avoid contact with the People's party workers or escape entirely the impact of party-mediated policies, the *etatiste* bourgeoisie at the provincial level joined with the party to discredit and suppress political expression of the rural majorities (see Karpat 1965, p. 477). As described by Frey, "The party was an organization for securing the necessary governmental and societal integration—a disciplined set of power and communication relations functioning mainly to implement certain decisions of top leaders." Occasionally in the role of monitor, the party also provided the "leadership with information not normally forthcoming through regular bureaucratic and military channels" (1965, p. 304). Not surprisingly then, Turkey's success in establishing a comprehensive, cohesive organization as an instrument of a national elite became a benchmark for similar efforts in the Islamic Middle East.

No regime, aside perhaps from Bourguiba's Tunisia, has in fact permitted so thorough a party monopoly of descending linkages. Moore describes how the Neo-Destour, in its integrating role, became the government's alter ego as a ruling institution (1965, pp. 105–06). Several parties in the region, moreover, have invited a more inclusive membership than the Kemalists and matched them in elaborate formal organization. The Neo-Destour of Tunisia and Morocco's Istaqlal enrolled about 10 percent of their nation's populations, including sizable rural groups, during the 1950s. With only the older bourgeois and feudal elements barred, Egypt recruited upwards of 20 percent of its total population and the major portion of eligible voters into the Arab Socialist Union in just a few months after its formation in 1962. Some parties, notably Algeria's National Liberation Front (FLN) and Syria's Baath, have also made periodically concerted, if less successful, efforts to swell party ranks in the hopes of extending their political education and surveillance of the masses. The determined efforts of Afghanistan's ruling Khalq party to protect its revolution through the building of grass roots loyalties furnish the best recent example of a party's personnel being entrusted with exclusive control over popular linkages.

To maintain contact with members and sympathizers, mass parties rely on a variety of mechanisms. Until displaced in 1964, the Neo-Destour leadership utilized regional "cadre conferences" to consult with local party branches, in some cases to educate activists and in others to hear provincial representations (Moore 1965, p. 120). Nearly every party of consequence in the region sponsors a newspaper as a means of transmitting the views of its leadership. Larger parties often circulate specialized journals targeted to particular interest and regional audiences. As a rule, these parties ally themselves with voluntary associations, many of them founded at the instigation of party leaders. Affiliated labor unions, guilds, and youth and professional associations, to mention the most obvious, assure a reliable pool of party recruits. Still more, joint memberships enable the party to borrow the usually more functional interaction patterns and communication systems of these groups to enhance its own organizational cohesion. Rallies, demonstrations, and ceremonial occasions offer the widest opportunities for contact with the masses. Frequently in conjunction with their affiliated groups, party activists assume prime responsibility for organizing and mobilizing enthusiastic crowds. Instructions go out by word-of-mouth, telephone, and sound trucks to both the committed and the more passive publics.

Party headquarters in many cases have merely replaced the homes of village or guild heads as places for individuals to congregate for political discussion and social diversion. But Turkey's People's Houses and Rooms remain the most ambitious scheme for bringing a party close to the people. Up to the time of their closing in 1950, the approximately 4,000 rooms in small towns and villages and the 500 houses in larger locales gave the public regular access to the government radio. A steady diet of party-supervised social and cultural activities similarly served to inculcate people in the principles of the Kemalist Revolution (Lewis 1961, p. 383).

In more recent years, local units of Turkish parties have served as listening posts for the purpose of monitoring the effects of government policies and hearing popular discontents. Roos and Roos report that 65 percent of the district governors surveyed in 1965 identified "politicians" as intermediaries with the public (1971, p. 186). Szyliowicz outlines the elaborate party hierarchy in rural Turkey and describes how local officials screen villagers' complaints before passing them up to the district level where requests are "considered, weighed and acted upon." Party officials may deal directly with local administrators at their own level to satisfy constituency demands. The most weighty decisions are forwarded to provincial level officials who typically mix with members of the party's central committee, deputies in parliament, and officials in the ministries (Szyliowicz 1966, pp. 146–50).

On a person-to-person basis, party leaders typically perform many of the client-patron activities normally associated with traditional influentials. Officials often attend to welfare needs and assist party members in securing minor government jobs. They are regularly asked for letters of introduction to government administrators and may intercede personally with the authorities. It is not uncommon for individuals, especially in the middle classes, to approach the party to arrange educational scholarships or army transfers. In fact, requests are received for exemptions from almost every kind of government regulation. Political parties naturally differ widely in their attention to particularistic, nonpolicy demands from nonelites. They also contrast in their means of processing and in their capacities to satisfy requests. Yet in virtually no nation in the region is the representational function wholly ignored by party operatives.

Where a parliament is active, much of this intermediary role may devolve on a locally-elected legislator. Even in chambers with little deliberative or rule-making powers, members are usually called upon to perform essentially ombudsman tasks; it may in fact be the only activity left to the parliamentarian that allows for some individual initiative. Those chambers dominated by class interests have been the most notorious in offering members and their clients built-in access to government ministries. With the substitution of lower status civil servants and professionals for landlords in the Iranian Majlis beginning in 1963, the Shah sharply diminished the bargaining power of legislators with the bureaucracy. Still, the expanded activity of party and parliamentary agencies did not entirely divert the flood of constituent petitions directed to deputies, nor were personal friendships and family connections eliminated as the principal determinants of a legislator's effectiveness. In the region's most exaggerated case, the pre-occupation of the pre-July 1973 Afghan House of the People with constituent and personal inverventions had left little time for even the appearance of law making. In the absence of either political parties or impelling institutional norms to regulate behavior, the deputies—mainly tribal and ethnic leaders—were active in the ministries either as petitioners against provincial administrative decisions, pleaders for exemptions to government rules, or advocates for increased local resources. In all three classes of mediation, however, the pursuit of general benefits was seldom carried on with the same perseverance as the quest for personal gain (Weinbaum 1972, pp. 61-64; 1977, pp. 110-14).

In several parliaments of the region, legislators also regularly channel broader constituency demands to higher elites. The relatively open politics of Turkey, pre-1975 Lebanon, and Israel offer favorable conditions for a legislative mediated feedback process. Kemalist doctrines had promised eventual popular participation and, as Frey points out, local forces sometimes managed to manipulate the party apparatus against the national elite. But not until the emergence of the multiparty system did "influence [begin] to flow reciprocally in two directions rather than one—up from lower levels as well as down from on high" (Frey 1965, pp. 304, 375). The immediate popularity of Democratic party organizers, beginning in 1948, confirmed the need for a breed of national politicians avowedly supportive of local, nonelite causes. The Anatolian masses were encouraged to look to the party and their deputies in the Assembly for alleviation of accumulated grievances. By 1950, the pressures of electoral competition induced the People's party to ease its paternalistic attitude and to more actively cultivate rural support. The masses won, in addition to policies that catered to their interests and values, a greater sense of their political importance and stake in government decisions (Payaslioglu 1964, p. 423). Except for a period in the late 1950s when Prime Minister Adnan Menderes could impose his will on the Democratic party, locals have played a decisive part in recruitment and nomination to the parliament in both major parties. Indeed, the disciplinary power of central party councils so weakened under the 1961 Constitution and election laws that local politicians and deputies increasingly determined legis-lative priorities and the fate of national party leaders.

Constituency-oriented legislators were a more constant reality of the Lebanese system. The burden of agency for a constituency had been pressed on legislators by popular experiences of bureaucratic unresponsiveness and well-articulated local demands for roads, water facilities, electricity, schools, and other programs of improvement. In identifying the Lebanese deputy as the prime broker between central governments and client groups, Hottinger observed, "He serves to channel whatever government favors are available to himself and to his group. For the government he is necessary because 'his' people trust their *zaim*, which makes it possible to reach the people through him and to obtain commitments from the group via his person. For the people he is also indis-pensable because they have little direct means of communication with a govern-ment viewed by many as alien, if not inimical" (1966, p. 91).

Close ties to the legislative constituency have also been apparent in Israel's Arab sector. The wasita of Arab Knesset deputies long offered the most effective channel to government ministries. Successful brokerage on behalf of community and individual interests was, at least until the mid-1970s, the measure of a deputy's reputation and popularity. While the proportional representation sys-tem and national issue preoccupations of the Jewish parties militate against legislative links with subgroups, the rising prominence of local leadership and the heightened awareness of constituency needs finds growing expression in the Knesset. The elaborate infrastructure of party organization in Israel, where all parties have mass memberships and about 40 percent of the population hold an affiliation, could in the future carry strong upward pressures to decision makers. The institution of popularly-elected mayors could also accelerate the process. But for the time being, the initiative lies with a small leadership circle whose primary links with public opinion are the electoral process and national-level intermediary associations.

Policy-related inputs are unanticipated in highly disciplined parliaments, though government leaders may look to deputies for subtle reference to public moods and policy preferences. Yet in periods of political relaxation, even docile legislatures can transform themselves into two-way channels with surprising ease. Following the forced abdication of Reza Shah in 1941, the Majlis moved aggressively to fill the domestic political vacuum. The regime's handpicked deputies took immediate advantage of the liberalization to air long-stifled polit-ical ideas and press public as well as personal complaints. Between 1965 and 1967, Egypt's National Assembly was given license by President Nasser to serve as a listening post and critic while it continued to carry official views to the public. Members of the parliament felt free to present grievances against admin-istrators and to spell out instances of mismanagement and corruption. Dekmejian concludes that the Assembly "served as a safety valve, and upward channel of communication and vehicle for popular education, all combined" (1971, p. 164).

The Assembly again briefly found its voice in late 1972 through the instrumentality of a parliamentary commission. Highly vocal, if not altogether unconstrained, debates also accompanied Sadat's multiparty experiment in 1976.

Examples of legislatures and parties deferential to provincial elites, themselves vehicles for popular prejudices and demands, are few enough in the Middle East. Even in Turkey, the military's interventionary activities for a time after March 1971 left the parliament and the influence of local politicians in doubt. Any conclusions about linkages through parties and legislatures in the region must therefore stress their fragility rather than their viability. On one hand, these institutions have given top elites a reasonably accurate picture of public attitudes, and parties have had no small part in creating a public opinion where none had previously existed. On the other hand, political elites have not penetrated nearly so far as it would appear from their participatory rhetoric or their mass organizations. In general, the effective voice of nonelites on policy makers is still feeble.

Responsibility for this state of affairs lies at the same time with national leaderships, intermediary elites, and the masses. Large elements in most countries exhibit a lingering distrust of party organizers as sincere advocates of popular causes. Outside of periods of general enthusiasm, few if any parties have fulfilled their stated mobilization and education goals, or more fundamentally, engendered the kind of personal, family, and community attachments that once exemplified Turkey's democratic party and its successor, the Justice party. The proportion of active members in most mass parties is often no more than 10 to 15 percent of the official party rolls. And the size of their militant cadres may be only a minor fraction of the activists. Energies that might have gone into mass recruitment or the upgrading of members' political competence have in many cases been exhausted in petty squabbling among party leaders.

A dedicated corps of party operatives, capable of reaching out to the lower classes while retaining the support of the educated middle classes, has been an elusive goal throughout the region. The Egyptian case is instructive. Halpern relates how the revolutionary leadership sought to mobilize millions of members for the Liberation Rally instead of first training a body of enterprising and disciplined organizers to give the movement direction and controls (1963, pp. 309-10). Many of the same mistakes were made by the Arab Socialist Union (ASU) in its formative period, however. By 1965, Nasser's fears that an elite corps would drive those excluded to communist or neo-Islamic organizations were dropped with the formation of a vanguard of fulltime professionals who would become "a self-reliant inter-communicating cadre" (Dekmejian 1971, p. 146). The plan called for the group to be highly selective and the identities of its members to be kept secret. At least a portion of their training was slated for the village level. But despite the government's claims that thousands of young men and women were schooled, after four years the experiment was announced a failure and the program allowed to expire (Peretz 1971, p. 223).

Anwar Sadat's efforts to diffuse ASU authority during 1971, in order to oust Nasserite groups, also weakened it as an instrument of population mobilization. By 1976, the Egyptian president recognized that the low level of party and political activity was incompatible with his new economic and political thrusts. The multiparty arrangement, allowed to replace the ASU, unleashed, however, a stream of criticism frustrating to the government and distracting from its goals. Forced to compete with the opposition, the ruling faction in the parliament devoted little of its energies to propagating the government's ideas and programs. A May 1978 referendum approved restrictions on parties of the Right and Left and promoted the founding of the National Democratic party. In personally assuming the party's chairmanship, Sadat expected to infuse it with some of his popularity and to give it ready access to the state-owned media. He was also determined to prevent the emergence of a party elite, such as existed in the 1960s, that might try to use the party apparatus to infiltrate the government bureaucracy and military.

Developments in Egypt point up the vacillation of many regimes over whether an open or more restrictive party organization better suits their purposes. The possible exploitative uses of a large, active membership and a skilled elite corps are viewed as having real drawbacks. There is the nagging fear that a too expansive participation in electoral politics will free older, antiregime elements to regain their influence. Also, as in most modernizing countries, ruling elites have had to consider, first, whether mass participation will overload the ability of mediating structures to deflect unwanted or unrealizable demands and, second, whether the failure to satisfy various interest publics will incline them to follow potential counterelites. At the level of organization, a highly inclusive membership usually leaves members' responsibilities ambiguous while taxing the party's capacity to offer meaningful recognition and rewards.

INTEREST ELITES

The weak reciprocity of party mediations carries over to the regions' voluntary associations. While mass interest groups are a growing phenomenon in Middle East politics, few hold a resemblance to western counterparts as demand-bearing groups. Most labor unions, youth and student groups, and business associations are appendages to political parties and thus share in the tasks of political education (that is, amplification and interpretation) and supervision (that is, monitoring and control). But such practices as the cultivation of popular support, the search for independent access to policy makers, and the open articulation of special interests are more rarely observable. A secular associational life is tolerated in many Middle East states only because organizational loyalties provide governments with a sometimes welcomed substitute for more traditional and less retrainable allegiances. It often happens that members of functional groups are willing to settle for largely symbolic and cathartic representations.

As concomitants of urbanization and industrialization, voluntary associations have proliferated in all but a few states in the region. A system of liberal politics quite naturally provides the best context for a vigorous interest group community, and organizations along vocational and class lines have been spawned in the several modernizing democracies. However, the emergence of mass interest groups in the Middle East is better explained by sheer political opportunity and colonial legacy (see Halpern 1963, pp. 318–39). Trade unions have flourished in Morocco, Tunisia, and the Sudan. And labor federations occupied a pivotal role in the politics of postindependence Algeria and postwar Iran, neither under predictably hospitable conditions.

Mass loyalties to trade unions were frequently forged in nationalist and independence movements in which organized labor furnished a readily mobilized force. Class consciousness and useful leadership skills had often been acquired through close contact with western examples. The organizations of European workers in the Maghreb along with France's frequent reluctance to place native labor on an equal footing spurred associational activity prior to independence. The Moroccan Workers Union (UMT), formally organized in 1955, succeeded once illegal societies that had grown to mass proportions following their participation in the nationalist agitation of 1952. At independence in 1956, the UMT was the country's lone labor federation with perhaps as many as 560,000 members (Waterbury 1970, pp. 197–98). In the wake of the colonists' departure from Algeria, the Workers Union (UGTA), with more than 200,000 members, remained as the only mass organization once the government had allowed the FLN to wither (see Ottaway and Ottaway 1970, pp. 206-07). In Tunisia, the General Union of Tunisian Workers (UGTT), also influenced by continental socialist models, had grown by the late 1970s to nearly 60 percent of the nation's total labor force.

Under a British Labour government, administrators in the Sudan abetted the formation of a powerful Railway Workers Union after 1946, and liberal trade union legislation in 1951 paved the way for a militant Workers Trade Union Federation. By the mid-1950s, the Sudan's communist-dominated Federation represented half of the nonagricultural wage earners in a country in which only about 200,000 people were employed in the industrial sector (Henderson 1965, p. 59; Halpern 1963, pp. 326-27). Nationalist and communist influences also contributed to the rapid organization of workers in Iran following the British and Russian wartime occupation. This small urban proletariat became an important component of an approximately 60,000-strong Tudeh party.

Aside from Morocco and Turkey, the region's major contemporary unions operate largely under the protective arm of established political parties. Morocco's UMT cast off an early association with the leading Istaqlal party. While it subsequently spearheaded an opposition party, the UMT has retained a largely independent posture, enabling it to inject workers' demands directly into a still-open competition for power in Morocco (see Amin 1970, p. 210). Turkey's largest labor federation, Turk Iş, was held captive by the autocratic Democratic party leadership during the 1950s. The liberal Turkish Constitution of 1961 furnished the legal bases and incentives to stand aloof from partisan politics. Through a unique blend of economic opportunism and political pragmatism, Turk Iş has withstood ideological challenges from the Left and held its grip over much of the urban work force (see Dodd 1969, pp. 176–79).

The more customary submersion of workers' groups by government parties is illustrated by Tunisia's UGTT, Algeria's UGTA, and in prerevolutionary Iran. Although not initially under the wing of the Neo-Destour, the UGTT was absorbed by the party, as were the several voluntary associations directly instigated by the Bourguiba regime. When, by early 1978, the union had freed itself to become a major vehicle for dissent, the government brutally crushed its general strike and again converted the UGTT into an organization suited to regime purposes. Algeria's UGTA had maintained a rough parity with the FLN during the revolutionary struggle. But following independence, the Federation's leaders fought a losing battle against Ben Bella to avoid subordination. The labor leaders tried again, unsuccessfully, to inject themselves into the policy processes after Boumedianne seized power (see Quandt 1969, p. 237). Iran's fledgling labor unions did not realize regime respectability until they had formally allied themselves with the Shah-sponsored Iran Novin party between 1963 and 1965. In exchange for an abdication of all initiatives to the government, the Iranian labor movement was permitted to grow to well over a million members by the mid-1970s. An independent course for labor appeared only with the collapse of authority in late 1978, taking the form of factory-centered workers' councils and militant, communist-oriented unions in the oil fields.

The mass mobilization of industrial and white collar workers is nowhere more complete than in Egypt and Israel. Union and ASU membership became virtually synonymous in Nasser's Egypt. The Israeli case is, as always, *sui generis*. Its European-oriented political leadership inherited an understanding of, if not deep sympathy for, trade unionism as a practical and ideological right. The existence of the labor federation, the Histadrut, as an integrating institution prior to the preindependence period gave it the status not only of workers' advocate but of employer, social welfare agency, and educator as well. Then as today, affiliation with the Histadrut is for most Jewish workers an economic necessity (see Fein 1967, pp. 195-96). Arab membership in local Histadrut units offers comparable social and economic benefits and, more than any other formal governing institution, touches the lives of Israel's Arab population. Even before the election of a right-wing Likud government in 1977, Histadrut leaders had begun to push more aggressively on behalf of working class interests.

In general, the region's political parties have balked at allowing the assertion of the kind of working class demands that might suggest divergent and incompatible national goals. With the exception of the periodically-suppressed

Turkish Labor party, no party of consequence in the Middle East mounts exclusively proletarian appeals. In other respects, however, labor movements are not so submerged that they should be written off. Most labor movements are numerically superior to their parent parties. As Halpern observes, unions are often more disciplined, with a better sense of common purpose than their affiliated mass parties (1963, p. 338). Unions not only provide the parties with a useful instrument of mass support, especially in bringing out a respectable vote in elections, but they can offer important psychological buffers for workers. Thus, membership in a union may give a worker a feeling of job security and communal-like protection analogous to a traditional guild and no less useful for a government seeking to monitor opinions. Labor hierarchies also promise channels to the government bureaucracy. Members often look upon their union leaders as people who can appreciate workers' special problems and who can argue their case persuasively in the ministries. The regular participation of union officials in grievance procedures and their usual attention to social welfare serves to mitigate the distrust that many workers feel for those leaders appointed by the party or the government. However, the nature of their intermediary role requires that union leaders not raise high expectations in the rank and file about their effectiveness as representatives and bargaining agents. Particularistic requests are handled more easily than collective demands, and the threat to agitate the membership is not a legitimate weapon in negotiations. On the occasion of strikes and other demonstrations, union leaders are ordinarily found to side quietly with the government employers.

Organized labor still encompasses only a minor proportion of all workers in many Middle East countries. Even where governments foster trade unions, the membership is mainly in the urban industrial sector. Moreover, labor solidarity in demands for more vigorous ascending mediations are frequently inhibited by traditional values and kinship ties. Workers arriving from rural areas of Turkey are probably typical. Most settle in urban enclaves among people from their own villages or clans, thereby perpetuating older loyalties and political prejudices. The survival of traditional patron-workers relationships in many Turkish enterprises is one consequence. By retaining personal sponsorship and obligation, this relationship inhibits accountable leadership and political action and precludes ideological trade unionism. The working classes in Turkey and elsewhere are notably more inclined to join militant brotherhoods and other extremist groups whose appeals are essentially religious and nationalistic.

Aside from attachments to religious orders and brotherhoods, there is little in the experiences of the rural masses that might prepare them for association along interest lines. Peasants had been kept deliberately ignorant of their common social and economic grievances by landlords and their agents. The first signs of an emerging consciousness have come with land reform and the rejection by modernizing regimes of mere passive consent by the rural masses. Inducements for peasant cooperation in development projects and encouragement to participation in electoral processes have begun to lessen the feelings of helplessness and indifference. That there can be political solutions to age-old hardships is gradually gaining acceptance in village populations throughout the Middle East. Peasants are increasingly, then, a distinct though hardly formidable demand-bearing group in national politics.

Over much of the region, the collective actions of peasants are carefully orchestrated by establishment political parties and related institutions. Turkey and Egypt illustrate differing versions of the same pattern: the incorporation of rural populations into the structure of mass parties, allowing for the political education and supervision of the peasantry to be mediated directly by party cadres. The formal alliance of separately identifiable peasant organizations with parties offers another practice. Iran's agricultural cooperatives became a major constituent of the Rastaqhiz party; in 1976, more than 5,500 cooperative societies, with a combined membership of 2.6 million, were affiliated. The General Union of Tunisian Farmers, encompassing 60,000 property-owning farmers, was similarly an offshoot of a ruling party (Halpern 1963, p. 96).

On the whole, peasants have not been easy converts to either parties or interest associations. The impermeability of the rural publics to organizers and nominal memberships are readily apparent, even in Morocco where unionized peasants and agricultural labor once theoretically comprised two-thirds of UMT (Waterbury 1970, pp. 197–98). Nowhere in the Middle East have peasants established their own party. Nor is any regime likely to tolerate an organized rural majority, inclined to conservative values, in a position to jeopardize industrial development goals. Populist peasant movements are also discouraged for fear they might offer a competing power base. The Shah's cashiering of his Minister of Agriculture in 1963 is a case in point. In the wake of land reform, Dr. Hasan Arsanjani was judged to have moved too quickly in informing peasants of their new rights. His personal ambitions were also suspect as he sought to organize the newly emancipated peasants into an audible interest bloc.

Student populations in the Middle East are the most conducive to organization and the least easily restrained. Although their tactics have occasionally overstepped the limits of government toleration, student associations have operated freely as pressure groups in Israel, Turkey, and, until recently, in Lebanon. One of the two major student groups in Turkey predates the Republic, and student organizations in all three countries have maintained a large measure of institutional independence. By contrast, students in less pluralistic systems are normally on the same footing as workers and peasants—subordinated to government parties. Student leadership is often installed by the state, and associations are made dependent on government subsidies. The organized student, whether university or secondary school, is an obvious target for indoctrination, and the heavy infiltration of their groups by government informers provides a valued source of intelligence about anti-system activities.

Student associations are nevertheless unreliable intermediary structures for ruling elites. Iranian university students were not uncharacteristic in their boycott of government-sponsored organizations and their continuous resistance to SAVAK's efforts to supervise student activities. Across the region, organized students of the Left or Right are likely to be in the vanguard of popular, anti-regime protests. As such, their interests range well beyond issues of job opportunity and academic reform. Egyptian students in January 1977 and in the Sudan in August 1979 were the dominant figures in urban riots against government-imposed cost-of-living increases, forcing major concessions by frightened regimes. Well before the conspicuous role of students in the broad coalition that toppled the Shah in January 1979, students spearheaded the fall of a military regime in the Sudan in 1964 and forced an Afghan government out of power the following year. Demonstrations in Turkey served as the catalyst for the military coup in 1960 and instigated the repressive military role between 1971 and 1974. As elsewhere, students in the Middle East have been more interested and skilled in expressive actions than in incremental policy change, their demands, in effect, non-negotiable.

Students, workers, and peasants are manifestly the region's largest and potentially most politically destabilizing interest communities. The professional, business, and veteran organizations, sport and literary societies, and the philanthropic and woman's associations that have also proliferated in many Middle East states are characteristically more apolitical. Organized increasingly along nontraditional lines, these interests have a conspicuously urban, middle class clientele. Their frequently calculated aloofness from politics is in some systems a token of the privileged status. More often, it reflects heavy doses of regime cooptation and intimidation. Yet by contrast to a traditional middle stratum of artisans, small merchants, and minor civil servants, whose common interests are normally hampered in finding organizational expression, the newer middle classes are less restricted. Their interest groups promise ruling elites highly specialized channels to particularly informed and influential publics and opportunities to divert energies and depoliticize demands. In some instances, these associations may be delegated self-regulatory powers as a means of easing the burden of direct supervision and control from above. By taking into account the anxieties of the new middle class and sanctioning an associated life, many governments have lessened the possibility that interests may coalesce more informally and that their demands will find unacceptable outlets.

ADMINISTRATIVE ELITES

Formal government bureaucracies afford the most pervasive and manifest links between citizens and the paramount elites of the Middle East. Administrators preempt most of the tasks of policy implementation and have only partially relinquished to parties and government-sponsored groups significant information-gathering and interpretative activities. Few transactions between mass publics and a national leadership escape mediation by a network of hierarchically-arranged administrators. While it is customary to single out as "strategic" those individuals just beneath the highest policy makers (see Deutsch 1963, p. 154), the normally lengthy bureaucratic chains that connect the leaders to a diversified citizenry permit critical mediations of rules and demands to occur at many junctures.

The intermediary roles of administrative elites do not call for impartiality. Nor are administrators expected to sustain a balanced flow of communications between the centers of power and the broad base of the society. Even government officials in regular contact with the masses ordinarily perceive of themselves as servants of the state rather than as representatives of the people. Civil servants, subject to the discipline of superiors and lacking vocational alternatives to government employment, have small incentive, aside from bribery, for ascending mediations, least of all on behalf of the lower classes. Socialist or populist rhetoric is usually a poor guide to the class orientation of administrators. In the inevitable expansion of governing apparatus in modernizing countries, the overpowering of a once-preeminent upper class has left most bureaucracies bastions of the educated middle classes.

The rationalization of bureaucratic processes has not kept pace with administrative growth. Bureaucracies over much of the region are widely criticized as uncoordinated and top heavy. Patterns of inefficiency, irresponsibility, and corruption are not difficult to uncover (see Binder 1964, p. 306; Jacobs 1966, pp. 44–45; Al-Marayati 1972, p. 137). Whether vertically through the society or horizontally across units of government, mediated communications are neither clear nor sensitive in bureaucratic channels. Information is colored and distorted by institutional practices and class perceptions. It is more profitable, even so, to conceive of mediation by administrative elites as a highly personal exercise, involving individual motives and fears.

The defensive tendencies exhibited by insecure administrators naturally inhibit the upward transmission of information inconsistent with the views and policies of their superiors. As Almond and Powell observe regarding most authoritarian systems, subordinate officials are regularly confronted with the choice of having to report unpleasant facts and face the consequences or to accept the risk of being discovered later to have deceived the policy makers (1966, p. 184). Jacobs' description of the strategies of Iranian bureaucrats is probably not atypical of administrative behavior in much of the Middle East. Officials will deliberately withhold intelligence gathered by the bureaucracy. In the event that it becomes impossible to suppress the transmission of information, those items of a positive nature, even if fictionalized, take precedence. Should the reporting of adverse intelligence through the chain of command become wholly inescapable, information is couched, wherever possible, in terms of the failings of individuals rather than the deficiencies of institutions or principles (Jacobs 1966, p. 45).

To counter bureaucratic defenses, top officials frequently devise means to improve the veracity of information and the speed of its transmission. Local officials may be given incentives to report directly to central authorities. Supplementary intelligence networks, created in the bureaucracy and the wider society, also promise to enhance the quality of decisions. Most practices designed to circumvent normal lines of authority and reporting are informal and of low visibility. Individuals of unquestioned personal loyalty are assigned to report directly to the highest echelons. Waterbury reveals that King Hassan of Morocco employs trusted informants in practically all the ministries (1970, p. 275), and Zonis described the Shah's practice of appointing individuals without official positions to monitor the activities of particular government units (1970, p. 170). The Shah also relied on the apparatus of the Imperial Inspectorate, an agency that was empowered to receive complaints from any source and to mount investigations into all corners of the bureaucracy. In general, the less conventional the mode of information gathering and the more numerous the channels, the better it serves top elites as instruments of bureaucratic and societal control.

No Middle East government offers anything so closely resembling an independent ombudsman as does Israel's State Comptroller, or the kind of quasi-official mediation offered by district Histadrut secretaries. All the same, opportunities for citizens' petitions to bypass local and lower-ranking administrators are almost universal. Along with these party and legislative channels, letters and personal visits to central government ministries are often well-institutionalized practices, even among the region's more authoritarian regimes. Ascending communications of this kind—typically involving complaints about the arbitrariness of bureaucrats, requests for exemptions from regulations, and pleas for employment—are rarely dealt with systematically or allowed to influence public policy. Still, any practices that raise the levels of elite mediation can carry systemwide consequences. Even the appearance of remedy through appellate means strengthens the image of the moral superiority of the national leadership among mass publics. Conversely, the belief that only those grievances able to short-circuit regular channels stand a chance of redress may increase cynicism about the bureaucracy.

Urban dwellers seeking satisfaction of various requests through bureaucratic channels frequently confront a broad array of possible contact points. Much of their time may be given over to locating a responsible civil servant or finding appropriate modes of approach. The appearance of government specialists among rural populations is obviously one hallmark of modernization. Health and agricultural officials and teachers have joined the more traditional specialists: the gendarmerie and the tax officials. Yet, whether in ascending or descending transactions with government, the prime axis of mediation for the rural masses runs through two sets of intermediaries: the district governor and the village headman. As Frey and Roos found in rural Turkey, each furnishes critical links between the rural populations and the national policy elites (1967, pp. 67–69).

The district governor varies across systems in terms of his authority and the extent of his contact with the population he oversees. Almost everywhere, however, he is identifiable as the lowest-ranking appointed official (with origins typically outside the community) holding general administrative responsibilities. In Turkey, the *kaymakam* exercises broad supervisory powers over specialized agencies of the Ankara government and is superior to a subdistrict chief or a village headman (*muhtar*). In turn, the kaymakam is answerable to the provincial governor, and through him, to the Ministry of Interior. Szyliowicz designates the kaymakam as the person in the best position to determine the observance of government regulations locally. As such, the district governor's willingness to intervene is a prerequisite for rural development in Turkey (1966, p. 130). Szyliowicz found the kaymakam "taking the lead in persuading local elites of the significance of new decrees" as well as "a source of new ideas." Additionally, the district governor in this study was observed to spend at least half of his time listening to complaints from the local populace and was called upon to adjudicate grievances between individuals and the state (1966, p. 130).

The Iranian *bakhshdar* (district governor) is clearly less pivotal in the administrative hierarchy. Bill describes how the bakhshdar has traditionally operated within a closed network of influence and graft and has usually earned the distrust of the peasantry. Many of these district governors were removed, however, when the Tehran government acted to tighten its control over the countryside in 1964. Appointed to replace them were recent university graduates, slated for on-the-job training prior to entry into the Ministry of Interior (Bill 1972, pp. 112–17). As could be anticipated, these young and often idealistic appointees attracted the resentment of local elites as well as some higher provincial officials. Many of the young bakhshdars resigned. But at least some persevered by drawing closer to the peasants and winning their confidence. The attempt of the educated bakhshdars to remain at the same time responsive to the pressures of the villagers and the demands of their superiors was unique in the history of administration in rural Iran.

Among the more specialized government agents, educators have recently become the most permanent fixtures in villages and lower class urban enclaves. At least in theory, the educational system is directly responsible for narrowing the social and ideological distances within societies. Programs to impart a functional literacy to the masses have been the most conventional means of closing the gap. More impressive headway has been realized in recent years in the transference of technical skills, especially when young, educated cadres have been assigned to rural areas. In a larger sense, everyone involved in mass secular education is part of a vanguard bringing an awareness and acceptance of modernizing goals and symbols. Their task has often proven an onerous one, and their efforts may sometimes be dysfunctional. Much of the frustrations of the newly

educated and their estrangement from established elites can be traced to out-
moded educational practices and an absence of job opportunities for the additional graduates. Educational growth has also heightened, if unintentionally, the
consciousness and impatience of the rural and urban masses and given them
potential political leaders. The result is not only a more authentic picture of
national requirements and demands for top policy elites, but also the occasion
for increased government vigilance and popular manipulation.

In turning to educators and other administrators to mediate system change,
formidable problems of bureaucratic structure and attitudes confront modernizing regimes. Major obstacles exist not only to the conscientious supervision of
government programs, but also to the gathering and interpretation of the kinds
of technological and political information on which realistic development plans
are based. The concentration of bureaucratic authority in a national capital,
once viewed as a necessary antidote to nonconformist and incompatible exercises of regional power, has made unwieldy and defensive bureaucracies commonplace in the Middle East. So long as national leaders were content simply to
sustain a privileged few through government employment and favors and deal
minimally with a citizenry, inefficient and insular bureaucracies were tolerable,
even desirable. But when governments have been ambitious to affect major social
and economic changes, they have usually found older administrative processes
and personnel an impediment. Practices designed to assure administrative discipline and hierarchy have stifled initiative, and administrators' fear of assuming
responsibilities have no doubt inhibited effective interactions with public clienteles. Because bureaucracies in the region have frequently proven resistant to
renovation in people and ideas, many of their mediate functions have necessarily
passed to political parties and related institutions. Decentralization provides an
alternate solution for bypassing bureaucratic networks of influence and reciprocity. The formal delegation of wider authority to newer government agencies in
the provinces and the creation of locally elected councils are stated policies of
several nations of the region. While these reforms are not likely, in the forsee-
able future, to draw off real decisional power from the center, decentralized
structures could conceivably improve the appetites and talents of local elites for
representation and bargaining with a national leadership.

MILITARY ELITES

Familiar distinctions between civilian and military bureaucracies quickly
break down in the Middle East. There is nothing comparable to the liberal
western notion of separate but unequal spheres, in which the serious intrusion of
the military upon civilian affairs is thought a temporary aberration of government. The blurring of military and civilian boundaries is hardly a new phenomenon. Islamic history abounds with examples of army chiefs serving as viziers in

the royal courts or gaining the ascendance over their masters without raising questions of legitimacy (see Khadduri 1955, pp. 171-72). Ataturk's determination to make the separation of military and civilian a matter of principle is almost without parallel. In most contemporary states of the region, members of the military regularly enter civilian officialdom, usually carrying with them their military frame of mind and obligations. (A reverse flow of teachers and other government employees into military careers is similarly observable.) Former army officers move easily into the national and secret police, and the administrative experiences of higher-ranking officers lead many to managerial posts in government-run enterprises (see Polk 1965, p. 228). Indeed, retired military officers are especially attracted to those government agencies directly in contact with and intermediary to large publics.

Peretz finds in Egypt that the bureaucratic ranks of local administration, labor, and youth ministries as well as the ASU are constantly replenished by former military officers (1971, p. 223). Hurewitz observes the efficacious use of the Egyptian army to train a civilian leadership (1969, pp. 161-62). Even so, the steady exchange of personnel does not obviate the fact that institutional rivalries between civilian and military bureaucracies overshadow cooperation in Egypt as in much of the Middle East. The impatience of ambitious officers with indolent and inept bureaucrats prompts coups aimed not only at conservative regimes, but also against military-dominated governments. Dissident officers are tempted to try their own hand at governing after contrasting the military's sense of mission and discipline with that of government ministries. As Halpern puts it, "Being closest to the ruling elite and knowing its faults so well, an army which failed to act would seem to implicate itself in the misdeeds of the elite" (1963, p. 260).

An earlier professional military had limited itself to periodic forays to pacify dissident populations, while a gendarmerie enforced the local authority of the landlord and other traditional leaders. Today, the military and the local police together operate to secure central government power and to mediate the implementation of national policies. The military is asked to assume direction of development projects, relief operations, and popular education of a rudimentary, technical, and political kind. Educational activities allow for the military's most extensive contacts with the rural masses and occasion its best opportunities for amplificatory and interpretative functions. To illustrate the Iranian military's intended "second stratum" role, translating the Shah's policies to nonelites, Zonis reports that 44,000 army recruits were participating in literacy instruction in some 22,000 villages during 1969 (1975, p. 196; 1971, p. 114). Further, with the advent of mass armies, many governments have seized on the military as a vehicle of modernization through the education of "captive" lower class recruits.

The notably middle class origins of the officer corps in the region go far to explain the military's extensive political involvement and its limits in an intermediary role. This also reflects the realities of class transformation in the Middle

East, even in those countries that pride themselves on socialist institutions and values. Aside from isolated cases of upward mobility, the military's upper echelons are normally a privileged group whose contempt for lower class recruits impairs their popular image as well as their combat effectiveness. Only the Algerian army, as a result of its protracted popular struggle against the French, can make claims to having promoted through the ranks many of peasant background. Still, efforts during the Boumediene regime to portray a "people's army" to the Algerian public were weakly credible in view of the army's relatively good pay and perquisites (Ottaway and Ottaway 1970, p. 97). Like the gendarmerie and secret police, the military has denied to it the confidence or the affection of the masses. However, increased activity as a mediator of control allows few people to be ignorant or indifferent to its presence.

Close ties between the military and particular sectors of a society are not uncommon. The Syrian army illustrates how a military establishment can serve as a bridge to national political power for economically-deprived ethnic and sectarian minorities (see Vatikiotis 1972, p. 230). The clan loyalties of bedouin officers in King Hussayn's army strengthen their control over the lower ranks and also assures the backing of Jordan's larger tribes. In Iran, the Tudeh party's strategically-located cells in the military provided clandestine, descending linkages to working classes until uprooted in the purges of 1954.

Yet Apter's general proposition that military and civilian bureaucracies "can manipulate power but cannot generate it" seems in the main applicable to mediation in the Middle East (1965, pp. 117–18). No military establishment has succeeded in matching the Turkish army in stoking mass political awareness, and none has exhibited the organizational skills necessary to substitute for the mobilizing potential of a mass party. Until it disintegrated early in the civil war, the small Lebanese army had furnished timely brokerage in resolving conflicts between major national groups when the delicate constitutional balances were threatened. But the region's military and police are rarely credited with an active role in interest aggregation. As Halpern argues, the military's talents for agitation and conspiracy among small groups are not duplicated in their use of persuasion and mediation among larger groups (1963, p. 273). And, for all their discipline and wide dissemination of commands downward, military bureaucracies seem poorly designed and motivated to monitor popular sentiments or to transmit them to national elites.

MEDIA ELITES

Occupying positions astride the major lines of vertical communication, mass media specialists in the Middle East are an increasingly indispensable elite. Journalists, television and radio personnel, cinema producers and writers, and experts in public relations are the managers and operatives in an overexpanding diffusion of messages through society. Lerner observes how "mediated experience through mass communications" has multiplied an earlier physical experience through transportation in spreading modern values (1958, p. 52). Even more than the agents of mass parties, media elites are offspring of a modernization process that looks to them, along with local opinion leaders, to link a nation's periphery with its center. No elite seems to have a greater stake or to be more intimately involved in rapid societal change.

Ottoman reformers of the late nineteenth century had been the first to rely on newspapers to spread ideas of modernization. It was left to Kemalist Turkey, however, to exhibit the region's first uninhibited use of the press and radio to fashion a public opinion and to construct a national identity. Karpat quotes Ataturk as saying that the media's extensive part in "indoctrination and information" has assumed no less importance than the army's role in winning over the people (1964, p. 170). The appeal of a controlled press for the would-be modernizer was even apparent in Afghanistan, where King Amanullah, a contemporary of Ataturk, tried vainly to employ a press to rally the nation's small literate public (see Gregorian 1969, p. 245). Today, no regime in the Middle East that seeks popular support and hopes to temper political expression is likely to depreciate the utility of the mass media for transmitting elite policies and expectations. While the printed media remain largely targeted for urban publics, radio, television, and the cinema are obviously not limited by conditions of literacy, and the size of their audience is decreasingly determined by economics.

The very thoroughness with which the mass media have permeated Middle East societies explains a tendency to exaggerate the impact of elite communications to the masses. As already noted, any notions of clear vertical channels rest on possibly-unwarranted assumptions about the receptivity of mass publics and usually overestimate the skills and sagacity of top leaders. More directly, assertions of media omnipotence usually ignore the participation of media intermediaries in the shaping and relaying of messages.

Ostensibly, most media specialists seem restricted to amplifying government news handouts and otherwise serving as siphons for regime demands on the larger society. The electronic media are everywhere a government monopoly and, with the notable and ephemeral exception of Turkey, all in recent years have been servile to government directives. A relatively independent press survives in Lebanon, Israel, and Turkey, but elsewhere in the region newspapers are either government-owned or carefully regulated, usually in the name of curbing sensationalism and irresponsibility. The sizable press in several countries that remains in private hands is ordinarily beset with censors or has been socialized to the permissible boundaries of discourse. While some media elites may earn honorific posts and even be invited to the inner circles, most are deliberately kept in an economically precarious and dependent position.

These realities do not obviate the proposition that intermediaries are integral to the transmission of messages through the mass media. The necessary translation of government policies into broadly communicative language and images injects the media specialist personally and often subjectively into the communication process. The expertise of national level media elites is regularly in demand for programming aimed at particular regional, ethnic audiences and for sharpening middle class attitudes. In possession of technological and political skills, these media elites help establish the credibility of messages and become natural allies of top elites in stimulating mass feelings. Much of the credit for the frenzied support governments are often able to generate among a citizenry results from the highly emotional rhetoric and use of analogies by radio commentators (see Harris 1958, pp. 99-100). Lerner points out how citizens of varied social classes are spurred to a continuous state of excitement by the "vibrant opinion" of newscasters (1958, p. 234).

Journalists and editorial writers are employed to float "trial balloons" for policy elites, and a controlled press may be invited to supply a system "auto-critique," intended to reveal wrongdoing among low-ranking officials and failures in low priority policies. The more rare occasions when media elites are authorized to reveal major policy setbacks and attach blame to high level officials usually herald changes in personnel and programs. Many commentators in the region develop national followings and are perceived as influentials in their own right. Mohammad Haykal, former editor of Al-Ahram, is probably the most glaring example. Haykal's status as unofficial spokesman for President Nasser brought him extraordinary prominence and influence, so much so that it became impossible to separate his views from those of Nasser—which probably argues for his placement among the highest of Nasser's policy elites rather than in a second stratum. Under Sadat, Haykal had increasingly to compete with other opinion makers, most notably the Akhbar group (Vatikiotis 1973, p. 8). Following Haykal's departure in 1974, no journalist was permitted to acquire the stature he had once enjoyed.

Distortions of government-initiated messages by national-level media specialists are illustrated in Turkey over two periods. Public countenance of a competitive press enabled anti-Menderes newspapers to circumvent many of the repressive press laws imposed by the prime minister between 1955 and 1960. Karpat relates how prior to the jailing of journalists and the permanent suspension of many newspapers, "the press could still inform the public of its position by mixing innuendo with news" (1964, pp. 279-80). During the 1960s, employees of the government-owned Turkish Radio and Television (TRT) made little effort to disguise their ideological biases in programming and commentary. Protected by constitutional provisions designed to safeguard against excesses of the Menderes regime, media elites sought to embarrass the Demirel government at every turn. Their boldness no doubt hastened the ruling party's fall in 1971, but it also helped to provoke the military's crackdown against the Left and to strip the TRT of its autonomous status.

Opportunities for manipulation and distortion predictably increase with the distance from the point of transmission and the number of mediators close to intended audiences. Earlier discussion has pointed out how politically-inattentive populations may rely on local elites for the amplification and interpretation of media communications. The degree and kind of modifications that occur logically vary with the identity of the intermediary and are not unrelated to the social context and the conditions of media accessibility. In rural Turkey, the empirical evidence of Frey and Roos (1967) shows that headmen stand at the center of village influence networks. While the investigators did not look specifically at the headman as mediator of media information, they discovered that as the general level of a village's acquaintance with radios, newspapers, and the cinema grew, the headman's influence *increased*. They also found that the headman could be distinguished from other villagers by his greater exposure to these same outside sources (1967, pp. 23, 40–41). It seems therefore reasonable to conclude that not only are the artifacts of modernity no threat to this traditional (but administratively-integrated) local official, but that the headman as opinion leader filters incoming information to simultaneously enhance his reputation and suit village prejudices.

However, findings that discount the importance of the two-step flow of descending messages are found in Harik's intensive study of rural communication behavior in an Egyptian village. Harik discovered that most peasants (48 percent) acquire their information on the major issues directly from the mass media; moreover, this link strengthens with the availability of radios and other channels. The same study also reveals that a substantial minority (37 percent), including a disproportionate number of illiterates, rely on mediators for their news (1971, pp. 732–35). Interestingly, Harik reports that these intermediaries are not traditional types, but are young, educated party representatives, professionals, and locally-elected officials, some of them outsiders to the village. By assuring conformity to government policies, most mediate "control" along with their highly purposeful interpretations of the media news (1971, p. 736). These findings fail to support the previous speculation that pressures for mediation may grow as incoming commands increase. The data do, all the same, demonstrate how local mediation occurs side by side with transmissions from above, much of it mediated nationally. The extent to which elites with modern values and resources have replaced older status types as opinion leaders sets Egypt apart from those Middle East countries in which less revolutionary changes have taken place at the community level.

The technical advances that tend to facilitate rapid and unimpeded transmissions from elites to masses are largely unidirectional. Media institutions seem poorly structured to handle a return flow of information to decision makers. The concentration of media specialists in the national capital and the major cities naturally limits the range of their possible representational and monitorial functions. Few media elites are recruited from the lower classes and, more importantly, professional norms do not encourage grass roots reporting. What feedback mechanisms the media elites do provide are therefore necessarily impressionistic, heavily subject to perceptual screens and editorial policies.

The most direct channels of ascending articulations are obviously through paid advertisements and letters to the editor. The former is mainly reserved for more affluent and organized citizens. Although the latter is also a vehicle for literate and attentive individuals, letters do frequently give a good picture of popular views. It is quite common for a newspaper in the Middle East to carry a letter berating a government ministry or calling attention to a community's need for a new road or school. More informally, specialized publics and interest elites frequently seek to cultivate friendly journalists and other media personnel. In countries in which publicists are largely unrestricted in selecting letters and other news items and may express editorial opinion freely, the press can be a strong if not always accurate mirror of public feelings. Overall, the level of bilateral communications between political elites and their publics through the media is one good measure of the openness of national policy processes. The more hierarchical the regime, the less likely it is to rely on media feedback and the more probable that it will turn to other mediating structures to provide the level of information necessary to keep abreast of popular expectations and demands.

CONCLUSION

The foregoing discussions of intermediary institutions describe communication structures all too often slighted in studies of mass-elite relations. It is frequently more convenient to lump together those identified here as mediating elites with primary policy makers or to associate them with mass publics. Admittedly, intermediary groups and individuals are at times initiatory of values and policies for a society and may feel the impact of authoritative decisions in a way indistinguishable from nonelites. But these discussions have sought to illustrate the broad middle ground for intermediary activity and the reality of several mediate functions. Besides the more familiar forms of intermediary behavior, a wider scope of activity, including the pervasive mediations of control, is described at length. In general, the six mediate functions are found both manifest and latent in Middle East political systems. Linkages assume variously direct and indirect forms, and communication channels are subject to high levels of interference and distortion as well as relatively clear, unimpeded transmissions.

This chapter differentiates levels of activity among intermediary elites and considers the interdependence of the several mediating institutions. Figure 6.1 summarizes these findings. The diagram calls attention to two structures, party and bureaucracy, that provide relatively strong descending and ascending medi-

FIGURE 6.1

Linkages Between Highest Policy Elites and Mass Publics
and Among Intermediary Elites (in Representative
Middle East Political Systems)

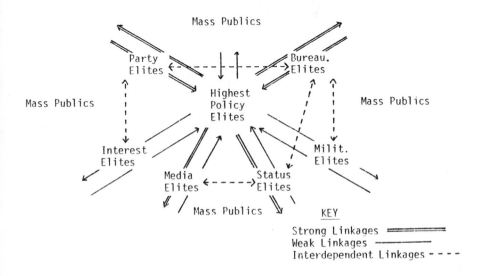

ations. It also indicates the comparatively weak ascending mediations for local status and media elites in the contemporary period. While the possibility of unmediated linkages between the public and primary elites is recognized, the weakness of these connections is also indicated. Figure 6.1, in addition, stresses the pivotal role of bureaucratic elites in the interdependence of the several mediation structures. It points out a subnetwork of party, bureaucracy, and local status elites, implying a high degree of functional overlapping and substitution. Other conspicuous interdependencies are pointed out, notably those between party and interest elites and between local status and media elites. Reliable coefficients of association naturally require focused empirical studies of communication patterns. All the same, the evidence assembled here suggests much about the direction and magnitude of these relationships.

TABLE 6.1

Level of Mediating Functions by Elites
(In Representative Middle East Political Systems)

Mediating Elites	Mediating Practices					
	Amplification	Interpretation	Control	Monitorial	Representational	Bargaining
Local status	Moderate	High	Moderate	Moderate	High	Moderate
Party	High	High	High	High	Moderate	Low
Interest	Moderate	Moderate	Moderate	Moderate	High	Low
Bureaucratic	High	High	High	High	Moderate	Low
Military	Moderate	Moderate	High	Moderate	Low	Low
Media	High	High	Low	Moderate	Low	Low

Note: Assessments are relative to the elites examined, rather than to some standard.

Source: Compiled by author.

Also by way of synopsis, Table 6.1 associates the general levels of mediate activity with the several intermediary structures. Each assessment is, of course, made relative to the elites examined, rather than against some absolute standards of mediate activity. Moreover, the levels are assigned by reference to clientele publics rather than for a larger system. Understandably, Table 6.1 condenses much that has already been observed, especially the greater weight of descending functions over ascending ones. Additionally, the table points out the often uneven nature of mediation. Most notably, party is not uniformly high, nor is military uniformly low. Similarly, and perhaps more expectedly, performance of some mediate functions differs markedly among elite structures. Representational mediations vary most among elites, whereas amplificatory and interpretative activities appear more alike.

That mediating elites are implicated in societal change is a constant theme throughout these discussions. Mass-elite linkages clearly mark the most sweeping changes in a nation's political culture, integration, authority structure, and technology. Because this chapter has focused on Middle East political systems, attention has been drawn to the widely observed transformation from communal societies. Traditional intermediaries, operating largely through primary relationships, have sometimes been found swept away, though the evidence more often points to their adaptation to modernizing processes. New, more impersonal, and specialized institutions have also emerged in what appears as an intensified demand for structures to mediate between the state and its citizens. But mediate elites have not always measured up to societal requirements. Moreover, mediating practices, adequate for some systems and periods, have at times proven unsuitable for others. Forms of representation and control that serve as appropriate instruments of modernization at an early phase of modernization may, for example, inhibit or deter change later.

The scope and intensity of mediate activity has, as is illustrated in Figure 6.2, risen with modernization in the Middle East. Figure 6.2 also indicates that the uneven expansion of the several functions with societal change has somewhat altered their relative salience. While amplification and control have generally shown the steepest increases with the passage to more complex societies, representational and bargaining functions have risen more slowly. Overall, more communication channels, many of them reciprocal, link elite and mass publics. Horizontal communications within each sector also tend to expand where liberalizing processes have accompanied change. Indeed, societies that move in pluralist or authoritarian directions often prescribe sharply differing intermediary relationships. As has been observed, intermediary structures may be absorbed by the largely inclusive policies of authoritarian regimes. Yet the features of change in the region are sufficiently homogeneous and intermediary elites sufficiently independent to permit some generalization about the systemic consequences of mediate activity.

FIGURE 6.2

Levels of Mediation under Conditions of Societal Change in Middle East

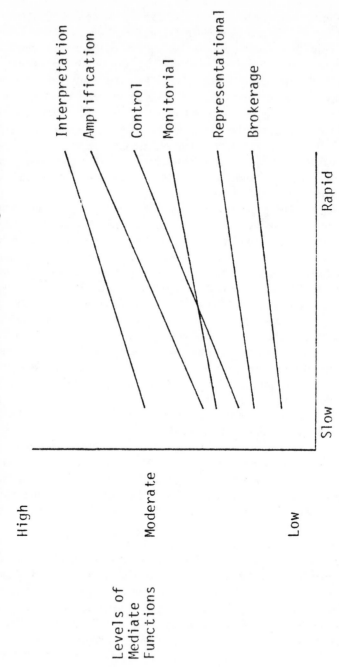

Problems of orderly and coherent system change cannot be separated from the conditions of over- and underdeveloped intermediary structures. More specifically, the analysis here bears out the proposition that *system instability and a low capacity for social and economic growth are associated with both autonomous mediating structures and atrophied or inactive ones. Highly mediated commands and demands increase distortion and reduce the chances of rational, coordinated activity. Weakly mediated communications may hinder the exposure of the masses to commands, reduce the clarity of information to policy makers, and overload their capacity to satisfy demands.* Logically, then, mediating elites that instead facilitate planned change in the Middle East tend to share the fundamental values and interests of primary elites without abdicating intermediary responsibilities. Highly independent intermediary institutions, which often secure nonelites in traditional societies and bring accountability of top elites in pluralistic ones, are thus likely to inhibit system change. Regimes that have, on the contrary, destroyed most intermediary structures in the process of directly mobilizing masses are often obliged to base development plans on unreal public attitudes and expectations and to tolerate ambiguously and inappropriately implemented policies.

The indispensability of mediating institutions ultimately rests on the enduring material and psychological gap that exists between masses and elites in the Middle East. It also reflects the generally slow progress toward national political and social integration that, for the time being, precludes a mass society in which elites and nonelites are directly exposed to one another or a mature totalitarian society with its elite dominance (see Kornhauser 1969, pp. 74–82). All the same, political relations in the Middle East have been radically transformed. Leaders are increasingly obliged to appeal for mass supports in order to retain power and to undertake desired economic development. Followers' heightened consciousness of their political roles and growing awareness of the opportunities to compete for expanding national resources encourage them to press for greater access to policy elites. As elites and masses reach out to one another, the necessary services of mediating institutions and actors become more apparent and the linkages they provide more critical to political development.

7

THE IMPACT OF ELITES AND
THEIR FUTURE STUDY

Russell A. Stone

Two "generations" of Middle Eastern elite studies have been identified in Chapter 1 of this volume. This chapter will attempt to suggest some directions for a third generation of research and theory construction. Much elite analysis to date received its current thrust from the work of Harold Lasswell and associates, beginning around 1950 (Lasswell, Lerner, and Rothwell 1952, Lasswell 1965). Many Middle Eastern elite studies have been carried out by followers of his ideas. These have concentrated on two of the three major approaches to elite study Lasswell outlined in an early work: the *contextual approach*, which highlights the social and political structures in terms of which the elite operate; and the *social process approach*, which stresses interactions among elite members and between them and their social and physical environment (Lasswell 1965, pp. 6-10). The former is similar to the analysis of processes of absorption and blockage, recruitment, promotion, and dismissal, and the latter resembles the analysis of socialization, social class background, training, and attitude formation. These concepts have been discussed in Chapter 1 as characterizing the major concerns of Middle Eastern elite analysis at the present time.

The third major approach indicated by Lasswell, the *decision process*, has received less attention. This should relate the elites themselves and the context in which they operate to the social consequences of elite existence and action (Lasswell 1965, pp. 10-12). Chapter 1 refers to these as policies, behaviors, and organizations established by elites. It is remarkable to recognize that students of Middle Eastern elites have closely followed Lasswell's agenda for research, in more-or-less chronological order (ibid.). We are beginning to have answers to questions such as: Who are they [elite participants]? What are their perspectives? In what arenas do they function? What base values are at their disposal? What strategies do they use? (The terminology has changed over the years, but the focus of inquiry has been followed.) However, to the last question in this context,

"How successful are they in influencing outcomes and effects," we have fewer and less satisfying answers.

Implicit in Lasswell's work is the suggestion that once we understand who elites are, how they emerged, and how they operate, this knowledge should lead us to study and ultimately to understand their impact on the societies they lead. Most studies of Middle Eastern elites do provide interesting descriptions of the composition of elite groups, informed by one or another theoretical perspective (attitudes, psychological factors, recruitment and socialization, or social class background). However, if one searches the conclusions of these studies for indications of how the findings relate to important decisions or policies, of how the composition of the elite affects the course of social or political change, the search yields few findings. Given the growing amount of available data and insight, this chapter will attempt to outline what kinds of new research approaches are necessary to answer the question posed in Chapter 1: "What do [elites] do with their power?" What are the consequences or implications of the background and composition of elite classes for the society as a whole? Can differences in these characteristics of elites be related to differences in government policies and programs, political stability, social change, or the effectiveness of attempts at modernization? This approach leads us into the fascinating area of prediction in the social sciences, the ability to move beyond descriptive or even explanatory research design to an ability to hypothesize about future events or predict possible alternative directions in social and political change.

The problem will be approached in three steps. The first section will summarize the theoretical perspectives used in Middle East elites studies to date, abstracting all the major variables used in the available studies. These will be organized into a scheme that suggests causal relationships among the variables, points to gaps in our knowledge, and focuses our attention on the dependent variables, which an understanding of elites can help explain. The second section will address some general methodological problems involved in bringing elite studies from their current concentration on single-shot and single-country inquiries to more general and/or comparative conclusions, which will also move our understanding in a future-oriented direction. The third section will introduce five specific study topics or methodological approaches that can be applied to Middle Eastern elites to help us find answers to the questions posed here.

THEORETICAL PERSPECTIVES

Four general approaches to the study of elites can be identified in the literature. These can be viewed as different groupings of independent variables, components of a general theoretical causal model that characterizes existing

Middle Eastern elites. Many studies do consider more than one of the four approaches. However, very few utilize all four dimensions.

The model will be sketched in terms of the abstract variables, with illustrative examples of Middle Eastern elites studies that exemplify different theoretical stresses. Then, a second, more detailed model will be presented, which can direct future research toward analysis of the consequences of elite characteristics for the society as a whole and for future directions of elite change.

The typology presented in Figure 7.1 shows the relationships among the four approaches. The top row, cells A and B, represents studies of the *political structures* in terms of which elites operate. The bottom row, cells C and D, represents studies of the *personal attributes or characteristics* of elite members, individually or aggregated into a collective portrait of elite characteristics. Viewing the same typology in terms of the columns, the first column, cells A and C, represents *historical or process dimensions* of elites, how they have circulated within the political structure (or how the structure itself has changed over time), and the background from which individuals have moved into elite positions. The second column, cells B and D, represents *current structures or characteristics* of elites, organized in such a way that they can be compared among countries in the region. A third column should be present, but few studies have attempted to include it. If the first column deals with the relevant past, and the second column with the *present* situation, then a logical addition would be *future trends* in political structures and elite characteristics. Later in this chapter, we will return to the possibilities for exploring this question.

FIGURE 7.1

Theoretical Perspectives: General Orientations

		Background Processes and Origins i	Current Conditions and Orientations ii	Future Directions and Viable Forms iii
Political Structures	I	A Recent History Elite Circulation	B Current Form of Political Structure	
Attributes of Elite Members	II	C Social Background and Preparation	D Attitudes Personality Motivation	

The role of elites in the recent history of political structures (cell A, Figure 7.1) can be discussed within the context of political groups (Sahelians in Tunisia, mujahidin in Algeria, army officers in Egypt or Syria, members of the Saudi royal family, and so on) or of political parties (where relevant), elections (Turkey's ruralizing election of 1950), coups, or cabinet shuffles. Analysis has usually focused on the causes of these changes and how they have affected the make-up of active elite groups. Few existing studies have investigated the consequences for society of elite composition or changes in membership, although it can be safely predicted that the 1979 revolution in Iran, led by religious leaders, will stimulate research of this nature.

To date, however, recent analyses with this theoretical orientation have focused on the abstraction of recognizable patterns of events from the day-to-day flow of political life as it cumulates into recent history. These abstracted patterns can then become building blocks in a general theory. Such a study is exemplified by Chapter 4, by Weinbaum's (1975) recent comparative analysis of changes in Middle Eastern elites, and by Hermassi's (1972) study of political leadership in the Maghreb. Among the political process variables identified through this approach are bunching within elite groups by people of similar age, education, or informal association ties, blockages of demands and needs, elite circulation, political generations, informal networks, mediation processes, and institution building. Moving outside the Middle East to other works on political modernization, the well-known early attempt at a general theory by Almond, Coleman, Pye, and others resulted in the identification of process variables such as interest articulation and interest aggregation. This form of analysis has lent itself to a few comparative studies aimed at deriving or testing the applicability of the abstracted patterns, including Moore's (1970) work on North Africa.

While the theory-building dimension of this approach is no doubt attractive, its ultimate usefulness is dependent upon pressing for answers to questions such as: When bunching within the elite results in blockages of demands from new need-bearing groups, what are the possible outcomes of need articulation? Do some historical patterns tend to result in different resolutions from other patterns? (For example: Are there similarities between the Alawite-dominated Syrian elite and the Sahelian-dominated Tunisian elite, similarities which will transcend the fact that one is a religious minority group and the other a regional entity? Do all military coups result in civilianization of the military elite or revolutionary command council? Will the military eventually be succeeded in countries where it is in power? How, and by whom?)

Current forms of political structure (cell B, Figure 7.1) refer to political organization frameworks rather than to processes and changes. Each individual country can be viewed as a case in an essentially comparative frame. Middle Eastern countries can be characterized along a number of crosscutting dimensions of structure. All of these can be used to compare countries, and together they form a multivariate model for comparative analysis. One approach could be to break down countries by monarchies versus republics. Republics in turn can be considered as monolithic (single party as Tunisia or military-dominated as Syria) versus pluralistic (Turkey, Israel). Alternately, the degree of military domination can be compared across monarchies and the two types of republics. Do differences exist between regimes in which the military does and does not play an active role in supporting a traditional monarch or king (Morocco or pre-1979 Iran versus Saudi Arabia or Jordan)? Are there differences between countries in which military leaders came to power through a coup or a series of coups (Syria, Iraq) and countries in which military leaders are national heroes in the fight for independence (Algeria) or were active in overthrowing the monarchy (Egypt, Libya)?

Other relevant structural characteristics include alternate centers of power, sources of new leaders or an elite pool within which the circulation of elites takes place, degree of stability, ruling elite composition, and rules or precedents for succession to power (peaceful or violent, predictable or unpredictable). Also relevant are bases for legitimacy of leadership, which might fall among the lines of monarchy, military, or nationalist movement as previously indicated, and the role of religion both as a focus for nationalism and as a basis for sub-group divisions within the elite. A final element in political structure is the extent and type of outside political influence in the internal political affairs of the various Middle Eastern countries. This includes the dimensions of East-West alliance or competition, sources of foreign exchange (oil income versus inter-national aid and World Bank loans), and the relationship between receiving for-eign military-technical assistance and having to accept foreign involvement in military defense on site or in foreign policy affairs.

Analysis of correlations among these variables in a study comparing all the countries of the Middle East can indicate which sets of variables tend to be associated together within one country and can answer questions such as: What structural features are more likely to emerge under military regimes? With which forms are they most consistent? Are there emerging predictable patterns of succession or circulation of elites? These questions all address themselves to the general issue of the nature of political modernization in the Middle East, based on models and events emerging in the area itself and not on an adapted idealized version of political development in the West.

Social class background of elites (cell C, Figure 7.1) refers to studies that have shifted the emphasis to the training, socialization, or preparation aspects of the elite members themselves, individually or aggregated, to indicate propor-tions within the elite class as a whole. Variables used here can include tribalism, ethnicity, religion or religious sect (for example, Christians versus Moslems in Lebanon, Alawites versus Sunnis in Syria), occupation, amount or type of edu-cation (such as law or engineering versus traditional religious studies; the faculty or school attended), political generation or cohort, informal networks, regional-ism (rural-urban, agrarian-nomadic, or specific regions of the country as mountains or plains), or social class (urban upper middle class versus peasant origin, against the social structure of the particular country) (Searing 1969).

These categories are obviously overlapping and repetitive as presented here. Thus, studies using this perspective have tended to choose from within this list a few mutually exclusive concepts specifically relevant to the particular country being studied. For an example from Egypt, see Moore (1974). Unfortunately, few studies use the same specific variables or, if they do, the variables are often conceptualized or measured in different ways. For instance, in an attitude survey section of the Roos and Roos study of Turkish administrative elites, "politicians" were viewed as a single occupational group, in contrast with business managers, lawyers, diplomats, engineers, and so on (1971, p. 162). However, in an earlier study in Turkey, Frey showed that only 296 of 1,988 (15 percent) of the studied "politicians" (National Assembly deputies) had no occupation other than government employ (1965, p. 96). All others could be identified with some other specific occupation. Thus, if a comparison were to be made, should the occupations of elites be considered "politician," or military, teacher, lawyer, doctor, business manager, religious leader, and so on?

The most interesting new use to which these kinds of variables can be put is to study the extent to which social background characteristics are associated with (or perhaps determine) the attitudes and interests of elite groups, then, in turn, whether these identified attitudes and interests can be used to predict future actions of elite groups. For instance, is a country whose elite has a relatively high proportion of people of rural origin more likely to institute agrarian reform? In a country with religious factions, does the religious group affiliation of the leader determine the affiliations of members of his cabinet, and does this result in disproportionate political and economic advantage to the religious group members involved? (These are longitudinal questions. By their nature, they cannot be solved with a one-time case study. A time lag is present between the formation of an elite and its access to power, with further time lagging between access to power and visible changes in the political and social structure.)

Finally, the attitudes, personality, and motivation of elite members (cell D, Figure 7.1) refer to studies based on collection of data from individual members of the elite class. This information can be aggregated to form portraits of the elite class as a whole, based on the measured attributes of the individuals, such as the Zonis (1971) study of Iran, or the study can focus on the impact of an individual elite personality on the society, such as parts of the Dekmejian study of *Egypt Under Nasir* (1971). Variables studied can include such personal characteristics as motivation, intelligence, ambition, attitudes, competence, or "charisma," as well as social background characteristics relevant to cell C, to the extent that they are determinates of individual traits. Note, for instance, the distinction between education as a personal characteristic (cell D)—highest degree achieved or academic record—and education as a social structural characteristic (cell C)—graduating from an "elite school" such as the Ankara Political

FIGURE 7.2

Theoretical Model with Variables

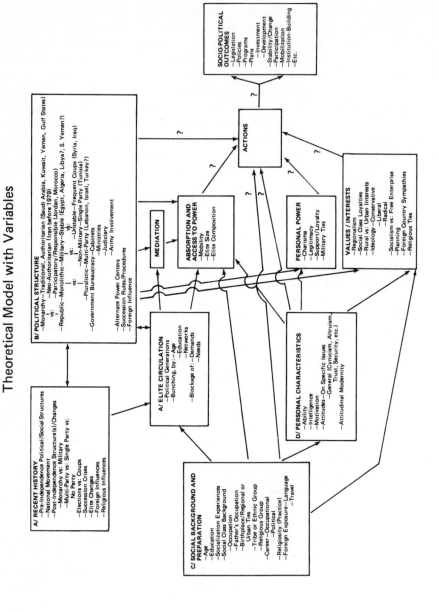

Science Faculty studied by Roos and Roos (1971). Traits such as achievement (*N Ach*), or media exposure, awareness, and empathy are also relevant here (Lerner 1958, McClelland 1961, Rogers 1969, Inkeles 1974). These character- istics of individuals result in attitudes toward political participation and, ulti- mately, in actions in the political and social arena. Few researchers may be as courageous as Zonis (1971) in revealing the insecurity, cynicism, mistrust, and exploitative attitudes of the former Iranian elite, but many other observers have commented, at least informally, on differences in "style" between elite groups or leaders in different countries, such as "cults of personality" (Moore 1970, p. 149). Others have attributed part of the problem in the ill-fated union between Egypt and Syria to differences in individual characteristics, not only between the heads of state, but between the respective elite classes more broadly defined (Dekmejian 1975, pp. 59, 62, 76, 105, 138). Clearly, personal ambition and style have stood in the way of Libyan President Kadaffi's many attempts to establish unions or looser federations with Egypt, Tunisia, Sudan, and Syria (First 1974).

Details of how the variables from the four theoretical perspectives can be aggregated into a block diagram that suggests a causal model of the determinants of elite characteristics and the impact of elites on society are presented in Figure 7.2. This model is preliminary and incomplete, while it is also much too complex. The variables included are those that have been used in the past and/or appear most fruitful for future analyses on the criteria of theoretical relevance, observability/measurability being subject to empirical research, and contribut- ing to new directions in elite research (to be suggested in the remainder of this chapter). In summarizing as much of the research as possible in block diagram format for compactness, we might be able to see possible relationships among variables that have not been associated in previous studies, but that might suggest fruitful re-analysis of existing data sets or the formulation of new studies based on combinations of existing methodologies.

The model highlights our meager knowledge of the *outcomes* of elite activities, or the extent to which knowledge about elites can be used to *predict* future events that elites are instrumental in bringing to pass. Concern for analysis of the backgrounds and make-up of elites in recent years must answer the question, "So what?" The model clearly indicates that attention must be turned to designing studies to settle issues such as those posed by Zartman: "We still have no idea why it matters to be among the 1917–37 cohort, to come from the Sahel, to have lower socioeconomic origins, or to have been a lawyer rather than a farmhand" (1975, p. 504). Before presenting examples of specific studies that are potentially fruitful for extending insights on the societal and political importance of elites, some more general changes in research methodol- ogy must be discussed.

METHODOLOGICAL APPROACHES

In the process of generating systematic knowledge about elites, the approach has generally been to focus attention on one country at a time. Given time and theoretical limitations, plus the problem of acquisition of language skills, this approach is quite understandable. Perhaps it is somewhat regrettable that researchers have chosen Turkey and Iran as early focuses of elite analysis, when choosing an Arabic-speaking country would have resulted in language skills more easily applied across a wider range of countries. However, the size and importance of those countries in the area is obvious justification. There is room for filling in studies of elites of many Middle Eastern countries that have not been the object of systematic research to date. While some information is available on virtually every state in the area, quality and quantity vary considerably, as do the perspectives of the researchers. Often elite analysis is a minor part of a more general work in politics or recent history.

Many researchers have also limited themselves to the analysis of one elite, or the group in power at a specific period of time. Some recent, ambitious elite analyses in the Middle East have moved beyond this problem by aggregating information over a very long period of time (Winder 1962-63, Frey 1965) or by comparing two groups at different points in time (Roos and Roos 1971). Generally, however, findings about change over time are rather meager in the literature, although many insights that do emerge are based in part on Middle Eastern sources (Quandt 1970, pp. 187-89). Again, changes in elites over time have not been related to consequential changes in the wider society.

In studies of one country or one time period, the unit of analysis tends to be the individual (elite member) or some subgroup, such as occupational class or age cohort within the elite. In the studies to be suggested, it is useful to shift concepts to a more macro level, using countries as units of analysis, or whole time periods in the case of longitudinal studies within one country. This shift will also give the studies a more regional emphasis, in the attempt to generate insights about Middle Eastern elites, rather than discrete national groups.

Comparative Analyses

Recognizing similarities and differences among elite structures in various countries of the Middle East permits the formulation of potential comparative studies to test the influence of different variables. Almost any concept from within the four sets of independent variables previously outlined can be chosen for comparison among countries in the area. The particular choice of a set of such variables would naturally be guided by pre-existing hypotheses, or failing that, by a factor analysis to determine which variables show the greatest variance among countries in the area. Often such studies, because they involve comparisons among different countries, will seek to draw upon existing data sets or characteristics of elites that can be determined without extensive field research.

For example, the question of whether a military government has predictable consequences for societal development can be evaluated in a paired comparison design that evaluates change patterns in Syria and Iraq, two countries with similar backgrounds of military regimes, and Egypt and Algeria, two more countries with similar experiences, but histories which differ from the first two. In the former case, military dominance in Syria and Iraq has survived despite series of military coups over an extended period of time in the immediate post-independence struggle for national solidarity. Both have military regimes in a true sense. Army officers compose most of the government elite, and the military plays an active role in many aspects of societal governance and control. Does this instability at the top within a military form of government result in more active military involvement in everyday life than would otherwise be the case? The contrasting situation emerges in Egypt and Algeria. The group of military leaders who led the fight for independence were able, within a short period of time, to establish a stable regime based on elite members who had been directly active in the struggle for independence. While many of the leaders are of military background, they have undergone a process of "civilianization" and, over the years, cease to be identified with the military, instead becoming a political elite. Nonmilitary elites have been recruited to high positions over the years, and the military is clearly subordinate to political control, rather than posing a potential threat to it. Thus one might hypothesize that the sooner a military regime stabilizes its leadership, overcoming resistance and establishing legitimacy, the more likely "civilianization" of the elite will occur. Given the well-established trend toward the initial emergence of military regimes in the Middle East and elsewhere in the Third World, this may be a more realistic line of inquiry than the previous stressing of participatory democracy by political development theorists.

Does this difference, in turn, have consequences for political stability, social change, or the emergence of new elites? Are subsequent coups less likely once the process of "civilianization" sets in? These questions can be investigated by examining the rates of access of new individuals to elite positions in countries that differ on the military-civilian variable. For instance, a study by Weinbaum (1975) could be re-analyzed to include crosstabulations showing whether changes in elites involved new people or merely reshuffling of existing members, to supplement the data presented on whether the new people moving in were of military or civilian background.

Differences between countries with young elite classes (Libya) versus more established elite groups (Egypt), elites of rural origin (Tunisia or Algeria) versus urbanized elites (Egypt or Lebanon), elites with traditional legitimation such as association with the royal family (Saudi Arabia, Iran, or Morocco) versus "new middle class" (Halpern 1963, pp. 51-78) elites (Turkey, Israel, Tunisia, or

Algeria) are all possibilities for comparative studies using the country at a given time period as the unit of analysis. Such studies would sort out the importance of the multitude of variables that analysts have used in the past (outlined in Figure 7.2), indicating which are most fruitful for further analysis, which can be abandoned as being irrelevant, and which are subsumed under or closely associated with others. By thus paring down the range of theoretically interesting and empirically relevant variables, theory building, systematic insights, and ideas for further research could be based on a more compact set of ideas. Also, such an approach might well point up surprising similarities or associations among countries in the area. In particular, the similarity of Israel, in many respects with many of the Arab countries in the area would undoubtedly emerge from such analysis (Dekmejian 1975, chap. 5). Perhaps similarities between Tunisia and Israel or between Algeria and Iran would highlight how scale of society or ecological conditions override differences in political structure or elite composition.

Ideally, such comparisons should be based on data gathered anew for the purposes of comparative study. From experience, attempts to use existing data sets, collected by different scholars and originally intended for disparate purposes, is seldom tractable for detailed, systematic comparative analysis (Stone 1973). Problems involved include differing definitions of variables, differing values or categories on variables (for instance, occupation categories seldom match exactly between studies), omitted data, varying time periods or dates of studies, and so on.

Unfortunately, the time and financial resources necessary to carry out a large scale comparative study, even in a limited geographical area such as the Middle East, limits the viability of the comparative approach based on all original data. Three alternate approaches to generating or obtaining good quality, comparable data can be envisioned.

First, new data can be collected on a few countries in a format to match previously existing data sets. This simply requires that researchers be aware of the details of previous questionnaires or data-collection instruments used in other Middle Eastern studies and design their own instruments to duplicate this data for a new country (or countries) at the stage of study design. Invariably, later researchers attempt to learn from the mistakes of previous studies, but improving the quality of data can be accomplished without ignoring the structure of existing data sets. More detail can easily be added while retaining pre-existing aggregated categories. The effort involves a willingness to build on the detailed work of others, rather than beginning conceptualization of variables anew with each study. Researchers tend to work with similar general theoretical concepts and ideas of what variables are relevant anyway. The added effort is in digging carefully into the early stages of the research of others and in previous researchers retaining and being willing to share the details of their instruments, which are not usually presented with research findings or even preserved when codebooks and data sets are stored in final "clean" format.

Second, comparative data can be generated from existing information not normally intended for such purposes. This may be in the form of government yearbooks, individual country statistics, events, biographical information, or even data from newspapers generated for use within a given country. The researcher's challenge is to locate information in similar format available from a large number of countries in the area. Two recent examples of such studies, one based on biographical data (Dekmejian 1975) and the other on political events (government changes) (Weinbaum 1975), indicate rising interest in the potential of this approach among Middle Eastern elites researchers.

Finally, some large data sets exist or are being compiled for use in comparative analysis. The first attempts were based on purely statistical sources. They were worldwide in scope and require "regionalization" if they are to be used for the Middle East alone. Later versions concentrated on political "events" and on political and social "indicators." Other sources were "regionalized" from the beginning, concentrating solely on the Middle East. Some provide a wide array of information, while others concentrate on one type of information, such as political and diplomatic documents. An excellent set of "yearbooks" (Europa) both update statistical data annually and provide in-depth analysis of current trends in the area as a whole and within individual countries of the Middle East. Some of these sources are in print only and must be converted to machine readable format for convenient comparative, multivariate analysis (Bacharach 1974, Hurewitz 1974). Other are already obtainable in computerized form (Banks and Textor 1963, Taylor and Hudson 1970). Once one researcher begins the comparative analysis process using these sources, hopefully his data and work will be available to others interested. Improvements in computer technology over the next few years should make this type of comparative data more easily accessible. Large data banks have operated for many years at the University of Michigan, the University of California at Berkeley, the University of Sussex, England, and in Holland (The Steinmetz Archives).

Many agencies of the United Nations have been paying considerable attention to the problem of gathering statistics from all the member nations and compiling and presenting them in a format that will facilitate comparisons. At present, the *United Nations Yearbook*, the *Demographic Yearbook*, and the *Yearbook of International Trade Statistics* provide some instructive methodological guidelines as well as data from which Middle Eastern subsets can be extracted. These can only provide background information to elite-related questions, but when combined with other data sets focusing on the elites, the potential for multivariate comparative analyses is enhanced. For instance, comparisons of rates of elite circulation can be related to country size, wealth, population growth rates, economic growth, or changes in rates of trade. The role of military elites can be related to rates of spending on the military or to political "events" that involve military readiness for violent confrontation.

Longitudinal Analyses

Longitudinal studies involve following a process of change over an extended period of time. Attempts have been made in some studies of Middle Eastern elites to monitor the group over a number of years (Frey 1965) or to compare attributes of elites at two points in time (Roos and Roos 1971). This approach does succeed in identifying patterns of change within the elite, emergent outcomes of the process of "circulation of elites," for what they are worth. For instance, ·Quandt identified increases, bell curves, decreases, and u-curves as patterns of change in levels of age and university education and proportions of various occupational groups in a comparative sample of elites (1970, p. 188). The value of this type of information, in and of itself, is questionable. A more fruitful form of longitudinal analysis would attempt to answer some of the questions implied in the causal diagram presented earlier.

An assumption that usually remains implicit in elite research is that the composition, background, interests, education, and/or attitudes of elites have consequences for their subsequent behavior and, more important, consequences that are reflected in political or social changes, policies, programs, and so on. No Middle Eastern elite study has actually succeeded in showing the links or relationships between the composition of an elite, studied in one time period, and the consequences of elite characteristics, which must be analyzed at a later period of time. Theoretically, this type of longitudinal design is more interesting than simple comparisons, as it explores questions of possible causality by identifying antecedents or independent variables in one time period and consequences, effects, outcomes, or changes in dependent variables that appear in a subsequent time period.

The time frame involved in longitudinal analysis with the implied expense, patience, and commitment on the part of the researcher, plus the vulnerability of research to political disruptions in the field, make such studies particularly difficult. Ways around this problem include involving Middle Eastern social scientists in studies in their home countries and designing studies that will yield valuable information at one point in time and then can be repeated in subsequent time periods by the same researchers or by other researchers following the same study design.

An example of the failure to examine the kind of longitudinal causal question suggested here can be drawn from the research on Turkish elites. Two detailed attempts to study elites over time have been carried out (Frey 1965, Roos and Roos 1971). Both researchers have discussed the "ruralizing election" in Turkey, yet neither has explored whether this election resulted in agrarian reform or changes in rural development policies of the Turkish government. Another example is a comparative study of the backgrounds of university students in six Middle Eastern countries that found that two of the countries had a higher proportion of students of rural background (Stone 1973). This resulted in a hypothesis that of the six countries in the study, these two might be more likely to favor agrarian reforms in the future, as the students move into positions of influence. The hypothesis is yet to be tested. The longitudinal element was missing, but it illustrates the kind of hypothesis potentially testable. Other hypotheses regarding the long-term viability of military regimes, the influence of wars as political events (for instance, mobility out of the army to high government posts in Israel, Egypt, and Algeria), and antecedents to or outcomes of succession crises (for instance, Tunisia after Bourguiba, Morocco after Hassan, Sadat's emergence after Nasser's death compared with Algerian succession after Boumedienne) would be fascinating to analyze in a longitudinal context.

Combination Design

The exploration of causality, a feature of both the comparative and longitudinal approaches, can be reinforced in a design that combines the two. For instance, consider an expansion of the question previously suggested. If more university students (future elites) are the children of farmers in one country than in another country, is the former country more likely to institute agrarian-oriented government policies, academic research, or economic development? Such a question involves both the comparative analysis of countries on the basis of composition of university-trained future elites and the aggregated actions of this elite over a considerable period. A lag must be built in to allow students time to complete their educations and find their ways into positions of influence in the political, social, and economic elite structures of the countries in question.

A less time-consuming approach to a comparative-longitudinal study would be to begin with the dependent variable and work back in time to identify the characteristics of relevant elites that can explain the observed range of outcomes in the dependent variable. For instance, almost all countries in the Middle East have undertaken some degree of agrarian reform. Can the types of reforms attempted and their relative successes to date be explained in terms of characteristics of the governing elites or those administrators responsible for instituting the reforms? Comparison of Iran's "White Revolution," land extension and irrigation projects in Iraq, Syria, Jordan, and Egypt, the multistep process of limiting land holdings in Egypt, and the cooperative movements in Tunisia and Algeria could reveal considerable differences among land reform models, procedures, and successes. Relating these differences to questions of elite composition, background, and interests could result in interesting explanations. Distinctions between the rural (Tunisia) and urban (Egypt) elites, between highly centralized (Iran) and participatory (Algeria) agrarian administrations, between politicized (Tunisia) and technocratic (Syria) elites, or even between military and civilian governments are examples of elite-related independent variables that could help explain agrarian reform as a dependent variable.

Predicting Future Trends

Successful comparative/longitudinal research should result in the understanding of trends and patterns of change in elites and elite "output" over time. Extrapolation of these trends can result in interesting and valid predictions of the possible range of future events. The intention should not be to arrive at specific predictions, which will inevitably prove inaccurate, but rather, following the ideas of the prominent French futurist, Bertrand de Jouvenel, to indicate a number of possible alternate futures, identify the variables and possible sequences of events that might lead to them, and analyze the implications of each alternate future for societal development in the Middle East. Such futuristic research also lays the basis for continued longitudinal study and hypothesis testing in subsequent years or even by subsequent generations of elite studies analysts. Over time, we should build up much more solid knowledge than now exists about what differences elite characteristics make for their subsequent actions and for the general process of social change and political development in the Middle East.

At present, the most crucial issue in the Middle East requiring a future study approach is the Palestine-Israel conflict. Among the Palestinians, the questions range from identification of the elites, including the composition of existing groups and the potential for emergence of new elite groups, to the analysis of the whole range of background, educational, religious, socioeconomic, political, and ideological characteristics and the relations between these and the consequences for society leadership, policies, decision making, political and military action. As a next step, the results of this analysis can be used for a comparative evaluation of the roles of elites from all the countries involved in potential settlements and/or conflicts. It is quite clear that in the conflict elites will shape future events, as decisions must be made quickly, in the context of intensive personal diplomacy or the pressures of battlefield strategy. Analysis of possible futures and alternative courses of elite actions and their consequences are not only fascinating scholarly undertakings, but might well be sources of applied knowledge, enabling the parties involved to arrive at mutual understanding of each others' characteristics, problems, and potential for change. This is a highly controversial, volatile subject. Research should be conducted with the greatest care for accuracy and strict adherence to the scientific ideal that knowledge is a public good that should be freely and understandably available to all.

For example, a study comparing the background, interests, and decision-making freedom of Israeli political elites with a similar analysis of extant and possible future Palestinian leaders would contribute greatly to the understanding of why groups feel so highly committed to their respective nationalistic causes and might reveal common grounds for understanding between them, rather than the present ideological impasse and conflict of national interests. At present, the two groups operate on different planes. Their experiences, life histories, and outlooks are entirely different, and their attitudes toward each other are based on fear rather than understanding. Analysis of the content of these differences and the possible alternate paths for reconciling them would be a constructive step toward resolution of this most volatile issue in the Middle East. The importance of these variables for understanding the peace agreement concluded between Egypt and Israel in 1979 is already obvious.

EMPIRICAL DIRECTIONS

Building on the summary of theoretical perspectives and inventory of variables used in previous Middle Eastern elite studies, plus the suggestions for directing research into a comparative/longitudinal and future-oriented vein, let us consider some specific models for possible studies. Care has been taken to suggest studies that can, in principle, be executed with relative success in the near future, taking into consideration the need for knowledge on this subject for the Middle East as an area, as well as the limitations on research prospects in the area. These studies should serve to broaden our insights on elites in the Middle East, and to systematically test hypotheses and answer questions posed in this chapter and elsewhere in this book. The ultimate aim is to make verifiable predictions about the consequences of elite characteristics and the structures in terms of which they operate and thus to understand future prospects for Middle Eastern societies. The examples below are in an early and crude stage of formulation. However, they will hopefully point out realistic possibilities for future research directions.

Integrating Theoretical Perspectives

It is important to understand the relationships among the four types of independent variables outlined in Figure 7.1, with more detail in Figure 7.2. Usually, elite studies focus on one or, at most, two of the sets of variables. As has been mentioned, each of the sets of variables represents a particular outlook or school of thought with regard to elites: background determinants versus currently observable characteristics, or political structures, frameworks for action versus attributes or attitudes of the elite actors. For instance, Quandt's (1969) study of Algeria focuses on political structure using a recent history or elite circulation approach, and Waterbury's study of Morocco, while actually covering a longer time period, views political structure as a sociopolitical framework, lasting tribal, geographical, and linguistic-social divisions forming a stable pattern within which elites operate and government functions (1970, p. 317). Now, obviously both countries undergo change and elite circulation, just as both have venerable sociopolitical frameworks. The question then arises as to why one approach "fits" Morocco and a different one is suited to Algeria. In particular, we should explore possible answers in other cells of Figure 7.1. Did Algeria's revolution (cell 1) reduce the importance of pre-existing sociopolitical interest groups (cell 2)? Does the answer lie in differing unaggregated attributes of elite members in the two countries, either in terms of background, occupation, military or nonmilitary, and so on (cell 3) or in terms of attitudes or structure of motivation (cell 4)?

To take another example that stresses other aspects, both Frey's (1965) study of Turkey and Zonis' (1971) study of Iran focused on the attributes of elites as individuals, aggregated to present a picture of elite characteristics. Frey, however, focuses on the social background and preparation of Turkish deputies over the years (cell 3) while Zonis focuses on the attitudes, motivations, and personality traits of the Iranian elite at the time of his study (cell 4).

While each of these studies provides an interesting picture of the elite in question, we are faced with the dual problem of determining whether differences among elites are due to different characteristics of the countries in the area or due to different theoretical orientations of researchers on Middle Eastern elites. This problem could form the basis of a systematic comparative analysis aimed at evaluating the relationships among, and relative validity of, the four theoretical perspectives identified in Figure 7.1.

For example, a study could investigate the following question, attempting to generalize to the Middle East as a whole. Were the personal traits of Iranian political leaders identified by Zonis (insecurity, cynicism, mistrust, and so on) related to the then-existing political structure (king, strong military and secret police, economic freedom, but little political liberty) or to the social backgrounds of the elite (education, culture, family traditions, occupations)? Answering this question would involve comparing other monarchies (Kuwait, Saudi Arabia, Jordan, Morocco) with nonmonarchies (Egypt, Algeria, Israel, Turkey) to determine if the personalities of elites differ noticeably. It would be desirable to control for and test alternate hypotheses involving education, occupation, traditionalism, family, and other elements of social background, which are available from other existing studies. This research would involve careful comparisons of matched elite samples, using similar interview instruments (an expensive and lengthy process), or deriving means of extracting insights on personality from existing documents or previous studies. As with other studies to be suggested, it is very important to build on existing research work, expanding its scope rather than repeating it, to meet new needs.

Outcomes of Elite Actions

There is a need to focus some research on the outcomes or effects of elite actions, the "decision process" in Lasswell's terms. Such research, in addition to filling in details missing from existing empirical work on Middle Eastern elites, would be of general theoretical importance. In terms of Figures 7.1 and 7.2, this involves identifying the "dependent" variables for which elite characteristics are the "independent," causal, or explanatory factors.

In Figure 7.2, it should be evident that we have much better data for variables on the left side of the figure than for those farther to the right. In fact, there is little clear discussion in the Middle Eastern elite literature as to what the important dependent variables are. They will be in the nature of political actions, social change, government policies or programs, and socioeconomic development visible on a local, regional, or national level and may encompass only a few people or social institutions or may be of such scope as to be felt throughout the country.

Also, little attempt has been made to analyze the extent to which outcomes are affected, determined, or caused by actions of the elite and, in turn, what explains or can predict these actions. Within the context of the Middle East, clear choices are made on cooperative versus free enterprise models for economic functioning, on how to allocate expenditure of income from petroleum revenues, on whether to institute agrarian reforms and what form these should take, on how much of government resources should be devoted to education, to medical care, and to agricultural improvement, and on how these expenditures should be allocated among competing demands from regions and cities versus rural areas, tribal groups, social classes, family, and other interest groups. Resources are almost always scarce in relation to needs, and decisions on priorities and allocation made by elites determine the course of change in all countries in the area.

The problem here is twofold. First is determination of which dependent variables are most important to study and, from among these, to identify those for which knowledge of elite characteristics is likely to be fruitful for enhanced understanding of outcomes. Second is to determine the extent to which elite characteristics are actually related to the outcomes (the existence, strength, and direction of the arrows in Figure 7.2).

An example already cited is the issue of agrarian reform. The populations of many countries in the area are predominately (60 to 75 percent) peasant or tribal agriculturalists or semi-nomads, depending for a livelihood entirely on farming and animals. The rest of the population, in turn, depends on these people for food supplies. The Middle East is an arid area, so most agriculture is subsistence-level. The ability of countries to feed themselves is thus a crucial problem, particularly in those countries with large populations relative to arable land. (Egypt is the prime example, but Israel, Lebanon, Iran, Algeria, as well as

Saudi Arabia, Kuwait, the Gulf States, and Libya also face the possibility of having to import food.)

Agricultural self-sufficiency, in turn, affects dependence on other nations and thus freedom in the area of foreign policy. Agricultural productivity can be left in private hands, but this is seldom the case any more. Thus government policies determine such basics as what technology, seeds, fertilizers, and so on are available, how land ownership is to be arranged, what scale units will be worked, and the extent of centralized agricultural planning of output as well as organization of inputs, especially fertilizer and water, when irrigation is possible. As elites make these general policy and resource allocation decisions, can knowledge of elite characteristics help us to predict what decisions will be made? If the elite come from rural backgrounds (Tunisia, Turkey after the "ruralizing election"), do agrarian-oriented decisions emerge? As centralized decision making is not suited to agriculture (Simmons 1970-71), do military governments and those with centralized economic development planning have problems with agricultural productivity?

Other aspects of development policy (industrialization, urban planning, internal migration, population policy) and foreign relations (political alliances, aid in various forms, United Nations activities) provide a wide range of other dependent variables that might be "explained," at least in part, by relating them to characteristics of elites or the structures in terms of which they operate. For example, the issue of population control/family planning is considered particularly sensitive in Moslem countries, yet there is considerable variation among countries in the Middle East with regard to official policies on the subject and in the extent to which contraceptives and family planning services are freely available, regardless of official policy. Egypt has long experimented with distributing contraceptives through doctors and public health officials. Tunisia has embarked on population policies more recently, but has been more thorough, more innovative, and more willing to "rationalize" Moslem tradition. Both medical and legislative elites are involved in determining and implementing population policies. Abortion laws require open legislative debate, and availability of contraceptives, birth control information, and medical services requires active involvement of large numbers of doctors and paramedical personnel. Can characteristics of these involved elites that are more likly to result in effective population programs be identified?

Multiple Correlation or Factor Analysis

Given the large number of variables assembled in Figure 7.2, plus the many more that could be added, it is obvious that the present state of the art of theorizing about Middle Eastern elites violates a basic tenet of theory construction: the principle of parsimony. The framework of variables, a potential causal model, is complex, confusing, and unwieldy. It must be simplified by eliminating unnecessary or irrelevant independent variables, determining which causal links are important and deleting those which are not, identifying steps (or circles) in causal chains, finding out which variables are determined, partially or wholly, by other variables, and seeing where covariation makes independent variables interchangeable. Reducing the complexity of the model will also clarify links and focus attention on questions of using elite analysis to predict future events or to predict states of important dependent variables.

For example, do elites from rural backgrounds have more "traditional" attitudes? Are they more religious? Does military background and, particularly, high military rank correlate with certain personality traits ("authoritarian personality")? Identification of variables that correlate strongly with others within a country or, even better, in comparative analysis across nations in the Middle East is interesting in itself and can help reduce the size of the causal model.

Discriminant Analysis

An important potential of causal modeling and path analysis for identifying systems of structurally interrelated relationships among sets of variables is discussed in Chapter 5. Successful isolation of models would be of immense methodological importance in demonstrating the potential for comparative-longitudinal analysis of political data, especially using existing data sets. However, such analysis continues to focus on relationships among sets of independent variables instead of evaluating their impact on dependent variables, which take different values among the countries in the area and/or in the same country over time. These issues might better be handled by a method that in essence reverses the reasoning of causal modeling or factor analysis.

Discriminant analysis begins with two or more countries or groups of countries that differ on a specific dependent variable (single party versus multiparty states, countries with and without rural cooperatives, and so on) and reasons back to identify the independent variables that account for this difference (various elite characteristics, such as those in Figure 7.2). The procedure is adaptable to nominal and ordinal as well as ratio data, which is important for most applications in Middle Eastern elite research, given the quality of available and conceivably obtainable data. It is explained in most recent books on multivariate analysis (Cooley and Lohnes 1971, Tatsuoka 1971, Van de Geer 1971) and is available in two widely-distributed packaged statistical programs, Statistical Package for the Social Sciences and Biomed.

Examples of relevant questions to which it could be applied in the area of Middle Eastern elites have been introduced previously. Taking the example of population policy as a dependent variable, two or more countries could be compared on independent variables such as education of elites, national educational curricula, the role of religion in politics or in the recruitment of elites, political structures (highly centralized, authoritarian regimes versus those allowing a wider range of personal choice), and so on to arrive at an explanation of differences in population policy. If agrarian reform was the dependent variable in question, the discriminant functions might include geographical or social class background of elite members, occupation of elite members' fathers, education, foreign exposure of elite members, and the economic development policies of the foreign countries with which the elites are familiar.

The virtue of this approach is that it stresses the *outcomes* of political process. Elite characteristics, political structure, or other variables are only included to the extent that they have explanatory power for dependent variables of interest. This approach provides a research operation for settling questions as to the importance of specific variables and, indeed, the importance of elite characteristics as an explanatory concept. If, for example, it is discovered that occupational composition of an elite bears no relationship to subsequent political processes, this variable can be abandoned in future research. Or, if it turns out that links with foreign countries determine political policy to a greater extent than the social class interests identifiable by education, occupation, or geographical origins of the elite members, the focus of elite analysis in the Middle East will be altered to a significant degree. For instance, given Egypt's recent turn back from ties with the Soviet Union to ties with the West, if this is a more powerful determinant of military or even economic and foreign trade policies than influence of other Arab countries or influence from elite attitudes (the elite has not changed), then it can be predicted that these policies will change noticeably within the next few years. This, in turn, will affect the probabilities of war in the Middle East and the flows of "petro-dollars" for investments in Egypt. (This example, first written in 1976, has been largely supported by events since that time.)

Social Psychology and Psychobiography

Another research topic, which involves different theoretical and methodological issues from the previous four, is the issue of personal characteristics of elite members. Individual leader traits are of crucial importance in Middle Eastern political systems, where power is centralized in one individual, be it a king or president, or in a small group of leaders forming the cabinet, executive council, or command council.

Earlier social psychological work on "authoritarian personality" (Adorno et al.. 1950), "Machiavellian personality" (Christie and Geis 1970), and authoritarian, democratic, and laissez-faire leadership styles (Hare 1962, chap. 11) has not been in vogue in recent years. It emerged out of a direct and immediate concern with leaders emerging in western Europe before and during World War II. While that era has passed for the Western world, centralized, authoritarian governments and powerful individual leaders characterize the political regimes of most Middle Eastern countries. Analysis of leadership styles in terms of these theoretical concepts is, therefore, not unsuitable, provided the approach can be made relevant to the societies and cultures involved. They are particularly suitable for the themes stressed in this chapter because the research reveals much about the effects leadership style have on satisfaction of followers and on willingness of followers to accept various styles of leadership. Thus the focus is on the impact of leaders on society as a whole, not just on the elite.

Another potentially promising field is that of "psychobiography," biographical studies of leaders from a psychoanalytic perspective, using as data writings, speeches, and accounts of interactions with other people, as well as the actions and personal histories of leaders. To date, the approach has been used primarily by historians (Brown 1959, Weinstein and Platt 1969 and 1973), and most analysis has focused on people now dead (Erikson 1958, Wolfenstein 1967, Mitzman 1970 and 1973, Wolman 1971), although intense interest in Richard Nixon's presidency has resulted in psychobiographical studies during his lifetime (Wills 1970, Barber 1972, Mazlish 1972). The challenge would be to carry out such studies on leaders or other Middle Eastern elite figures while they are active and in power, based on those materials available before they retire and have time to write autobiographies.

Some Middle Eastern leaders have been particularly cooperative in beginning autobiographical writings early in their careers (Nasser 1955, Hussein 1962 and 1969). However, for most elites of interest, materials will be fragmentary, and considerable inventiveness is required on the part of the researcher in order to produce a creditable study in time for its use in predicting future characteristics, actions, or viability of leaders while they are in power.

These suggestions are only tentative. They highlight the difficult but crucial question of how to analyze the individual competence of elite members and, as a further step, the relative competence among possible incumbents to leadership roles. To what extent do personality, intelligence, ambition, experience, individual vested interests, and placement in a social network make one individual more suitable for leadership than another? If the answers to this question are relative rather than absolute, as is likely, then what personality types give what results in what situations? Can we explain or predict how one individual, rather than another, actually gains political power? Given the predominance of centralized power and authoritarian political leadership in Middle Eastern nations, they are now, and will undoubtedly continue to be, led by individuals or small groups of elite who are interesting figures. The shaping of Tunisia by Bourguiba and Libya by Kadaffi are current examples. From the recent past, the Shah in Iran, Nasser in Egypt, Faisal in Saudi Arabia, and, slightly more distant, Ataturk in Turkey can be added to the list. A better understanding of the dynamics of their leadership roles, of the examples they have set for future leaders, and of the way they have shaped the futures of their countries, both by building political frameworks and by setting a "style" for elite interaction and acceptable behavior, could be a key element in analyzing the part elites will play in the future of the Middle East.

CONCLUSION

This chapter has had two aims. The first was to summarize briefly the approaches that have been taken to the study of Middle Eastern elites, with a view toward organizing the variables into a comprehensive theoretical model that draws attention to questions of relationships among variables. The second was to indicate new directions, approaches, and methods that could be used to extend the analysis of Middle Eastern elites beyond individual case studies to comprehensive comparisons among countries in the area and beyond single time orientations to questions of change and future studies. New studies are continually emerging that come close to fulfilling the intentions of suggestions presented here. However, care has been taken to suggest studies that have not been undertaken to date, to my knowledge. Examples and illustrations are all based on issues or events in the Middle East or directly relevant to that area of the world, although with some adjustment in the facts, the general principles are probably relevant to most parts of the Third World. The examples and research directions are presented in the most sketchy of terms. Full elaboration of the ideas, followed by implementation of the studies, could well be the better part of several years' labor. The more modest intention of this chapter was to make suggestions that will hopefully be of value to researchers pursuing continuing interests in the nature and impact of Middle Eastern elites.

BIBLIOGRAPHY

Abrahamian, Ervand. 1968. "The Crowd in Iranian Politics 1905–1953." *Past and Present* 41, pp. 184–210.

Adam, Andre. 1955. "Naissance et developpement d'une classe moyenne au Maroc." *Bulletin Economique et Social du Maroc* 68, pp. 489–92.

Adorno, T. W., E. Frenkel-Brunswik, D. H. Levison, and R. N. Sanford. 1950. *The Authoritarian Personality*. New York: Harper.

Ahmad, Feroz. 1969. *The Young Turks*. New York: Oxford.

Ajami, I. 1969. "Social Classes, Family Demographic Characteristics and Mobility in Three Iranian Villages." *Sociologus Ruralis* 9, pp. 62–72.

Akzin, Benjamin. 1961. "The Knesset." *International Social Science Journal* 13, pp. 567–83.

Alexander, Alec P. 1960. "Industrial Entrepreneurship in Turkey: Origins and Growth." *Economic Development and Cultural Change* 8, pp. 349–63.

Alfarabi. 1964. *Kitāb al-Siyāsah al-Madaniyyah (The Political Regime)*. Edited by Fauzi M. Najjar. Beirut: Imprimérie Catholique.

———. 1968a. *Kitāb al-Millah wa Nusūs Ukhrā (Book of Religion)*. Edited by Muhsin Mahdi. Beirut: Dār al-Machrecq.

———. 1968b. *Ihsa'al-'Ulūm (Enumeration of the Sciences)*. In *Kitāb al-Millah wa Nusūs Ukhrā (Book of Religion)*, edited by Muhsin Mahdi, chap. 5. Beirut: Dār al-Machrecq.

Algar, Hamid. 1970. *Religion and State in Iran 1785–1906: The Rule of the Ulama in Qajar Period*. Berkeley and Los Angeles: University of California Press.

Alibert, Jean-Louis. 1966. "L'Opposition en Afrique noire." In *Forces Politiques en Afrique Noire*, edited by Pierre Lampuéi. Paris: Presses Universitaires Française.

Al-Marayati, Abid A. 1972. *The Middle East: Its Government and Politics*. Belmont: Duxbury.

Almond, Gabriel, and G. B. Powell, Jr. 1966. *Comparative Politics*. Boston: Little, Brown.

Al-Qazzaz, Ayad. 1970. "Power Elite in Iraq 1920–1958: A Study of the Cabinet." Unpublished paper delivered at the Fourth Annual Conference of the Middle East Studies Association. Mimeographed.

Althauser, Robert P. 1974. "Inferring Validity from the Multitrait-Multimethod Matrix." In *Sociological Methodology, 1973–1974*, edited by Herbert L. Costner. San Francisco: Jossey-Bass.

Alwin, Duane F. 1974. "Approaches to the Interpretation of Relationships in the Multitrait-Multimethod Matrix." In *Sociological Methodology, 1973–1974*, edited by Herbert L. Costner. San Francisco: Jossey-Bass.

Alzobaie, A., and M. El-Ghannam. 1968. "Iraqi Student Perceptions of Occupations." *Sociology and Social Research* 52, April, pp. 231-36.

Amin, Samir. 1970. *The Maghreb in the Modern World*. Baltimore: Penguin.

Anise, Ladun. 1974. "Trends in Leadership Succession and Elite Change in African Politics Since Independence." *African Studies Review* 17, pp. 507-24.

Apter, David. 1965. *The Politics of Modernization*. Chicago: University of Chicago Press.

Arian, Asher. 1977. "Israeli Elections: A Mechanism of Change?" *Jerusalem Quarterly* 3, pp. 17-27.

———. 1978. "The Electorate: Israel 1977." In *Israel at the Polls*. Washington: American Enterprise Institute.

Armstrong, L., and G. Hirabayshi. 1956. "Social Differentiation in Selected Lebanese Villages." *American Sociological Review* 21, pp. 425-34.

Aron, Raymond. 1951. *Tes guerres en chaine*. Paris: Gallimard.

Ashford, Douglas E. 1964. *Second and Third Generation Elites in the Maghreb*. Washington: State Dept. (Excerpts in Zartman 1971.)

———. 1965a. "Bureaucrats and Citizen." *The Annals of the American Academy of Political and Social Science*, March, pp. 89-100.

———. 1965b. *Morocco-Tunisia: Politics and Planning*. Syracuse: Syracuse University Press.

———. 1965c. "Neo Destour Leader and the 'Confiscated Revolution.'" In *French Speaking Africa: the Search for Identity*, by W. H. Lewis. New York: Walker.

———. 1966. *Perspectives of a Moroccan Nationalist: An Attitudinal Analysis of Local Leadership in the Istiqial Party*. Totowa: Bedminster.

———. 1967. "Elite Values and Attitudinal Change in the Maghreb (Morocco, Algeria, Tunisia)." Bloomington: The Carnegie Seminar on Political and Administrative Development, Dept. of Government, Indiana University.

Ashraf, Ahmad. 1969. "Historical Obstacles to the Development of a Bourgeoisie in Iran." *Iranian Studies*, Spring-Summer, pp. 54-79.

Averroes. 1562. *Libros Decem Moralium Nicomachiorum Expositio*. In *Aristotelis Opera cum Averrois Commentariis*, Vol. 3. Venice: Apud Junctas.

———. 1954. *Tahāfut al-Tahāfut (The Incoherence of the Incoherence)*. Translated by Simon van den Bergh. London: Luzac.

———. 1959. *Kitāb Fasl al-Maqāl (The Decisive Treatise)*. Edited by George F. Hourani. Leiden: E. J. Brill.

———. 1960. *Talkhīs al-Khatābah*. Edited by 'Abd al-Rahmān Badawī. Cairo: Maktabat al-Nahdah al-Misriyyah.

———. 1963. *Kitāb al-Kashf 'an Manāhij al-Adillah fī 'Aqā' id al-Millah (The Book of Un-covering the Clear Paths of the Signs about the Beliefs of the Religious Community)*. Edited by Mahmoud Kassem. Cairo: Maktabat al-Anglū al-Misriyyah.

———. 1974. *Averroes on Plato's Republic*. Edited and translated by Ralph Lerner. Ithaca: Cornell University Press.

Avery, P. 1965. *Modern Iran*. London: Ernest Benn.

Awad, Mohammed H. 1971. "The Evolution of Landownership in the Sudan." *Middle East Journal* 25, Z, pp. 212–28.

Axelrod, Robert. 1970. *Conflict of Interest*. New York: Markham.

Bacharach, Jere. 1974. *A Near East Studies Handbook*. Seattle: University of Washington Press.

Baer, Gabriel. 1970. "The Administrative Economic and Social Function of Turkish Guilds." *International Journal of Middle East Studies* 1, 1, pp. 28–50.

Bagley, F. 1968. "Technocracy in Iran." *Der Islam* 44, June, 230–42.

Bailes, K. E. 1977. *Technical Elites and Soviet Society*. New York: Columbia.

Bailey, C. 1970. "Cabinet Formation in Jordan, 1950–1970." *New Outlook* 13, November, pp. 11–23.

Bailey, F. G. 1969. *Stratagems and Spoils: A Social Anthropology of Politics*. New York: Schocken.

Baldwin, George. 1963. "The Foreign Educated Iranian—A Profile." *The Middle East Journal* 17, Summer, pp. 238–44.

Banfield, Edward C. 1961. *Political Influence*. New York: Free Press.

Banks, A. S., and R. B. Textor. 1963. *A Cross-Polity Survey*. Cambridge: Massachusetts Institute of Technology.

Barber, James David. 1972. *The Presidential Character*. Englewood Cliffs: Prentice-Hall.

Barker, Ernest, ed. 1962. *Social Contract*. New York: Oxford University Press.

Bechtold, Peter. 1976. *Politics in the Sudan*. New York: Praeger.

Beck, Carl, and J. M. Malloy. 1966. *Political Elites: A Mode of Analysis*. Pittburgh: Archives on Political Elites in Eastern Europe (occasional paper), University of Pittsburgh.

Beck, Carl, et al. 1973. *Comparative Communist Political Leadership*. New York: McKay.

Be'eri, Elezar. 1966. "The Egyptian Army Officer Class." *Asian and African Studies*, pp. 1–40.

———. 1969. *Army Officers in Arab Politics and Society*. New York: Praeger.

Bent, F. 1969. "The Turkish Bureaucracy as an Agent of Change." *Journal of Comparative Administration*, pp. 47–64.

Berger, Morroe. 1957a. *Bureaucracy and Society in Modern Egypt: A Study of the Higher Civil Service*. Princeton: Princeton University Press.

———. 1957b. "Bureaucracy East and West (Egypt)." *Administrative Science Quarterly* 1, pp. 518–29.

———. 1958. *The Middle Class in the Arab World*. Princeton University Conference 9, p. 15.

———. 1960. *Military Elite and Social Change: Egypt Since Napoleon*. Princeton: Princeton University, Center for International Studies (research monograph).

———. 1962. *The Arab World Today*. New York: Doubleday.

Berque, Jacques. 1957. "L'univers politique des arabes. 4.-Institutions. 6.-Perspectives." *Encyclopedia Française* 9, pp. 36.4–38.7.

———. 1972. *Egypt: Imperialism and Revolution*. New York: Praeger.

Berrea, Jean. 1962. *Integration Politique Exterieure*. Paris: Nauwaelerts.

Bertsch, G. K., R. P. Clark, and D. M. Wood. 1978. *Comparing Political Systems*. New York: Wiley.

Bill, James A. 1963. "The Social and Economic Foundations of Power in Contemporary Iran." *The Middle East Journal* 17, pp. 400–13.

———. 1969. "The Politics of Student Alienation: The Case of Iran." *Iranian Studies* 2, pp. 8–26.

———. 1972a. *The Politics of Iran*. Columbus: Charles E. Merrill.

———. 1972b. "Class Analysis and the Dialectics of Modernization in the Middle East." *The International Journal of Middle East Studies* 3.

———. 1973. "The Plasticity of Informal Politics." *The Middle East Journal* 27, 2, pp. 131–58.

Bill, J. A., and C. Leiden. 1979. *Politics in the Middle East*. Boston: Little, Brown.

Binder, Leonard. 1964. *Iran: Political Development in a Changing Society*. Berkeley: University of California.

———. 1966a. "Political Recruitment and Participation in Egypt." In *Political Parties and Political Development*, edited by Joseph La Palombara and Myron Weiner. Princeton: Princeton University Press.

———. 1966b. "Egypt: The Integrative Revolution." In *Political Culture and Political Development*, edited by L. W. Pye and S. Verba. Princeton: Princeton University Press.

———. 1978. *In a Moment of Enthusiasm: Political Power and the Second Stratum in Egypt*. Chicago: University of Chicago Press.

Binder, Leonard, et al. 1971. *Crises and Sequences in Political Development*. Princeton: Princeton University Press.

Black, Donald. 1976. *The Behavior of Law*. New York: Academic Press.

Blalock, H. M., Jr. 1960. *Social Statistics*. New York: McGraw-Hill.

———. 1970. "A Causal Approach to Nonrandom Measurement Errors." *American Political Science Review* 65, December, pp. 1,099–111.

———. 1971. *Causal Models in the Social Sciences*. Chicago: Aldine-Atherton.

———. 1974. "Beyond Ordinal Measurement: Weak Tests of Stronger Theories." In *Measurement in the Social Sciences*, edited by H. M. Blalock, Jr. Chicago: Aldine.

Blau, Peter, and O. D. Duncan. 1967. *The American Occupational Structure*. New York: Wiley.

Bodman, Herbert L. 1965. *Political Factions in Aleppo 1760--1826*. Chapel Hill: University of North Carolina Press.

Bonilla, Frank. 1968. *The Failure of Elites*. Cambridge: MIT Press.

Bonilla, Frank, and J. A. S. Michelena, eds. 1967. *Strategy for Research on Social Policy*. Cambridge: MIT Press.

Bottomore, T. B. 1964. *Elites and Society*. Baltimore: Penguin.

Bousquet, G. 1953. "Les elites gouvernantes en Afrique du Nord depuis la conquête française." *Welt des Islams* 3, pp. 15–33.

Box, G. E., and G. M. Jenkins. 1970. *Time Series Analysis: Forecasting and Control*. San Francisco: Holden Day.

Box, G. E., and G. C. Tiao. 1965. "A Change in Level of a Non-Stationary Time Series." *Biometrika* 52, 1, pp. 181–92.

Brewer, M. B., D. T. Campbell, and W. D. Crano. 1970. "Testing a Single-Factor Model as an Alternative to the Misuse of Partial Correlations in Hypothesis-Testing Research." *Sociometry* 33, pp. 1–11.

Brown, L. Carl. 1974. *The Tunisia of Ahmed Bev*. Princeton: Princeton University Press.

Brown, Norman D. 1959. *Life Against Death: The Psychoanalytic Meaning of History*. Middleton: Weslyan.

223

Brunner, R. D., and G. D. Brewer. 1971. *Organized Complexity*. New York: Free Press.

Brunner, R. D., and K. Liepelt. 1972. "Data Analysis, Process Analysis, and System Changes." *Midwest Journal of Political Science* 16, November, pp. 538–69.

Bujra, A. S. 1970. "Urban Elites and Colonialism: Nationalist Elites of Aden and South Arabia." *Middle East Studies* 6, pp. 189–211.

Bulliet, Richard W. 1972. *The Patricians of Nishapur*. Cambridge: Harvard University Press.

Burnham, W. Dean. 1970. *Critical Elections and the Mainsprings of American Politics*. New York: Norton.

Caiden, E., and N. Raphaeli. 1968. "The Image of the Israel Civil Service among University Students in Israel." *Public Administration in Israel and Abroad* 9, pp. 161–75.

Campbell, Donald T. 1969. "Reforms as Experiments." *American Psychologist* 24, 2 pp. 409–29.

————. 1970. "Natural Selection as an Epistemological Model." In *A Handbook of Method in Cultural Anthropology*, edited by R. Naroll and R. Cohen. Washington: National History Press.

————. 1975. "'Degrees of Freedom' and the Case Study." *Comparative Political Studies* 8, pp. 178–93.

Campbell, Donald T., and D. W. Fiske. 1959. "Convergent and Discriminant Validation by the Multitrait-Multimethod Matrix." *Psychological Bulletin* 66, pp. 81–105.

Campbell, Donald T., and J. Stanley. 1963. *Experimental and Quasi-Experimental Designs for Research*. Chicago: Rand McNally.

Cankaya, A. 1972. Yeni Mulkiye Tarihi ve Mulkiyeliler (New History of the Civil Service School and Its Graduates). Ankara: Mars Basimevi.

Caporaso, James A. 1973. "Quasi-Experimental Approaches to Social Science: Perspectives and Problems." In *Quasi-Experimental Approaches*, edited by James A. Caporaso and Leslie L. Roos, Jr. Evanston: Northwestern University Press.

Caporaso, James A., and Leslie L. Roos, Jr., eds. 1973. *Quasi-Experimental Approaches*. Evanston: Northwestern University Press.

Chaliand, Gerard. 1977. *Revolution in the Third World*. New York: Viking.

Chambers, Richard L. 1964. "Civil Bureaucracy in Turkey." In *Political Modernization in Japan and Turkey*, edited by Robert Ward and Dankwart Ruston. Princeton: Princeton University Press.

Christie, R., and F. L. Geis, eds. 1970. *Studies in Machiavellianism*. New York: Academic Press.

Le Coeur, Ch. 1936. "Metiers et classes sociales d'Azzemour." *Revue African* 79, pp. 933–56.

Coleman, J. S. 1955. "The Emergence of African Political Parties." In *Africa Today*, edited by C. Grove Haines. Baltimore: Johns Hopkins University Press.

————. 1972. *Policy Research in the Social Sciences*. Morristown: General Learning.

Coleman, J. S., ed. 1965. *Education and Political Development*. Princeton: Princeton University Press.

Cooley, W. W., and P. R. Lohnes. 1971. *Multivariate Data Analysis*. New York: Wiley.

Cook, T. D., and Donald T. Campbell. 1976. "The Design and Conduct of Quasi-Experiments and True Experiments in Field Settings." In *Handbook of Industrial and Organizational Research*, edited by M. D. Dunette. New York: Rand McNally.

Coser, Lewis. 1956. *The Functions of Social Conflict*. New York: Free Press.

Cottam, Richard. 1964. *Nationalism in Iran*. Pittsburgh: Pittsburgh University Press.

Cottingham, Clement. 1974. *Contemporary African Bureaucracy: Political Elites, Bureaucratic Recruitment, and Administrative Performance*. Morristown: General Learning Corp.

Crecelius, D. 1966. "Al-Azhar in the Revolution." *The Middle East Journal* 20, Winter, pp. 31–49.

Czudnowski, M. 1970. "Legislative Recruitment under Proportional Representation in Israel: A Model and a Case Study." *Midwest Journal of Political Science* 14, May, pp. 216–48.

————. 1972. "Socio-Cultural Variables and Legislative Recruitment." *Comparative Politics* 4, pp. 561–87.

Dahl, R. A. 1960. *Who Governs?* New Haven: Yale University Press.

Dahrendorf, Ralf. 1967. *Society and Democracy in Germany*. Garden City: Anchor.

————. 1970. *Modern Political Analysis*. Englewood Cliffs: Prentice-Hall.

————. 1971. *Polyarchy*. New Haven: Yale University Press.

Davies, James C. 1962. "Toward a Theory of Revolution." *American Sociological Review* 27, 1, pp. 5–19.

Davison, Roderic H. 1963. *Reform in the Ottoman Empire*. Princeton: Princeton University Press.

Dawn, C. E. 1962. "The Rise of Arabism in Syria." *Middle East Journal* 16, 1, pp. 145–67.

————. 1971. "The Legacies of the Modern Historical Era: The Independent Countries." *People, Power and Political Systems: Prospects in the Middle East*. Washington, D.C.: The Middle East Institute.

Debbasch, Charles, et al. 1970. *Ponvoir et Administration au Maghreb: Etudes sur les elites.* Paris: Centre National de Recherche Scientifique.

Dekmejian, R. H. 1970. "Egyptian Power Elite." *University of Toronto Graduate* 3, pp. 39–45.

———. 1971. *Egypt Under Nasir.* Albany: State University Press of New York.

———. 1974. "Elite Recruitment, Markov Chains and Path Analysis: Israel, Egypt and Lebanon." Paper presented at the annual meeting of the American Political Science Association.

———. 1975. *Patterns of Political Leadership: Egypt, Israel, Lebanon.* Albany: State University Press of New York.

Demeersenman, A. 1951. "Elites Tunisiennes en progression." *IBLA* 16, 54, pp. 125–49.

deTmaz, Jose Luis. 1970. *Los Que Mandan (Those Who Rule).* Albany: New York State University Press.

Deutsch, K. W. 1963. *The Nerves of Government.* Glencoe: Free Press.

Djilas, Milovan. 1957. *The New Class.* New York: Praeger.

Dobkin, Marlene. 1967. "Social Ranking in the Women's World of Purdah." *Anthropological Quarterly* 40, pp. 65–72.

Dodd, C. D. 1969. *Politics and Government in Turkey.* Berkeley: University of California Press.

Dodd, C. H. 1964. "Social and Educational Background of Turkish Officials." *Middle East Studies* 1, 3, pp. 468–76.

Dozy, R. 1932. *Histoire des Musulmans d'Espagne*, Vol. 3. Leiden: E. J. Brill.

Duchac, René, et al. 1973. *La formation des élites maghrébines.* Paris: Librairie generale de droit et de juris prudence.

Duncan, Otis D. 1966. "Path Analysis: Sociological Examples." *American Journal of Sociology* 72, pp. 1–16. (Reprinted in Blalock 1971).

———. 1972. "Unmeasured Variables in Linear Models for Panel Analysis." In *Sociological Methodology, 1972*, edited by Herbert Costner. San Francisco: Jossey-Bass.

———. 1975. *Introduction to Structural Equation Models.* New York: Academic Press.

Duncan, Otis D., D. L. Featherman, and B. D. Duncan. 1972. *Socioeconomic Background and Achievement.* New York: Academic Press.

Dupre, Louis. 1969. "Democracy and the Military Base of Power." *Middle East Journal* 22, Winter, pp. 29–44.

Duvall, Raymond, and M. Welfing. 1973a. "Social Mobilization, Political Institutionalization and Conflict in Black Africa: A Simple Dynamic Model." *Journal of Conflict Resolution* 17, December, pp. 673–702.

——. 1973b. "Determinants of Political Institutionalization in Black Africa." In *Quasi-Experimental Approaches*, edited by J. Caporaso and L. Roos. New York: Academic Press.

Eberhard, Wolfram. 1954. "Change in Leading Families in Southern Turkey." *Anthropos* 49, pp. 992–1003.

——. 1962. "Afghanistan's Young Elite." *Asian Survey* 12, pp. 3–22.

——. 1972. "Landlords in a Democracy: The Adaptability of a Traditional Elite." In *The Developing Nations*, edited by F. Tachau. New York: Dodd, Mead.

Edinger, Lewis J., and Donald Searing. 1967. "Social Background in Elite Analysis." *American Political Science Review* 62, 2, pp. 428–45.

Eisenstadt, S. N. 1951. "The Place of Elites and Primary Groups in the Absorption of New Immigrants in Israel." *American Journal of Sociology* 57, pp. 221–31.

——. 1956. "Patterns of Leadership and Social Homogeneity in Israel." *International Social Science Bulletin* 8, 1, pp. 37–54.

——. 1965. "Political Development." In *Social Change*, edited by Amitai Etzioni. New York: Basic.

El-Bushra, S. 1969. "Occupational Classification of Sudanese Towns." *Sudan Notes and Records* 50, 1, pp. 75–96.

Elizur, Youval, and Eliahu Salpeter. 1973. *Who Rules Israel?* New York: Harper & Row.

Elon, Amos. 1971. *Israelis: Founders and Sons*. New York: Holt, Rinehart and Winston.

Entelis, John. 1974. "Ideological Change and an Emerging Counter-Culture in Tunisian Politics." *Journal of Modern African Studies* 12, pp. 543–68.

Erikson, Eric. 1968. *Identity*. New York: Norton.

——. 1958. *Young Man Luther*. New York: Norton.

Etzioni, Amitai. 1959. "Functional Differentiation of Elites in the Kibbutz." *American Journal of Sociology* 64, March, pp. 476–87.

——. 1965. *Political Unification: A Comparative Study of Leaders and Followers*. New York: Holt, Rinehart and Winston.

Faksh, Mahmud. 1971. "Education for Development: Dysfunctional Trends in Egypt." Paper delivered to Middle East Studies Association.

Faris, Robert. 1960. "The Middle Class from a Sociological Viewpoint." *Social Forces* 39, pp. 1–5.

Fein, L. J. 1967. *Israel*. Boston: Little, Brown.

Feith, Herbert. 1962. *The Decline of Constitutional Democracy in Indonesia*. Ithaca: Cornell University Press.

Feuer, Lewis S. 1968. *The Conflict of Generations*. New York: Basic.

Findikoglu, Z. F. 1958–59. "Social Stratification Related to Turkish Social Changes." *Revue de la Faculte de Science Economique, Universite d'Istanbul* 20, pp. 374–88.

Findlay, Carter. 1970. "The Legacy of Tradition to Reform: Origins of the Ottoman Foreign Ministry." *International Journal of Middle East Studies* 4, pp. 354–57.

Finer, S. E. 1961. *The Man on Horseback*. New York: Praeger.

First, Ruth. 1974. *Libya: Elusive Revolution*. Baltimore: Penguin.

Fisher, S. N. 1962. "Community Power Studies: A Critique." *Social Research* 29, Winter, pp. 449–66.

Flis-Zonabend, Française. 1968. *Lycéens de Dakar*. Paris: Maspero.

Frey, F. W. 1963. "Political Development, Power and Communications in Turkey." In *Communications and Political Development*, edited by L. W. Pye. Princeton: Princeton University Press.

———. 1965. *The Turkish Political Elite*. Cambridge: Massachusetts Institute of Technology.

———. 1975. "Patterns of Elite Politics in Turkey." In *Political Elites in the Middle East*, edited by George Lenczowski. Washington: American Enterprise Institute.

Frey, F. W., and L. L. Roos. 1967. "Social Structure and Community Development in Rural Turkey: Village and Elite Leadership Relations." In *Rural Development Research Project*, Report No. 10. Cambridge: Center for International Studies, Massachusetts Institute of Technology.

Friedman, John. 1972. "A General Theory of Polarized Development." In *Growth Centers in Regional Economic Development*, edited by Niles Hansen. New York: Free Press.

Friedrich, Carl J. 1950. *Constitutional Government and Democracy*. Boston: Beacon.

Gable, R. W. 1961. "Public Administration in Iran: Sketches on Non-Western Transitional Bureaucracy." *Philippine Journal of Public Administration* 5, July, pp. 226–34.

Galindo, E. 1959. "Jeunesse et sport." *Revue de l'Institut des Belles Lettres Arabes* 24, pp. 349–62.

Gehlen, M. P., and M. McBridge. 1968. "The Soviet Central Committee: An Elite Analysis." *American Political Science Review* 62, p. 1241.

Gibb, H. A. R. 1932. *Whither Islam?* London: Gollancz.

Glass, G. V., V. L. Willson, and J. M. Gottman. 1975. *Design and Analysis of Time-Series Experiments*. Boulder: Colorado Association University Press.

Goldberg, H. 1968. "Elite Groups in Peasant Communities: A Comparison of Three Middle Eastern Villages." *American Anthropologist* 70, pp. 718-31.

Goldhammer, H. L. 1968. "Social Mobility." In *International Encyclopedia of the Social Sciences* 14, edited by D. L. Sills, pp. 429-38. New York: Macmillan.

Goldziher, Ignaz. 1903. *Mohammed Ibn Toumert*. Translated by G. Demombynes. Algiers: Fontana.

Goodrich, Daniel. 1966. *Sons of the Establishment*. New York: Rand McNally.

Gordon, David C. 1962. *North Africa's French Legacy, 1954-62*. Cambridge: Harvard University Press.

Gouldner, Alvin W. 1979. *The Future of Intellectuals and the Rise of the New Class*. New York: Seabury.

Graham and K. H. Roberts, eds. 1972. *Comparative Studies in Organizational Behavior*. New York: Holt, Rinehart and Winston.

Greenstein, Fred. 1969. *Personality and Politics*. Chicago: Markham.

Gregorian, V. 1969. *The Emergence of Modern Afghanistan*. Stanford: Stanford University Press.

Greiner, L. 1972. "Evolution and Revolution as Organizations Grow." *Harvard Business Review* 50, July–Aug., pp. 37–46.

Grunebaum, Gustave E. von. 1961. *Medieval Islam*. Chicago: University of Chicago Press.

Gurr, Ted R. 1970. *Why Men Rebel*. Princeton: Princeton University Press.

Hacker, Andrew. 1975. "What Rules America?" *The New York Review of Books* 22.

Hagen, Everett E. 1960. "The Entrepreneur as a Rebel Against Traditional Society." *Human Organization* 19, pp. 185-87.

Hall, D. T. 1976. *Careers in Organizations*. Pacific Palisades: Goodyear.

Halpern, Manfred. 1962. "Middle Eastern Armies and the New Middle Class." In *The Role of the Military in Underdeveloped Countries*, edited by J. J. Johnson, pp. 277-316. Princeton: Princeton University Press.

———. 1963. *The Politics of Social Change in the Middle East and North Africa*. Princeton: Princeton University Press.

———. 1969. "Egypt and the New Middle Class: Reaffirmation and New Explorations." *Comparative Studies in Society and History* 11, pp. 97-108.

Halstead, John P. 1967. *The Origins and Rise of Moroccan Nationalism*. Cambridge: Harvard University Middle East Center.

Hamady, Sania. 1960. *Temperament and Character of the Arabs*. New York: Twayne.

Hannan, Michael T., R. Robinson, and J. T. Warren. 1974. "The Causal Approach to Measurement Error in Panel Analysis: Some Further Contingencies." In *Measurement in the Social Sciences*, edited by H. M. Blalock, Jr. Chicago: Aldine.

Hannan, Michael T., and Alice A. Young. 1977. "Estimation in Panel Models: Results on Pooling Cross-sections and Time Series." In *Sociological Methodology, 1977*, edited by David R. Heise. San Francisco: Jossey-Bass.

Harbison, Frederick, and Charles Myers. 1964. *Education, Manpower, and Economic Growth*. New York: McGraw-Hill.

Hare, A. Paul. 1962. *Handbook of Small Group Research*. New York: Free Press.

Harik, I. F. 1968. *Politics and Change in a Traditional Society: Lebanon, 1711-1845*. Princeton: Princeton University Press.

———. 1971. "Opinion Leaders and the Mass Media in Rural Egypt." *The American Political Science Review* 65, pp. 731–40.

———. 1972a. "The Ethnic Revolution and Political Integration in the Middle East." *The International Journal of Middle East Studies* 3, 3, pp. 303–23.

———. 1972b. *Mann Yahkum Lubnan?* Beirut: Dar al-Nahar.

———. 1973. "The Single Party as a Subordinate Movement: The Case of Egypt." *World Politics* 26, 1, pp. 80–105.

———. 1974. *The Political Mobilization of Peasants: A Study of an Egyptian Community*. Bloomington: Indiana University Press.

———. 1975. "The Lebanese Political Elites." In *Political Elites in the Middle East*, edited by George Lenczowski. Washington: American Enterprise Institute.

Harrington, C. W. 1958. "The Saudi Arabian Council of Ministers." *Middle East Journal* 12, Winter, pp. 1–19.

Harris, Christina. 1964. *Nationalism and Revolution in Egypt*. The Hague: Mouton.

Harris, G. L. 1958. *Jordan: Its People, Its Society, and Its Culture*. New York: Grove Press.

Harris, George S. 1965. "The Role of the Military in Turkish Politics." *Middle East Journal* 19, pp. 54–66, 169–76.

Heise, D. R. 1970. "Causal Inference from Panel Data." In *Sociological Methodology, 1970*, edited by E. F. Borgatta and G. W. Bohrnstedt. San Francisco: Jossey-Bass.

Henderson, K. D. D. 1965. *Sudan Republic*. New York: Praeger.

230

Hermassi, Elbaki. 1972. *Leadership and National Development in North Africa*. Berkeley: University of California Press.

Heyd, Uriel, ed. 1961. *Studies in Islamic History and Civilization*. Jerusalem. (Esp. Gabriel Baer's "The Village Shaikh in Modern Egypt.")

Hibbs, Douglas A., Jr. 1977. "On Analysing the Effects of Policy Interventions: Box-Jenkins and Box-Tiao versus Structural Equation Models." In *Sociological Methodology, 1977*, edited by David R. Heise. San Francisco: Jossey-Bass.

Higley, John, G. Lowell Field, and Knut Grøholt. 1977. *Elite Structure and Ideology*. New York: Universitetsforlaget through Columbia University Press.

Himberg, Harvey A. 1972. *Social and Political Dimensions of Recruitment in Tunisia*. Boston: African Studies Association.

Hirsh, James, et al. 1975. *Approaches to Elite Analysis*. Washington: Mathematica.

Hobbes, Thomas. 1968. *Leviathan*. Edited by C. B. Macpherson. Harmondsworth, England: Penguin.

———. 1972. *De Cive*. In *Man and Citizen*, edited by Bernard Gert. Garden City: Anchor.

Hodgkin, Thomas. 1962. *African Political Parties*. Baltimore: Penguin.

Hoffman, B. G. 1967. *The Structure of Traditional Moroccan Rural Society*. The Hague: Mouton.

Holtzman, A. 1963. *The Townsend Movement*. New York: Bookman.

Hopkins, Raymond. 1971. *Political Roles in a New State*. New Haven: Yale University Press.

Hopper, Jerry R., and Richard L. Levin, eds. 1967. *The Turkish Administrator: A Cultural Survey*. Ankara: U.S. Agency for International Development.

Hoselitz, Bert. 1966. "Investment in Education and its Political Impact." In *Education and Political Development*, edited by James S. Coleman. Princeton: Princeton University Press.

Hottinger, A. 1966. "Zu'ama in Historical Perspective." In *Politics in Lebanon*, edited by L. Binder. New York: Wiley.

Hourani, Albert. 1962. *Arabic Thought in the Liberal Age 1798-1939*. New York: Oxford University Press.

Hudson, Bradford B. 1959. "Cross Cultural Studies in the Arab Middle East and United States: Studies of Young Adults." *Journal of Social Issues* 15.

Hudson, Michael C. 1966. "The Electoral Process and Political Development in Lebanon." *Middle East Journal* 20, pp. 173-86.

———. 1969. *Precarious Republic*. New York: Random House.

———. 1977. *Arab Politics*. New Haven: Yale University Press.

Huntington, S. 1968. *Political Order in Changing Societies*. New Haven: Yale.

Hurewitz, J. C. 1969. *Middle East Politics: The Military Dimension*. New York: Praeger.

———. 1974. *The Middle East and North Africa: A Documentary Record*. New Haven: Yale University Press.

Hussein, King of Jordan. 1962. *Uneasy Lies the Head*. London: Heinemann.

———. 1969. *My War with Israel*. New York: Morrow.

Hussein, Mahmud. 1975. *L'Egypte*. Paris: Maspero.

Hyman, H. H. 1964. "Research Design." In *Studying Politics Abroad*, by R. E. Ward et al. Boston: Little, Brown.

———. 1972. *Secondary Analysis of Sample Surveys*. New York: Wiley.

Hyman, H., A. Payaslioglus, and F. W. Frey. 1958. "The Values of Turkish College Youth." *The Public Opinion Quarterly* 20, Fall, pp. 275–91.

Inkeles, Alex. 1974. *Making Men Modern*. Cambridge: Harvard.

Issawi, Charles. 1955. *The Entrepreneur Class*. Ithaca: Cornell University Press.

Jacobs, Norman. 1966. *The Sociology of Development: Iran as an Asian Case Study*. New York: Praeger.

Jazi, Mohammed Dali. 1971. *L'orientation des parlementaires en Tunisie*. University of Paris. Paris: memoire de D.E.S.

Jreisat, J. 1970. "Administrative Change of Local Authorities: Lessons from Four Arab Countries." *Journal of Comparative Administration* 2, December, pp. 377–85.

Kahn, R. L. 1972. "The Meaning of Work: Interpretation and Proposals for Measurement." In *The Human Meaning of Social Change*, edited by A. Campbell and P. E. Converse. New York: Russell Sage Foundation.

Kaplinsky, Z. 1954. "The Muslim Brotherhood." *Middle Eastern Affairs* 5, December, pp. 377–85.

Karpat, Kemal H. 1964. "The Mass Media: Turkey." In *Political Modernization in Japan and Turkey*, edited by D. A. Rustow and R. E. Ward. Princeton: Princeton University Press.

———. 1965. "Recent Political Developments in Turkey and Their Social Background." In *The Contemporary Middle East*, edited by Benjamin Rivlin and Joseph S. Szyliowicz. New York: Random.

Ka'ūs, Kai. 1951. *A Mirror for Princes, The Qābūs-Nāma*. Translated by Reuben Levy. London: The Cresset Press.

Kautsky, John. 1962. *Political Change in Underdeveloped Countries*. New York: Wiley.

———. 1972. *Political Consequences of Modernization*. New York: Wiley.

Kazamias, A. M. 1966. "Potential Elites in Turkey." *Comparative Education Review* 10, pp. 470–81.

———. 1967. "Potential Elite in Turkey: Exploring the Values and Attitudes of Youth." *Comparative Education Review* 11, February, pp. 22–37.

Kearns, Kevin C. 1963. "Perspectives on a New Capitol." *Geographic Review* 63, 2, pp. 147–69.

Keddie, Nikkie. 1969. "The Roots of the Ulama's Power in Modern Iran." *Studia Islamica* 29, 1, pp. 31–54.

———. 1970. *Al-Afghani*. Berkeley: University of California Press.

———. 1971. "The Iranian Power Structure and Social Change 1800–1969: An Overview." *International Journal of Middle Eastern Studies* 2, January, pp. 3–70.

Kelley, J. 1973. "Causal Chain Models for the Socioeconomic Career." *American Sociological Review* 38, August, pp. 481–93.

Kendall, Patricia L. 1956. "The Ambivalent Character of Nationalism among Egyptian Professionals." *Public Opinion Quarterly* 20, pp. 277–92.

Kenny, D. A. 1975. "A Quasi-Experimental Approach to Assessing Treatment Effects in the Non-equivalent Control Group Design." *Psychological Bulletin* 82, 3, pp. 345–62.

Kerlinger, F. N. 1973. *Foundations of Behavioral Research*. New York: Holt, Rinehart and Winston.

Kerstiens, Thom. 1966. *The New Elite in Asia and Africa*. New York: Praeger.

Key, V. O. 1975. "A Theory of Critical Elections." *Journal of Politics* 17, 1, pp. 1–22.

Khadduri, M. 1953. "The Role of the Military in Middle East Politics." *American Political Science Review* 47, pp. 511–24.

———. 1955. *War and Peace in the Law of Islam*. Baltimore: Johns Hopkins University Press.

———. 1968. "The Army Officer: His Role in Middle Eastern Politics." In *Social Forces in the Middle East*, edited by S. N. Fisher. New York: Greenwood.

———. 1969. *War and Peace in the Law of Islam*. Baltimore: Johns Hopkins.

———. 1970. *Political Trends in the Arab World*. Baltimore: Johns Hopkins.

233

———. 1973. *Arab Contemporaries: The Role of Personalities in Politics*. Baltimore: Johns Hopkins.

Khallaf, A., and E. Schwayri. 1966. "Family Firms and Industrial Development: The Lebanese Case." *Economic Development and Social Change* 15, pp. 59–69.

Kirkpatrick, Jeane. 1976. *The New Presidential Elite*. New York: Basic.

———. 1971. *Leader and Vanguard in Mass Society*. Cambridge: Cambridge University Press.

Kornhauser, W. 1969. *The Politics of Mass Society*. New York: Free Press.

Lacouture, Jean. 1970. *The Demi-Gods: Charismatic Leadership in the Third World*. New York: Knopf.

Land, K. C. 1969. "Principles of Path Analysis." In *Sociological Methodology, 1969*, edited by E. F. Borgatta. San Francisco: Jossey-Bass.

Landes, David. 1969. *Bankers and Pashas: International Finance and Economic Imperialism in Egypt*. New York: Harper and Row.

Laoust, Henri. 1970. *La politique de Gazālī*. Paris: Paul Geuthner.

Lapidus, Ira M. 1967. *Muslim Cities in the Later Middle Ages*. Cambridge: Harvard University Press.

LaPalombara, Joseph, and Myron Weiner, eds. 1966. *Political Parties and Political Development*. Princeton: Princeton University Press.

Lasswell, Harold. 1930. *Psychopathology and Politics*. Chicago: University of Chicago Press.

———. 1936a. *Politics, Who Gets What, When, How*. Hightstown: McGraw-Hill.

———. 1936b. *World Politics and Personal Insecurity*. Hightstown: McGraw-Hill.

———. 1948. *Power and Personality*. New York: Norton.

———. 1965. "The Comparative Study of Elites." In *World Revolutionary Elites*, edited by H. D. Lasswell and Daniel Lerner. Cambridge: Massachusetts Institute of Technology.

Lasswell, Harold, Daniel Lerner, and C. E. Rothwell. 1952. *The Comparative Study of Elites*. Stanford: Hoover.

Lasswell, Harold, with Abraham Kaplan. 1950. *Power and Society*. New Haven: Yale University Press.

Leites, Nathan C. 1953. *A Study of Bolshevism*. Glencoe: Free Press.

Lenczowski, George, ed. 1975. *Political Elites in the Middle East*. Washington: American Enterprise Institute.

Lerner, Daniel. 1958. *The Passing of Traditional Society: Modernizing the Middle East*. Glencoe: Free Press.

———. 1960. "Swords and Ploughshares: The Turkish Army as a Modernizing Force." *World Politics* 12, pp. 19–44.

LeVine, Victor T. 1967. *Political Leadership in Africa*. Stanford: Hoover.

———. 1973a. "Problems of Political Succession in Independent Africa." In *Africa in World Affairs*, edited by Ali Mazrui and B. Patel. New York: Third Press.

———. 1973b. "Leadership Transition in Black Africa." Paper presented to African Studies Association.

Levy, R. 1969. *The Social Structure of Islam*. Cambridge: Cambridge University Press.

Lewis, B. 1961. *The Emergence of Modern Turkey*. New York: Oxford.

Lieberman, S. S., R. Gillespie, and M. Loghmani. 1973. "The Isfahan Communications Project." *Studies in Family Planning* 4.

Lijphart, Arend. 1968. *The Politics of Accommodation: Pluralism and Democracy in the Netherlands*. Berkeley: University of California.

Lipset, S. M. 1966. "Elections: Expression of Democratic Class Conflict." In *Class, Status and Party*, edited by Reinhard Bendix and S. M. Lipset. New York: Free Press.

———. 1970. *Revolution and Counter Revolution*. New York: Doubleday.

Lipset, S. M., and A. Solari. 1967. *Elites of Latin America*. New York: Oxford.

Lloyd, Lord. 1933–34. *Egypt Since Cramer*. New York: Macmillan.

Lloyd, Peter C. 1966. *New Elites in Tropical Africa*. New York: Oxford.

Locke, John. 1960. "The Second Treatise of Government." In *Two Treatises of Government*, edited by Peter Laslett. New York: Mentor.

Lowi, Theodore. 1963. "The Case of Innovation in Party Systems." *American Political Science Review* 57, 3, pp. 570–83.

Machiavelli, Niccolò. 1950. "The Prince." In *"The Prince" and "The Discourses,"* edited by Max Lerner. New York: The Modern Library.

———. 1961. "Letter to Francesco Vettori, 10 December, 1513." In *Lettere*, edited by Franco Gaeta. Milan: Feltrinelli.

Magnarell, J. 1967. "Regional Voting in Turkey." *The Muslim World* 57.

Mahdi, Muhsin. 1964. "Averroes on Divine Law and Human Wisdom." In *Ancients and Moderns*, edited by Joseph Cropsey. New York: Basic.

Makarius, Raul. 1960. *La Jeunesse intellectuelle d'Egypte de la deuxieme mondiale*. Paris: Mouton.

Manaster, G. J., and R. J. Havighurst. 1972. *Cross National Research: Social-Psychological Methods and Problems*. Boston: Houghton Mifflin.

Mannheim, Karl. 1952. "The Social Problems of Generations." In *Essays in the Sociology of Knowledge*, edited by Paul Kecskemeti. New York: Oxford.

Marais, Octave. 1964. "La Classe dirigeante au Maroc." *Revue Française de Science Politique* 14, pp. 709–37. Translated in Zartman 1973.

Mardin, Serif. 1962. *The Genesis of Young Ottoman Political Thought*. Princeton: Princeton University Press.

Marr, Phebe Ann. 1970. "Iraq's Leadership Dilemma: A Study in Leadership Trends, 1948–1968." *Middle East Journal* 24, Summer, pp. 283–301.

Marrākushī, 'Abd al-Wāhid ibn 'Ait al-. 1893. *Histoire des Almohades*. Translated by E. Fagnan. Algiers: Jourdan.

Māwardī, Abū al-Hasan al-. 1966. *Al-Ahkām al-Sultāniyyah*. Cairo: Mustafā al-Bābī al-Halabī.

Mayer, Adrian. 1967. *"Pīr* and *Murshid*: An Aspect of Religious Leadership in West Pakistan." *Middle East Journal* 3, January, pp. 160–69.

Mayhew, Bruce. 1975. "Sociological Perspectives on the Structure of Elite Systems." In *Approaches to Elite Analysis*, by Robert Slater et al. Washington: Mathematica.

Mazlish, Bruce. 1972. *In Search of Nixon*. New York: Basic.

McClelland, David. 1961. *The Achieving Society*. Princeton: Princeton University Press.

Mead, Margaret. 1970. *Culture and Commitment: A Study of the Generation Gap*. New York: Natural History Press.

Meckstroth, T. W. 1975. "'Most Different Systems' and 'Most Similar Systems'—A Study in the Logic of Comparative Inquiry." *Comparative Political Studies* 8, 2, pp. 132–57.

Memmi, Albert. 1967. *The Colonizer and the Colonized*. Boston: Beacon.

Meyer, A. J. 1958. "Entrepreneurship and Economic Development in the Middle East." *The Public Opinion Quarterly* 20, Fall, pp. 391–96.

Micaud, Charles, L. Carl Brown, and C. H. Moore. 1964. *Tunisia: The Politics of Development*. New York: Praeger.

Michels, Robert. 1962. *Political Parties*. New York: Free Press.

Mihçioglu, C. 1972. *Daha Iyi Bir Kamu Kizmeti Için (Toward a Better Public Service)*. Ankara: Universitesi Başimevi.

Miller, William G. 1969. "Political Organization in Iran: From Dowreh to Political Power." *Middle East Journal* 23, 2, pp. 159–67.

Mitzman, Arthur. 1970. *The Iron Cage: An Historical Interpretation of Max Weber*. New York: Knopf.

———. 1973. *Sociology and Estrangement: Three Sociologists of Imperial Germany*. New York: Knopf.

Montague, R. 1952. "Le proletariat marocain." In *Industrialisation de l'Afrique du Nord*, edited by J. Leduc. Paris: Colin.

Montety, Henri de. 1957. "Le developpement des classes moyennes en Tunisie." In *Developpement d'une classe moyenne dans les pays tropicaux et subtropicaux*, pp. 131-39. Brussels: International Institute of Different Civilizations.

Moore, Clement H. 1965. *Tunisia Since Independence*. Berkeley: University of California.

———. 1967. "Mass Party Regimes in Africa." In *The Primacy of Politics*, edited by Herbert Spiro. Englewood Cliffs: Prentice-Hall.

———. 1970. *Politics in North Africa*. Boston: Little, Brown.

———. 1974. "Professional Syndicates in Contemporary Egypt." *American Journal of Arabic Studies* 3, 1, pp. 60–82.

———. 1980. *Dreams of Development: Egyptian Engineers in Politics*. Cambridge: Massachusetts Institute of Technology.

Moore, Clement H., and A. Hochschild. 1968. "Student Unions in North African Politics." *Daedalus* 87, pp. 21–50.

Morgenthau, Ruth Schachter. 1964. *Politics in French-Speaking West Africa*. New York: Oxford.

Morris-Jones. 1976. *Making of Politicians*. Atlantic Highlands: Humanities.

Morse, Chandler, et al. 1969. *Modernization by Design*. Ithaca: Cornell.

Mosca, Gaetano. 1923. *Elementi di Scienza Politica*. Turin: Fratelli Bocca.

———. 1939. *The Ruling Class*. New York: McGraw-Hill.

Mosteller, F., and J. W. Tukey. 1968. "Data Analysis, Including Statistics." In *The Handbook of Social Psychology*, Vol. II, edited by G. Lindzey and E. Aronson. Reading, Mass.: Addison-Wesley.

Muhlman, W. E. *Messianismes revolutionnaires au Tiers Monde*. Paris: Gallimard.

Mulk, Nizām al-. 1960. *Siyāsat-Nāma (Book of Government)*. Translated by Hubert Darke. London: Routledge and Kegan Paul.

Mushtaq, Ahmad. 1963. *Government and Politics in Pakistan*. New York: Praeger.

237

————. 1964. *The Civil Servant in Pakistan: A Study of the Background and Attitudes of Public Servants in Lahore* New York: Praeger.

Nagle, J. D. 1977. *System and Succession.* Austin: University of Texas.

Naraghi, E. 1951. "Elite ancienne et élite nouvelle dans l'Iran actual avec une note sur le systeme d'éducation." *Revues etudes islamiques* 25, pp. 69–80.

Naroll, R. 1970. "Data Control in Cross-Cultural Surveys." In *A Handbook of Method in Cultural Anthropology*, edited by R. Naroll and R. Cohen. Washington: Natural History Press.

Nasser, Gamal Abdel. 1955. *Egypt's Liberation: Philosophy of the Revolution.* Washington: Public Affairs Press.

Newell, R. S. 1972. *The Politics of Afghanistan.* Ithaca: Cornell.

Newman, K. J. "The New Monarchies of the Middle East." *Journal of International Affairs* 13, Spring, pp. 157–68.

Nezami, A. 1968. *Legislative Elites in Persia.* Chicago: University Thesis.

Nie, N. H., et al. 1975. *Statistical Package for the Social Sciences*, second ed. New York: McGraw-Hill.

Nordlinger, E. 1970. "Political Development: Time Sequences and Rates of Change." In *Politics and Society: Studies in Comparative Political Sociology*, edited by E. Nordlinger. Englewood Cliffs: Prentice-Hall.

Olson, M. 1968. *The Theory of Collective Action.* New York: Schocken.

Ottaway, D., and M. Ottaway. 1970. *Algeria: The Politics of a Socialist Revolution.* Berkeley: University of California Press.

Ovid. 1960. *Metamorphoses.* Translated by Frank Justus Miller. London: William Heinemann,

Oualoulou, Fathallah. 1975. *Le Tiers Monde et la troisième phase de domination.* Rabat: Editions Maghrebines.

Owen, J. 1968. "Social Structure in East Pakistan: A Case Study in Change." *Middle East Forum* 44, pp. 27–33.

Ozbudun, Ergun, and Frank Tachau. 1975. "Social Change and Electoral Behavior in Turkey: Toward a 'Critical Realignment'?" *International Journal of Middle East Studies* 6, 4, pp. 460–80.

Palmore, Erdman. 1975. *The Honorable Elders.* Chapel Hill: Duke University Press.

Pareto, Vilfredo. 1916. *Trattato di Sociologia Generale.* Florence: Barbera.

————. 1964. *Cours d'Économie Politique.* Geneva: Droz.

Parry, Geraint. 1970. *Political Elites*. New York: Praeger.

Patai, R. 1965. "The Dynamics of Westernization in the Middle East." In *The Contemporary Middle East*, edited by B. Rivlin and J. S. Szyliowicz. New York: Random House.

Payaslioglu, A. T. 1964. "Political Leadership and Political Parties: Turkey." In *Political Modernization in Japan and Turkey*, edited by D. A. Rustow and R. E. Ward. Princeton: Princeton University Press.

Paxton, Robert O. 1973. *Vichy France: Old Guard and New Order*. New York: Knopf.

Pelz, Donald C., and Robert A. Lew. 1970. "Heise's Causal Model Applied." In *Sociological Methodology, 1970*, edited by Edgar F. Borgatta and George W. Bohrnstedt. San Francisco: Jossey-Bass.

Peretz, D. 1971. *The Middle East Today*. New York: Holt, Rinehart and Winston.

Perlmutter, Amos. 1968. "The Israeli Army in Politics: The Persistence of the Civilian over the Military." *World Politics* 20, July, pp. 559–92.

Peters, Emrys L. 1963. "Aspects of Rank and Status among Muslims in a Lebanese Village." In *Mediterranean Countrymen*, edited by Julian Pitt-Rivers. Paris: Mouton.

Plato. 1956. *Symposium*. Translated by Benjamin Jowett. Indianapolis: The Liberal Arts Press.

———. 1968. *The Republic of Plato*. Translated by Allan Bloom. New York: Basic.

Polk, W. R. 1965. *The United States and the Arab World*. Cambridge: Harvard University Press.

Polk, W., and R. Chambers, eds. 1968. *Beginnings of Modernization in the Middle East*. Chicago: University of Chicago Press.

Polsby, Nelson W. 1963. *Community Power and Political Theory*. New Haven: Yale.

Potter, A. 1966. "The Elite Concept." *Political Studies* 14, October, pp. 373–75.

Presthus, Robert V. 1973. *Elite Accommodation in Canadian Politics*. Cambridge: Cambridge University Press.

———. 1975. *Elites in the Policy Process*. Cambridge: Cambridge University Press.

Presthus, Robert V., with Serda Erem. 1958. *Statistical Analysis in Comparative Administration: The Turkish Conseil d'Etat*. Ithaca: Cornell.

Price, M. P. 1948. "The Parliaments of Turkey and Persia." *Parliamentary Affairs* 1, Summer, pp. 43–50.

Przeworski, A., and H. Teune. 1970. *The Logic of Comparative Social Inquiry*. New York: Wiley.

Putnam, J. K. 1970. *Old Age Politics in California*. Stanford: Stanford University Press.

Putnam, Robert D. 1971. "Studying Elite Political Culture." *American Political Science Review* 65, 3, pp. 651–81.

———. 1976. *The Comparative Study of Political Elites*. Englewood Cliffs: Prentice-Hall.

Pye, L. W., ed. 1963. *Communications and Political Development*. Princeton: Princeton University Press.

Quandt, William B. 1969. *Revolution and Political Leadership: Algeria, 1954-1958*. Cambridge: Massachusetts Institute of Technology Press.

———. 1970. "The Comparative Study of Political Elites." *Sage Professional Papers in Comparative Politics*. Beverly Hills: Sage.

Rae, Douglas, and Michael Taylor. 1970. *The Analysis of Political Cleavages*. New Haven: Yale University Press.

Raiffa, H. 1953. "Arbitration Schemes for Generalized Two Person Games." In *Contributions to the Theory of Games*, vol. 2, edited by H. W. Kuhn and A. W. Tucker. Princeton: Princeton University Press.

Raoof, A. H. 1970. "The Kingdom of Saudi Arabia." In *Government and Politics of the Contemporary Middle East*, edited by T. Y. Ismael. Homewood: Dorsey Press.

Raphaeli, N. 1970. "The Senior Civil Service in Israel: Notes on Some Characteristics." *Public Administration* 48, 1, pp. 169–78.

Rashiduzzaman, M. 1968. "Pakistan's Local Bodies and Social Change: The Emerging Pattern of Local Leadership." *Orient* 9, August, pp. 125–28.

Renan, Ernest. 1949. *Averroès et l'Averroisme*. In *Oeuvres Complètes*, vol. 3. Paris: Calmann-Levy.

Riker, William. 1962. *The Theory of Political Coalitions*. New Haven: Yale University Press.

Robins, Robert S. 1976. *Political Institutionalization and the Interaction of Elites*. Beverly Hills: Sage.

Rogers, Everett E. 1969. *Modernization Among Peasants*. New York: Holt, Rinehart and Winston.

Roos, Leslie L., Jr. 1972. "Politics, Organizations and Choice." *Administrative Science Quarterly* 17, 4, pp. 529–43.

———. 1973. "A Rotation Design: Administrative Influence in Turkey." In *Quasi-Experimental Approaches*, edited by J. Caporaso and L. Roos. Evanston: Northwestern University Press.

———. 1978. "Institutional Change, Career Mobility, and Job Satisfaction." *Administrative Science Quarterly* 23, 2, pp. 318–30.

Roos, Leslie L., Jr., and Noralou P. Roos. 1971. *Managers of Modernization*. Cambridge: Harvard University Press.

Roos, Leslie L., Jr., et al. 1968. "Students and Politics in Turkey." *Daedalus* 97, pp. 184–203.

Rose, Arnold M. 1967. *The Power Structure: Political Processes in American Society*. New York: Oxford.

Rosen, Larry. 1972. "Muslim-Jewish Relations in a Moroccan City." *International Journal of Middle East Studies* 3.

Rosenthal, E. I. J. 1958. *Political Thought in Medieval Islam*. Cambridge: Cambridge University Press.

Rousseau, Jean-Jacques. 1959. *Dialogues*. In *Oeuvres Complètes*, vol. 1. Paris: Gallimard.

———. 1964a. *Discours sur les Sciences et les Arts*. In *Oeuvres Complètes*, vol. 3. Paris: Gallimard.

———. 1964b. *Discours sur l'Inégalité*. In *Oeuvres Complètes*, vol. 3. Paris: Gallimard.

———. 1964c. *Du Contrat Social*. In *Oeuvres Complètes*, vol. 3. Paris: Gallimard.

———. 1969. *Lettre à Christophe de Beaumont*. In *Oeuvres Complètes*, vol. 4. Paris: Gallimard.

Ruf, Werner K., et al. 1976. *Rapports de Dependance au Maghreb*. Paris: Centre National de Recherche Scientifique.

Rugh, William. 1973. "The Emergence of a New Middle Class in Saudi Arabia." *Middle East Journal* 27, 1, pp. 1–24.

Runciman, W. G. 1969. *Social Science and Political Theory*. Cambridge: Cambridge University Press.

Rustow, Dankwart. 1966. "The Study of Elites: Who's Who, When and How." *World Politics* 18, pp. 690–716.

———. 1969. "Ataturk's Political Leadership." In *Near Eastern Round Table, 1967-68*, edited by R. Bayly Winder. New York: New York University Press.

———. 1971. *Middle Eastern Political Systems*. Englewood Cliffs: Prentice-Hall.

———, ed. 1970. *Philosophers and Kings*. New York: Brazilier.

Safran, N. 1972. "How Long Will Sadat Last? Moscow's Not-so-Secret Wish." *New Middle East*.

Safran, Nadar. 1961. *Egypt in Search of Political Community*. Cambridge: Harvard University Press.

Salem, Elie. 1965. "Local Election in Lebanon: A Case Study." *Journal of Political Science* 9, November, pp. 376–87.

Sanua, V. 1969. "The Psychology of the Egyptian Fellahin." In *The Mind of Man in Africa: An Integrated Anthologia Relating to Psychiatry and Mental Health*, edited by E. Margetts. New York: Pergamon.

Sayigh, Yusul A. 1962. *Entrepreneurs of Lebanon*. Cambridge: Harvard University Press.

Schein, E. H. 1971. "The Individual, the Organization, and the Career: A Conceptual Scheme." *Journal of Applied Behavioral Science* 1, 4, pp. 401–26.

Schlesinger, Arthur M. 1939. "Tides of American Politics."

——. 1949. *Paths to the Present*. New York: Macmillan.

Schmidt, Charles F. 1975. "A Spatial Model of Authority-Dependency Relations in South Africa." *Journal of Modern African Studies* 8, pp. 483–95.

Schoenberg, R. 1972. "Strategies for Meaningful Comparison." In *Sociological Methodology, 1972*, edited by Herbert L. Costner. San Francisco: Jossey-Bass.

Schonfeld, William R. 1975. "The Meaning of Democratic Participation." *World Politics* 28, 1, pp. 134–58.

Schramm, W. 1964. *Mass Media and National Development*. Stanford: Stanford University Press.

Schultz, Ann. 1973. "A Cross National Examination of Legislators." *Journal of Developing Areas* 7, pp. 571–90.

Scott, R. E. 1967. "Political Elites and Political Modernization." In *Elites in Latin America*, by S. M. Lipset and A. Solari. New York: Oxford.

Seale, Patrick. 1965. *Struggle for Syria*. New York: Oxford University Press.

Searing, Donald B. 1969. "The Comparative Study of Elite Socialization." *Comparative Political Studies* 4, pp. 471–500.

Seligman, Lester. 1950. "The Study of Political Leadership." *The American Political Science Review* 44, December, pp. 904–16.

——. 1964a. "Elite Recruitment and Political Development." *The Journal of Politics* 26, pp. 612–26.

——. 1964b. *Leadership in a New Nation: Political Development in Israel*. New York: Atherton.

Seller, Charles. 1965. "The Equilibrium Cycle in 2-Party Politics." *Public Opinion Quarterly* 29, 1, p. 30.

Selznick, Philip. 1966. *TVA and the Grassroots*. New York: Harper and Row.

Sereno, Renzo. 1968. *The Rulers*. New York: Harper and Row.

Sertel, Ayşa. 1970. "A Study of Power Conceptions in a Turkish Village." *Hacettepe Bulletin of Social Science and the Humanities* 2, June, pp. 49–83.

Sewell, William, and Robert M. Hauser. 1975. *Education, Occupation and Earnings*. New York: Academic Press.

Shaji'i, Zahra. 1965. *Namayandigan-i Majlis-i Shoray-i Melli Dar va yek Doure-yi Qanun-Gozari: Mottal'e Az Nazar jam'e Shenasiyi Siyasi (Members of the Majlis in Twenty-One Sessions: An Investigation from the Viewpoint of Political Sociology)*, Tehran: University of Tehran Press.

Shamir, S. 1962. "Changes in Village Leadership." *New Outlook* 5, 2.

Shapiro, Yonathan. 1979. "Sabras in Politics." *Jerusalem Quarterly* 11, pp. 112–27.

————. Pending. *The Party System and Democracy in Israel*.

Sharabi, Hisham. 1962. *Government and Politics in the Middle East in the Twentieth Century*. New York: Van Nostrand.

————. 1965. "The Transformation of Ideology in the Arab World." *Middle East Journal* 19, 4, pp. 471–86.

Shaw, Stanford. 1969. "The Origin of Representative Government in the Ottoman Empire: An Introduction to the Provincial Council, 1830–1876." In *Near Eastern Round Table, 1967-68*, edited by R. Bayly Winder. New York: New York University Press.

Shepsle, Kenneth. 1971. "Review of Rae and Taylor (1970)." *American Political Review* 65, 3, pp. 790–92.

Sherwood, W. B. 1967. "The Rise of the Justice Party in Turkey." *World Politics* 20, 1, p. 65.

Shils, Edward. 1963. *The Intellectual in Political Development*. Paris: Mouton.

Shouby, E. 1951. "Influence of Arabic Language on the Psychology of the Arabs." *Middle East Journal* 5, pp. 284–303.

Simmel, Georg. 1955. *Conflict and the Web of Group Affiliations*. New York: Free Press.

Simmons, John. 1970–71. "Agricultural Cooperatives and Tunisian Development." *Middle East Journal* 24, pp. 455–65, and 25, pp. 45–57.

Simon, H. A. 1969. *The Sciences of the Artificial*. Cambridge: Massachusetts Institute of Technology.

Singer, Marshall. 1964. *The Emerging Elite*. Cambridge: Massachusetts Institute of Technology.

Sloane, Ruth, et al. 1962. *The Educated African*. New York: Praeger.

Smith, Peter. 1975. *Argentina and the Failure of Democracy: Conflict Among Political Elites*. Madison: University of Wisconsin Press.

Springborg, Robert. 1975. "Patterns of Association in the Egyptian Political Elite." In *Political Elites in the Middle East*, edited by George Lenczowski. Washington: American Enterprise Institute.

Stephens, Richard. 1971. *Wealth and Power in Peru*. Metuchen: Scarecrow.

Sternberg-Sarel, Benno. 1969. "Revolution per le haut dans les campagnes de l'Egypt." *Temps Modernes* 24, 274, pp. 1772–802.

Stewart, Frank Henderson. 1977. *Fundamentals of Age-Group Systems*. New York: Academic Press.

Stinchcombe and J. C. Wendt. 1975. "Theoretical Domains and Measurement in Social Indicator Analysis." In *Social Indicator Models*, edited by K. C. Land and S. Spilerman. New York: Russell Sage Foundation.

Stirling, Paul. 1953. "Social Ranking in a Turkish Village." *British Journal of Sociology* 4, 1, p. 31ff.

———. 1963. "The Domestic Cycle and the Distribution of Power in Turkish Villages." In *Mediterranean Countrymen*, edited by J. Pitt-Rivers. The Hague: Mouton.

———. 1965. *Turkish Village*. London: Weidenfeld and Nicolson.

Stone, Russell. 1973. "Anticipated Mobility to Elite Status Among Middle Eastern University Students." *International Review of History and Political Science* 10, pp. 1–17.

Strauss, Leo. 1958. *Thoughts on Machiavelli*. Glencoe: Free Press.

Suleiman, M. W. 1967. *Political Parties in Lebanon*. Ithaca: Cornell.

———. 1970. "Lebanon." In *Government and Politics of the Contemporary Middle East*, edited by T. Y. Ismael. Homewood: Dorsey.

———. 1972. "Crisis and Revolution in Lebanon." *The Middle East Journal* 26, Winter, 1, pp. 11–24.

Sullivan, John L., and Robert E. O'Connor. 1972. "Electoral Choice and Popular Control of Policy." *American Political Science Review* 66, 4, pp. 1256-1268.

Sundquist, James L. 1973. *Dynamics of the Party System*. Washington: Brookings.

Sween, J., and Donald T. Campbell. 1976. "A Study of the Effect of Proximally Auto-Correlated Error on Tests of Significance for the Interrupted Time Series Quasi-

Experimental Design." Psychology Dept., Evanston: Northwestern University. Mimeographed.

Szyliowicz, Joseph. 1966. *Political Change in Rural Turkey, Erdemli*. The Hague: Mouton.

———. 1970. "Students and Politics in Turkey." *Middle Eastern Studies* 4, May, pp. 150–62.

———. 1971. "Elite Recruitment in Turkey." *World Politics* 23, pp. 371–98.

Tachau, Frank, with M. J. Good. 1973. "The Anatomy of Political and Social Change: Turkish Parties, Parliaments, and Elections." *Comparative Politics* 5, 4, pp. 551–73.

———. 1975a. "Social Backgrounds of Turkish Parliamentarians." In *Commoners, Climbers and Notables: Social Ranking in the Middle East*, edited by Christoffel Anthonie Oliver van Nieuwenhuijze. Leiden: E. J. Brill.

———, ed. 1975b. *Political Elites and Political Development in the Middle East*. Boston: Schenkman.

Tachau, Frank, and Jacob Landau, eds. 1980. *Electoral Politics in the Middle East*. Stanford: Hoover Institute.

Tannous, A. 1955. "Dilemma of the Elite in Arab Society." *Human Organization* 14, Fall, pp. 11–15.

Tatsuoka, M. M. 1971. *Multivariate Analysis*. New York: Wiley.

Taylor, C. L., and M. C. Hudson. 1970. *World Handbook of Political and Social Indicators*. New Haven: Yale.

Teitler, Marcel, et al. 1973. *Elites pouvoir et legitimite au Maghreb*. Paris: Centre National Recherche Scientifique.

Tessler, Mark A. 1976. "Political Generations in Tunisia." In *Change in Tunisia*, edited by Russell Stone and John Simmons. Albany: State University Press of New York.

———. Pending. "Acculturation, SES and Attitude Change in Tunisia."

Thucydides. 1954. *The Peloponnesian War*. Translated by Rex Warner. Harmondsworth, England: Penguin.

Tilly, Charles. 1973. "Does Modernization Breed Revolution?" *Comparative Politics* 5, 3, pp. 425–47.

Time. 1974. Special Issue on "Leadership in America," July 15.

Treiman, D. J. 1970. "Industrialization and Social Stratification." In *Social Stratification: Research and Theory for the 1970's*, edited by Edward O. Lauman. Indianapolis: Bobbs-Merrill.

Tufte, E. R. 1969. "Improving Data Analysis in Political Science." *World Politics* 21, 4, pp. 641–54. Reprinted in *The Quantitative Analysis of Social Problems*, edited by E. R. Tufte, 1970. Reading, Mass.: Addison-Wesley.

Ulman, A. Haluk, and Frank Tachau. 1965. "Turkish Politics: The Attempt to Reconcile Rapid Modernization with Democracy." *The Middle East Journal* 19, 2, pp. 153–68.

Upton, Joseph. 1960. *The History of Modern Iran, an Interpretation*. Cambridge: Cambridge University Press.

Van de Geer, J. P. 1971. *Introduction to Multivariate Analysis for the Social Sciences*. San Francisco: Freeman.

Van Nieuwenhuijze, C. A. O. 1965. *Social Stratification and the Middle East: An Interpretation*. Leiden: Brill.

———, ed. 1977. *Commoners, Climbers and Notables*. Leiden: Brill.

Vatikiotis, P. J. 1961a. "Dilemmas of Political Leadership in the Arab Middle East: The Case of the U.A.R." *The American Political Science Review* 55, pp. 103–11.

———. 1961b. *The Egyptian Army in Politics: The Pattern for New Nations*. Bloomington: Indiana University Press.

———. 1972. "The Politics of the Fertile Crescent." In *Political Dynamics in the Middle East*, edited by P. Y. Hammond and S. S. Alexander. New York: American Elsevier.

———. 1973. "Egypt Adrift: A Study in Disillusion." *New Middle East*.

Verba, S., N. Nie, and J. Kim. 1971. "The Modes of Democratic Participation: A Cross-National Comparison." *Sage Professional Papers in Comparative Politics*. Beverly Hills: Sage.

Vidich, Arthur J., and Joseph Bensman. 1958. *Small Town in a Mass Society*. Princeton: Princeton University Press.

Vorys, Karl Von. 1959. "The Legislators in Underdeveloped Countries." *Political Research, Organization and Design*, pp. 23–26.

Wallerstein, Emanuel. 1965. "Elites in French Speaking West Africa." *Journal of Modern African Studies* 3, 1, pp. 1–34.

———. 1967. "Class, Tribe and Party in West African Politics." In *Party Systems and Voter Alignments*, edited by S. M. Lipset and Stein Rokkan. New York: Free Press.

Walzer, Richard. 1962. *Greek into Arabic*. Cambridge: Harvard University Press.

Ward, Robert, and Dankwart Ruston, eds. 1964. *Political Modernization in Japan and Turkey*. Princeton: Princeton University Press.

Waterbury, John. 1967. "Marginal Politics and Elite Manipulation in Morocco." *European Journal of Sociology* 8, pp. 94–111.

————. 1970. *The Commander of the Faithful*. New York: Columbia.

Webb, E. J., D. T. Campbell, R. D. Schwartz, and L. Sechrest. 1966. *Unobtrusive Measures*. New York: Rand-McNally.

Webber, R., ed. 1969. *Culture and Management*. Homewood: Richard D. Irwin.

Weiker, W. F. 1963. *The Turkish Revolution, 1960–61*. Washington: Brookings.

Weinbaum, M. G. 1972. "Afghanistan: Nonparty Parliamentary Democracy." *Journal of Developing Areas* 7.

————. 1973. "Iran Finds a Party System." *Middle East Journal* 27.

————. 1975. "Dimensions of Elite Change in the Middle East." Presented at Middle East Studies Association annual meeting, November.

————. 1977. "The Legislator as an Intermediary in Afghanistan." In *Legislators in Plural Societies*, edited by A. F. Eldridge. Durham: Duke University Press.

Weingartner, R. 1968. "The Quarrel About Historical Explanation." In *Readings in the Philosophy of the Social Sciences*, edited by May Brodbeck. New York: Macmillan.

Weinstein, Fred, and Gerald M. Platt. 1969. *The Wish to be Free*. Berkeley: University of California.

————. 1973. *Psychoanalytic Sociology*. Baltimore: Johns Hopkins.

Welfing, M. B. 1975. "Models, Measurement and Sources of Error: Civil Conflict in Black Africa." *American Political Science Review* 69, pp. 871–88.

Wheaton, Blair, Bengt Muthen, Diane F. Alvin, and Gene F. Sumers. 1977. "Assessing Reliability in Panel Models." In *Sociological Methodology, 1977*, edited by David R. Heise. San Francisco: Jossey-Bass.

Wiley, D. E., and J. A. Wiley. 1970. "The Estimation of Measurement Error in Panel Data." *American Sociological Review* 35, pp. 112–17. Reprinted in *Causal Models in the Social Sciences*, edited by Hubert M. Blalock, Jr., 1971. Chicago: Aldine-Atherton.

Wilkinson, Rupert. 1969. *Governing Elites*. New York: Oxford.

Wills, Garry. 1970. *Nixon Agonistes*. Boston: Houghton Mifflin.

Winder, R. Bayly. 1962–63. "Syrian Deputies and Cabinet Ministers, 1919–1959." *Middle East Journal* 16, pp. 407–29; 17, pp. 38–54.

Wolfenstein, E. Victor. 1967. *The Revolutionary Personality*. Princeton: Princeton University Press.

Wolman, Benjamin, ed. 1971. *The Psychoanalytic Interpretation of History*. New York: Basic.

Wood, A. D. 1935. *A History of the Levant Company*. London: Oxford University Press.

Xenophon. 1965. *Recollections of Socrates*. Translated by Anna S. Benjamin. Indianapolis: Bobbs-Merrill.

Zartman, I. William. 1964. *Morocco: Problems of New Power*. New York: Atherton.

———. 1970. "The Algerian Army in Politics." In *Soldier and State in Africa*, edited by Claude Welch. Evanston: Northwestern University Press.

———, ed. 1973. *Man, State and Society in the Contemporary Maghreb*. New York: Praeger.

———. 1974. "The Study of Elite Circulation." *Comparative Politics* 6, 3, pp. 465–88.

———. 1975a. "Algeria: A Post-revolutionary Elite." In *Political Elites and Political Development in the Middle East*, edited by Frank Tachau. Boston: Schenkman.

———. 1975b. "The Elites of the Maghreb." *International Journal of Middle East Studies* 6, pp. 495–504.

———. 1976. "Political Science." In *The Study of the Middle East*, edited by Leonard Binder. New York: Wiley.

———. 1978. "Coming Political Problems in Africa." In *The United States and Africa*, edited by Jennifer Whitaker. New York: New York University.

———. 1979. "Political and Social Trends." In I. W. Zartman et al., *Continent in Crisis: Africa in the 1980s*. New York: McGraw-Hill.

———. Pending. "The Rise and Passing of the Algerian Military Regime." In *Radical and Reformist Military Regimes*, edited by Jon Kraus. Berkeley: University of California Press.

Zartman, I. William, John Pierre Entelist, and James Paul. 1971. "An Economic Indicator of Socio-Political Unrest." *International Journal of Middle East Studies* 2, pp. 293–310.

Ziadeh, Farhat. 1968. *Lawyers, The Rule of Law, and Liberalism in Modern Egypt*. Stanford: Hoover.

Zonis, M. 1970. "Iran." In *Governments and Politics of Contemporary Middle East*, edited by T. Y. Ismael. Homewood: Dorsey Press.

———. 1971. *The Political Elite of Iran*. Princeton: Princeton University Press.

———. 1975. "The Political Elite of Iran: A Second Stratum?" In *Political Elites and Political Development in the Middle East*, edited by Frank Tachau. New York: Wiley.

INDEX

LIST OF CONTRIBUTORS

I. WILLIAM ZARTMAN is Professor of Politics and former department head at New York University.

CHARLES BUTTERWORTH is Associate Professor of Government and Politics at the University of Maryland, College Park.

ILIYA HARIK is Professor of Political Science at Indiana University, Bloomington.

LESLIE ROOS, Jr. is a Professor in the Faculty of Administrative Studies, University of Manitoba, Winnipeg, Canada.

RUSSELL STONE is Associate Professor of Sociology at the State University of New York, Buffalo.

MARVIN WEINBAUM is Associate Professor of Political Science at the University of Illinois, Champaign-Urbana.